Fanged Fan Fiction

Fanged Fan Fiction

Variations on *Twilight*,
True Blood and
The Vampire Diaries

MARIA LINDGREN LEAVENWORTH
and
MALIN ISAKSSON

McFarland & Company, Inc., Publishers
Jefferson, North Carolina, and London

LIBRARY OF CONGRESS CATALOGUING-IN-PUBLICATION DATA

Lindgren Leavenworth, Maria, 1969–
    Fanged fan fiction : variations on Twilight, True Blood and The vampire diaries / Maria Lindgren Leavenworth and Malin Isaksson.
        p.   cm.
    Includes bibliographical references and index.

    ISBN 978-0-7864-7044-0
    softcover : acid free paper ∞

    1. Fan fiction — History and criticism.   2. Vampires in literature.   3. Literature and the Internet.   I. Isaksson, Malin, 1970–   II. Title.
PN3377.5.F33L43 2013
809.3—dc23   2013022283

BRITISH LIBRARY CATALOGUING DATA ARE AVAILABLE

© 2013 Maria Lindgren Leavenworth and Malin Isaksson. All rights reserved

No part of this book may be reproduced or transmitted in any form or by any means, electronic or mechanical, including photocopying or recording, or by any information storage and retrieval system, without permission in writing from the publisher.

Cover photograph © 2013 Nejron Photo

Manufactured in the United States of America

McFarland & Company, Inc., Publishers
  Box 611, Jefferson, North Carolina 28640
    www.mcfarlandpub.com

Acknowledgments

Our interest in the literary aspects of fan fiction began several years ago. On the one hand, it offered us the chance to develop previous research interests (intertextuality in Maria's case, reception studies in Malin's), and, on the other, the excitement of moving in directions which were new to us and offered opportunities to explore an emerging academic field. With colleagues similarly interested in fanfic we organized an international symposium, "Textual Echoes," in Umeå, Sweden, in February 2010. The contributions provided analyses of fanfic texts from various perspectives and solidified our belief that close readings of the text form contribute valuable knowledge about contemporary creativity and about the place fanfic has in a longer history of transformative practices.

In 2011, our project *FAN(G)S: Fan Fiction and the Vampire Trope* received funding from the Swedish Research Council which enabled us to work on this book. The specific call for applications within a program called "The Uses of Fiction" resulted in seven funded projects and a research network. The network group, coordinated by Professor Danuta Fjellestad and Professor Lars-Håkan Svensson, has met twice a year to discuss methodological and theoretical issues which sometimes divide this interdisciplinary group, and which sometimes show how much we have in common. We are thankful for support and criticism from the coordinators and from our fellow researchers working with the human need for and uses of fiction.

The Department of Language Studies at Umeå University has a very active higher seminar where colleagues have given us valuable feedback on chapter drafts and asked crucial questions regarding terminology, theory and interpretations. We thank you, one and all, and hope that the finished book accurately reflects our response to your careful readings and answers at least some of your remaining queries. We are particularly grateful to Professor Heidi Hansson and Dr. Van Leavenworth, thoughtful and meticulous readers, who commented on the finished manuscript and were critical and supportive in equal measure. Here as well, it is our hope that the end result bears out your constructive comments. In cases where it does not, the responsibility is all ours.

Finally, our warmest thanks to family and friends who have put up with us and our incessant talk about vampires (with or without bite).

Table of Contents

Acknowledgments v
Preface 1

Introduction: Transfusions, Transformations, Transgressions 3
1. Single White Females and Sympathetic Vampires:
   The Canons 17
2. Vampiric Prosumption: Archives, Genres and Fans'
   Negotiations of Rules 44
3. The Archive of New Stories 68
Interlude: The Normal Discussion 112
4. Canon-Transgressive Lemony Goodness: Sexual Norms
   and Undead Desires 118
5. Something Wicked This Way Comes: Ethics, Monstrosity
   and Issues of the Soul 158
Conclusion: The Vampire Archived and Re-Fanged 200

Chapter Notes 205
Works Cited 211
Index 223

Preface

The desire to add to an existing story, to ensure the continued "lives" of its characters, or to enter into a dialogue with a preexisting narrative for purposes of acclaim or criticism is by no means unique to the text form of fan fiction, but finds a particular contemporary expression in it. We have been drawn to fanfic, online-published stories taking as their starting point an already existing fictional text, as much for the similarities with other types of intertextual works as for the transformative differences which make each reading challenging and productive. Our sustained close readings of a selection of fanfic address what has been perceived as missing in scholarship, and move away from ethnographic explorations of fandoms and fan practices toward a view of fan fictions as literary artifacts in their own right. As written readings of a preexisting text, fan fiction often illustrates very complex relationships between authorial power and subversion, between mainstream messages and individual interpretations.

Our selected fanfics come from contemporary, popular culture source texts featuring vampires as central characters. In *Our Vampires, Ourselves* (1995), Nina Auerbach suggested that "at the end of the twentieth century, vampirism is wearing down and vampires need a long restorative sleep" (192). Vampires did not, however, sleep very long (if they slept at all), but made their reappearance in the paranormal romance genre. Among the plethora of contemporary vampire texts are Stephenie Meyer's novels in the Twilight series and the film adaptations of these, Charlaine Harris' Sookie Stackhouse novels and the TV series *True Blood*, and novels by L.J. Smith which have been loosely adapted for television in the series *The Vampire Diaries*. What the vampires have in common in these texts is that, like fans, they are communal rather than solitary, and the traditional threat of the undead is downplayed through their lasting and romantic bonds with humans. The lure of these kinds of vampires, and the active fandoms formed around the fictional worlds, have resulted in an enormous output of transformative writings, the primary material for our study.

Previous scholarship about fans has contributed valuable information about identity-making processes (individual and communal), about forms of resistance to and compliance with trends and tendencies in written and visual fictions. Scholarship about vampires has variously discussed ethnographic aspects and psychological readings, considered the ways in which vampire fiction adheres to genre limitations or exceeds these, and stressed the symbolic implications of past and contemporary takes on the vampire trope. While indebted to both academic fields, in this book we read the vampire through the lens of fan fiction, particularly regarding how the trope is used to subvert norms established in the source texts which structure depictions of sexuality, sexual practices, and monstrosity. But our interest also lies in exploring types of fanfic texts commonly overlooked in discussions because they are not readily subversive. Of special interest in this case is the identification of primary narrative strategies in the fanfic production which illustrate particular transformative processes.

To fans, fan scholars, and scholar-fans, parts of our discussions will in all likelihood seem redundant since we outline the structure of fanfic sites and explain fanfic-specific terms. To fans of vampire fiction, and vampire scholars, other parts of the book may seem to only state the obvious. To literary critics, finally, our delineation of genre and discussions about intertextuality may appear either too detailed or too shallow. Our purpose, however, is to bring together theories and methods from several academic fields and supply enough information to serve as a background to our close readings. It is our hope that our findings, in turn, will contribute to fan studies and to vampire scholarship, and will firmly establish that fan fiction has an important function to fill within literary studies.

Introduction: Transfusions, Transformations, Transgressions

> *I sit at the desk with my back to the window, and there, behind me, I feel an eye that sucks up the flow of the sentences, leads the story in directions that elude me. Readers are my vampires.* — Italo Calvino, *If on a Winter's Night a Traveler*

"Bella is gone. She [...] is dead." So says Edward Cullen to Bella Swan's father Charlie in shoefreak37's fan fiction *The Strange Design of Comfort*. In this story both Bella and the child she has carried have died and Edward's vampiric venom, which in Stephenie Meyer's last installment in the Twilight series, *Breaking Dawn*, saved her (and turned her), has proven ineffective. In the fanfic, the death of Bella becomes a vehicle for deepening and eroticizing the homosocial bond between Edward and the werewolf Jacob Black and for exploring issues connected to grief. The access to Edward's thoughts and feelings in addition means increased opportunities for internal reflections on monstrosity. Does life without Bella, arguably a drastic revision, mean that the Edward we meet in the fanfic is not the Edward of Meyer's creation? What remains to link the fanfic to the "original" story? The use of quotation marks here is deliberate because in the contemporary media and culture climate, lines are increasingly blurred between what is perceived as original and derivative writing. Edward in shoefreak37's version may be modeled on sexually transgressive or more clearly predatory instantiations of the vampire trope, and Meyer's version, in turn, has close derivative ties to the traditional romance hero, albeit with paranormal character traits. At the same time, Edward's grief in the fanfic acquires a deeper meaning when read against the backdrop of his and Bella's love in Meyer's novels, and the intimacy between him and Jacob follows logically from the conflicted but intense emotions they have there. Close readings of fan fiction repeatedly lead to considerations of where inspiration may come from, which intertextual links are retained, and explorations of in which new directions the story is led.

In some discussions, fan fiction is considered vampiric as the source text is appropriated, invaded, even seen as drained of life. Authors of novels and producers of visual texts may be aware, like Calvino's narrator in our epigraph, of an unsettling presence behind the dark window pane, of the anonymous minds ingesting the primary material only to take it in new directions in their own imaginations and in their own stories. In other discussions, to which we hope to contribute, the use of the vampire imagery can be turned on its head because there is also a sense of metaphorical turning, a rebirth of the source text into a new state of being. Rather than leading to the textual equivalent of the increased weakness of the vampire's victims, the vampiric reader's figurative siphoning of blood suggests the opposite. Something is taken, something else is given back; the figurative blood exchange goes both ways.

The analogy, of course, comes naturally to this project. We are concerned with contemporary American vampire text worlds, and particularly with how the fanged beings are read, re-written and altered in fan fictions: texts which test the limits of an already existing fictional work and explore gaps and discrepancies within it. By sustained textual analyses of a selection of vampire fanfics we trace themes connected to romantic and sexual loves and to issues of good and evil, in the process discussing what other venues of symbolic transfusion are used by fanfic authors, what additional past and contemporary texts are used as sources of sustenance. We investigate what narrative and textual strategies are employed in fan fiction to explore the potentialities which remain unrealized in the source material. And while not claiming that our findings are generalizable to all vampire fan fiction, we still identify and comprehensively discuss some of the main tendencies in contemporary online creativity.

Our close readings come at a time when remixes and transformative works are accepted, sometimes celebrated, forms of expression. Elizabeth Bennet battles the undead in Seth Grahame-Smith's novel mash-up *Pride and Prejudice and Zombies* (2009) and Amanda Grange envisions Mr. Darcy's resistance to marriage as a result of being a vampire in *Mr Darcy, Vampyre* (2009). In *Abraham Lincoln, Vampire Hunter* paranormal elements are superimposed on historical events (Grahame-Smith 2010) and versions of classics such as Bram Stoker's *Dracula* are amped up with sex scenes and republished (and "co-authored," in this case, by Scarlett Parrish 2012).[1] Just like these examples, and seldom simply about imitating the source text, fanfics complement and diversify mainstream contemporary media products and messages and are increasingly noted for these (and other) reasons. In a 2011 article, Lev Grossman writes that "[r]ight now fan fiction is still the cultural equivalent of dark matter: it's largely invisible to the mainstream, but at the same time, it's unbelievably massive" (n. pag.). A year after Grossman's article, mainstream publishing came to a rather rude awakening to the existence of this dark matter with the much discussed publication of E.L. James' *Fifty Shades* trilogy. The novels were originally published as *Master of the Universe*, a fan fiction inspired by the Twilight novels. Written under the pseudonym Icequeens Snowdragon, Icy for short, the fanfic initially appeared in chapter installments on FanFiction.net and, after its removal from this general site (possibly because of the story's too-explicit content), on the author's own homepage. Already at the outset, Icy removed the paranormal element (she creates a story which in fanfic terminology is All Human, or AH) and recast Meyer's Edward as a businessman and Bella as a twenty-two-year-old university student. The fanfic is also categorized as an Alternate Universe (AU) — a what if-story — and in this highly sexualized version of events, Bella is initiated as a Submissive to Edward's Dominant. The fanfic received a lot of attention and many online reviews, cited by numerous commentators as a strongly contributing reason for the novels' subsequent publication.

For traditionally published they have been, with the characters' names changed to Christian Grey and Anastasia Steele and with additional details which anchored the fanfic in the Twilight universe removed. The trilogy first appeared as e-books, published by Writer's Coffee Shop Publishing House in 2011.[2] In April 2012 it was also published as both hardcover and paperback by Vintage, set off an unprecedented consumerism, and made James the most sold author on Amazon.com, surpassing even J.K. Rowling (Meredith n. pag.). With this commercial success came attention from both readers and critics. Discussions online and in articles branched off in different directions. One debate focused on the fact that fan fiction is often created communally, and that comments and feedback from readers may profitably influence the text, published as it is in installments. When a work is pulled and published, and in the process often also sanitized to better fit the mainstream print market, the non-commercial aspect of fan fiction is negated and the text's participatory "provenance" is lost; the latter aspect often seen as a betrayal of other fans' involvement in the process (Litte n. pag.). Another aspect of the debate was whether or not the printed works could be seen as plagiarizing the previously published fan fiction or Meyer's copyrighted work. The latter worry was assuaged by comparisons with other derivative texts with some commentators subscribing to Grossman's view that although "[a] writer's characters are his or her children ... even children have to grow up sometime and do things their parents wouldn't approve of" (n. pag.). Once a text is published, the author loses complete control. The reader behind his or her shoulder is already perusing not only characters but also plot lines, central events, and perspectives, pondering the alternative directions the narrative might take.

Reading fan fiction requires knowledge of its genres, categories and conventions, as does reading any other text form. The question posed and aside answer provided by Laura Hazard Owen, "How similar is *50 Shades of Grey* to *Twilight* (not very unless *Twilight* contains a major bondage and sadomasochism element that I missed)" (n. pag.), reveal a rather shallow understanding of fan fiction categories such as All Human and kinkfic (stories depicting kinky sexual practices). Seen in the light of these, a story in which Edward is no longer a vampire but a sexy multi-millionaire CEO with a predilection for sexual domination and Bella is his enamored sexual submissive in training, is a not uncommon example of a reworking of Twilight relationships. Even though Twilight does not feature bondage or BDSM practices, issues of excessive control and submission are central. That is, the similarity is certainly there on a thematic level and an elaboration of the dynamics between the characters along explicitly sexual lines is hardly surprising to fanfic readers. On the level of genre, both the fanfic and the novel are driven by Edward's/Christian's love and care for Bella/Anastasia. In Twilight, Edward (over)protects Bella because of their fated romance and in *Fifty Shades of Grey*, Christian's education of Anastasia stems from a desire to be all she needs. However, the sanitizing process a work goes through when it is pulled from a fanfic site and traditionally published does make questions and answers such as Owen's understandable. If *Fifty Shades of Grey* is read as an example of female-authored, straight erotica, no longer connected to Twilight through the use of character names and familial relationships, it loses something in the process. Christian Grey's "control freak" behavior (James 205) and Anastasia Steele's gradual acknowledgement of the sexually pleasurable aspects of being dominated are then no longer seen as a comment on aspects of the source text, such as Edward's stalking of Bella, his control over whom she sees and when, his violence in sexual situations (with the couple's wedding night as a prime example), as well as Bella's lack of self-confidence and seeming willingness to regard herself as inferior. Our contention, therefore, is that whereas it is quite possible to read and enjoy James's published novel on its own, a close reading of it as a fan fiction lends it an important critical edge.

Not surprisingly, *Fifty Shades of Grey* has resulted in new readings and, consequently, new fan fictions. Among these are stories which fill in missing moments in the novel and its sequels, those that shift perspectives, those that outline the future adventures of Anastasia and Christian, and those that transform the heteronormative plot into a same-sex tale of dominance and submission. In short, fanfic authors do the same with this text as they do with others of a less complicated origin. An interesting metatextual response within the Twilight fandom is Heyl13's fanfic *The Blue Book of Pain*. This story (whose title is an intertextual reference to Christian Grey's Red Room of Pain) is labeled All Human, and pairs Bella with Jacob, thus giving her a different outlook on life than she has in the relationship with Edward and in a paranormal setting. Jacob returns home from work to find a distressed Bella, for the first time in her life unable to finish a book, and guess which one it is? It is not only the poor writing, the lack of plot, the clichéd representation of power resting in the man's hands, and the "[b]ad sex" of *Fifty Shades of Grey* that offend Bella in the fanfic, but the characters as well. The "overly judgmental" heroine has "no backbone," Bella complains, and the hero is a "controlling, manipulating, abusing, borderline sadistic *prick*."[3] Jacob tries to calm her down by reminding her that it is, after all, a work of fiction, but Bella remains agitated by the fact that the book has become such a success and that Anastasia might be seen as "a role model" when, in fact, she is "a doormat." We may be stating the obvious here, but of interest in this fanfic is not only the criticism of James' novel, but the fact that one version of Bella (the fanfic one) chastises another, earlier, version. And in this, she is not alone. In fact, there is a whole subset of Twilight fan fictions which are described with the phrase "Bella with a backbone," and which similarly to Heyl13's story considerably enhance the female protagonist's agency and independence, thus critiquing the whole premise of Twilight.

As mechanisms and strategies employed in the fanfic production are examined through close readings, the text form can profitably be seen as contributing to ongoing meaning-making processes, and findings can complement the expanding area of fan studies. By now, the fan has become a carefully studied phenomenon within ethnography and cultural studies through the work of critics who can broadly be placed into three at times overlapping stages of scholarship.[4] Taking inspiration from Michel de Certeau and John Fiske, critics' emphasis in the first wave was often on delineating how and in what ways fans constituted an active audience in opposition to dominant readings, and on how their artifacts and discussions could be read as subversive and as examples of collective attempts to gain some form of power. Henry Jenkins' early work *Textual Poachers* (1992) exemplifies this approach but so does later work such as Sheenagh Pugh's *The Democratic Genre* (2005). In the second wave, with focus on media forms and technologies enabling different varieties of fan expression, scholarly emphasis shifted to seeing fans as part of the mainstream and their patterns of consumption, read through the lens of Pierre Bourdieu's work, as illustrative of their (individual or collective) cultural capital (see, for example, Harris and Alexander's collection *Theorizing Fandom* 1998). "These Bourdieuian perspectives," Jonathan Gray, Cornel Sandvoss and C. Lee Harrington argue, "aimed to unmask the false notion of popular culture as a realm of emancipation," resulting in queries about the worth of or future for fan studies (6). However, fan studies has moved into a third wave "distinguished by a greater self-reflexivity about the theorist's own motives and positions and by a shift in emphasis toward exploring the contributions of fans to contemporary culture" (Thomas 4). Issues of aesthetics within fandoms are raised, and the detached position of the critic is abandoned in favor of a re-positioning as "fan scholar" (Hills *Fan Cultures*) or as "aca-fan" (Jenkins "Confessions"). In the third wave, scholars have also come to acknowledge and address the fact that the vast majority of Internet users make a rather trivial everyday use of Web 2.0, while simultaneously stressing that such trivial practices are worthy of academic attention. Through "Critical Internet Theory," scholars further question the concept of participatory culture by emphasizing the fact that far from all media users participate by offering their own creative work and, importantly, that amateur work of various kinds can be seen not only as individual expressions of creativity or knowledge but also as free labor (Fuchs). Important to note in any discussion about contemporary media practices which require Internet access is of course also that large parts of the world's population are excluded, even from trivial or non-participatory use. By extension, fan fiction can therefore be a "democratic genre" only in a limited sense.

The predominant focus on fans and fandoms does not mean that fan fiction has been neglected in critical discussions. However, brief analyses of fanfics are often used to illustrate tendencies within a larger fandom. One example is *"Star Trek* Rerun, Reread, Rewritten" (1988), Jenkins' article which grew into *Textual Poachers*. Early criticism was often focused on female-authored fanzine-published slash (homoerotic pairings of male characters who are not romantically linked in the source text), in line with the first wave's focus on resistive readings. Among these are Joanna Russ's "Pornography by Women, for Women, with Love" (1985), Patricia Frazer Lamb and Diane Veith's "Romantic Myth, Transcendence, and *Star Trek* Zines" (1986) and works by Camille Bacon-Smith and Constance Penley (*Enterprising Women* 1992 and *NASA/Trek* 1997, respectively). Many of these scholars combine readings of fanfic with ethnographic research, and one conclusion reached is that fan writing of all kinds attracts predominantly female authors. Referring to an earlier work by Bacon-Smith, Jenkins, for example, argues that "more than 90%" of fan writing is authored by women ("*Star Trek*" 90).[5]

While interest in slash continued in articles published in the late 1990s and early 2000s, Kristina Busse and Karen Hellekson note that critics read "fanfic as an interpretative gesture, thus using fan fiction to gain further insight into a particular source text," the latter falling into the genres of science fiction or fantasy (20). Hellekson and Busse's edited collection *Fan Fiction in the Age of the Internet* (2006) stresses the importance of third-wave autoethnography in fanfic studies, although, because of the individual contributions to the volume, it is of "an ephemeral, provisional, and contingent [rather than] self-reflexive" kind (24). The chapters provide useful historical comparisons and discussions of various categories of fan fiction draw attention to both material affordances of the online environment and to ways in which fanfic conforms to the mainstream rather than only resisting tendencies. The latter line of inquiry also comes to the fore in discussions by, for example, Christine Scodari ("Resistance Re-Examined" 2003) and Anne Kustritz ("Slashing the Romance Narrative" 2004). Critical considerations of fan fiction thus ride the same waves as more general discussions in fan studies.

As literary scholars and media consumers, we approach fan fiction from a perspective akin to that which Matt Hills proposes as beneficial to media and cultural studies when trying to resolve tensions between "critical scholar anti-fans and celebratory scholar fans" ("Media Academics" 46). We are consumers of the same popular culture texts as the fanfic authors we study. We have our own reactions to and interpretations of these texts and do not distance ourselves from them. Rather, we take a deep interest in mainstream media and their ability to engage audiences and spark off fan activities. However, we do retain a critical distance to the texts we examine (both source texts and fanfic) and we are not active in any of the fandoms we study. We do not profess to have the inside knowledge of fans of the source texts, nor will we engage in the kind of autoethnography often encouraged in the third wave of fan studies. Our discussions in this book therefore do not seek to contribute to an increased knowledge about the identities or motivations of fans beyond what is evident in their texts. We do not claim that fans' situatedness in cultural, national, and class identities at a particular historical moment is irrelevant, and we find no reason to contest findings indicating that the overwhelming majority of fanfic authors are female. Nor do we argue that material benefits and limitations of technology do not impact on the production. On the contrary, our own analyses would be impoverished without the ethnographic and cultural studies work that precedes us. However, our contribution addresses what is still missing in fan studies in general: a depth of knowledge about the actual artifacts, acquired by sustained close readings of fan fiction. By seeing the text form alongside other types of intertextual works, we approach the stories from a literary perspective, while still paying attention to the particularities of responses to contemporary concerns and a media climate which encourages rather than dissuades audience participation.

Our focus on fan fictions as literary artifacts owes a great deal to discussions by Milly Williamson, whose book *The Lure of the Vampire* shares our focus on vampire fiction and fan practices. Firstly, Williamson contends "that there is value in attempting to objectively understand the dynamics and logics of phenomena" (94). Secondly, in her discussions about potential readings of *Dracula* which emanate from other perspectives than the privileged white, male, heterosexual, upper class reading position, Williamson refers to Franco Moretti's idea of "the *Zeitgeist* fallacy," that is "the notion that the spirit of any age is shared by all members of society," which often results in a tendency to make generalizations concerning the text itself but also to over- or predetermine the reactions of its readers, assuming all to have similar responses (5).[6] We want to stress that we see the selected fan fictions as individual responses to the canon, as particularized written readings. We do not proclaim that all our findings are valid for a particular generation of readers, a particular type of readers, or even of a fandom. Our arguments build on a selection of fan fictions and just as we would not attempt to draw conclusions about the text form drama on the basis of a handful of Elizabethan plays, we would not claim that the tendencies and patterns identified here apply to the entire vast field that is fan fiction.

The official conceptual materials which the fans respond to are in fanfic vernacular referred to as *canon*.[7] Canon, although linked to the traditional usage denoting texts in a cultural heritage, is here seen as specifically connected to fan fiction and in relation to *fanon*: the fans' interpretations. Along these lines, then, the canon is the "original" work, and the fanon is composed of interpretations and associations found in fan fiction and in other types of fan art and fandom discussions. Even when appearing very detailed and closed, fans find virtualities and potentialities to explore in the canon materials. A narrative perspective may be shifted, a minor character may be developed, and a new relationship may be mined for its potential. For some fanfic authors, writing becomes a testing ground and a creative workshop, for others, writing fanfic can be a highly political activity where issues that are deemed unsuitable for mainstream media can be debated and explored.

The canons which the fanfic authors studied in this book start from will be referred to as Twilight, True Blood and The Vampire Diaries, and while they encompass both written and visual material, we have made delimitations.[8] When referring to Twilight we are concerned with Stephenie Meyer's novels *Twilight* (2006), *New Moon* (2006), *Eclipse* (2007) and *Breaking Dawn* (2008), as well as with the film adaptations *Twilight* (Hardwicke 2008), *New Moon* (Weitz 2009), *Eclipse* (Slade 2010) and *Breaking Dawn* Parts 1 and 2 (Condon 2011, 2012). The canon we refer to as True Blood consists of the twelve hitherto published novels in Charlaine Harris' Sookie Stackhouse series (the last novel is scheduled for publication in the spring of 2013, and falls outside the scope of this study). The novels, published yearly between 2001 and 2012, are *Dead Until Dark, Living Dead in Dallas, Club Dead, Dead to the World, Dead as a Doornail, Definitely Dead, All Together Dead, From Dead to Worse, Dead and Gone, Dead in the Family, Dead Reckoning*, and *Deadlocked*. This canon also includes the first five seasons of the HBO series *True Blood* (Ball 2008–2012). Finally, the canon texts grouped together under The Vampire Diaries consist of L.J. Smith's novels *The Awakening, The Struggle, The Fury* and *The Reunion* (all published in 1991), her continuation in *Nightfall* (2009), *Shadow Souls* (2009) and *Midnight* (2010), and the first three seasons of the CW Television series *The Vampire Diaries* (Williamson and Plec 2010–2012). Where it is relevant we will point out that an argument only relates to, for example, Harris' novels and not the TV series, but when we use the non-italicized terms Twilight, True Blood, and The Vampire Diaries, we are referring to the canon in a more general sense.

Twilight, True Blood and The Vampire Diaries emerged at roughly the same time and are part of a larger trend in publishing and broadcasting in which vampires are in focus, often featured in the paranormal romance genre.[9] Our interest in these canons results from the highly active fandoms which have formed around them and specifically from the varied output of fan fiction. But there are also a number of textual elements which illustrate both differences and similarities between the canons and which have been of particular importance to our project. First of all, we are interested in the development of the vampire into a humanized figure that elicits sympathy. This development, although variously figured in the canons, signals an increased interest in relatable forms of Otherness but can simultaneously be read as a defanging of the vampire. Of significance is therefore to see how these competing tendencies — relatability and marginalization — are negotiated by fanfic authors. In what ways do fanfic authors create their own versions of Otherness and what does it signify? When the vampire's bite is recuperated, why and how is this done? The texts' participation in the romance genre is our second point of interest since romantic and sexual relationships are central in fan fiction generally. How do fanfic authors comply with or contest heteronormative genre structures and limitations and what role does the specificities of vampire/human interactions play in their stories? Finally, we want to explore fanfic re-allocations of agency and narrative perspective. The main protagonist in all three canons is a human female, in different ways circumscribed by cultural and gendered structures, and in the written texts it is her narrative perspective which is dominant. How do fanfic authors resist or comply with gendered and interspecies inequalities in their own stories? In which ways do altered points of view result in new views of the canon narrators, and how do these shifts enhance the agency of characters not awarded narrative perspectives in the canons? In the analyses chapters of this book, we come back to the argument that canon and fanfic contribute to the same imagined archive. Canon works occasion fanfic in the first place and fanfic, in turn, deposits interpretations and associations into the archive which may influence any new reading of the canons. Similarities and differences between the canons when it comes to Otherness and defangedness, romance and sexuality, narrative and individual agency, are thus very productive when investigating the spin fanfic authors put on these issues by adding alternative vampires and human protagonists to the ever-expanding archives.

Our readings in the coming chapters variously pick up different strands and themes prevalent in the preceding waves of fanfic studies. On the one hand, our analyses show that fan fiction is in many instances still resistive, be this to genre constraints, heteronormativity, or mainstream depictions of good and evil. On the other hand, there are also clear tendencies to participate in the maintenance of hierarchical structures, connected to genre, gender and discourses of normalization, and often, fan fictions intertwine defiance to some elements with adherence to others. Authors are active in some aspects, passive in others, and their written readings illustrate the competing tendencies of hetero- and homogeneity. To designate readings as defiant or subversive further seems to presuppose that there is an overarching, easily determined dominant ideology at work in all texts, which readers and viewers would then either conform to or oppose. The reality is rather that each canon contains a multitude of ideological messages, which may differ between the written and visual media, and that individual members of its audience can react to some but not others and negotiate the former in various ways. To see fan fictions as literary artifacts in their own right and to approach them with the methodological and theoretical tools used in other forms of literary analysis make fanfic author's responses to the complexity and polyphony of contemporary popular texts exceedingly clear. To combine analyses of fan fictions which illustrate a deep fidelity to the canon with those which represent a questioning of the cultural norms expressed through sometimes radical re-workings results, we argue, in a more profound understanding of both the text form and of the vampire trope as it is figured in the stories.

* * *

The first chapter, "Single White Females and Sympathetic Vampires," explores the importance of genre which in the case of the canon texts is different variations on the popular romance. By outlining the basic structure of the romance format, with emphasis on the sub-genre paranormal romance, we give a brief introduction to canon plot lines and central events which will be of particular importance in the ensuing analysis chapters. As the paranormal romance (like all forms of romance) is intensely character driven, we also examine the female protagonists and the main male vampires against the background of genre. We end this chapter by discussing transmediality and seriality, and how these formal specificities have implications for fanfic production. In transmedial texts where the same (or similar) story is told in different media formats, the authority of the originator is diminished, at times to the point that it is difficult to precisely determine who the originator is. This vagueness appears particularly conducive to fanfic production. Fans also evince an interest in the extended middles of serialized texts — parts which explore minor plot developments and where different obstacles have to be overcome. As the serialized narrative often works according to a repetitive structure, it offers fanfic authors possibilities of creating stories which just as well could have been part of the canon, and where little or no background or exposition is necessary.

Chapter two, "Vampiric Prosumption," opens with a presentation of the methodological choices made when working with this book and with how archives, categorizations and paratextual conventions which apply to fan fiction have helped us meet specific methodological challenges. We further discuss the hybrid genres of the fanfic text form, as well as levels of signification in the canons which are then negotiated and variously used in fan fiction. This chapter ends with close readings of three fanfics which in differing ways exhibit close intertextual ties to their respective canon, while simultaneously playing with its "rules." The analyses also forge links with chapter one as we examine instances of resistance to the paranormal romance format.

In the third chapter, "The Archive of New Stories," we analyze fanfics which exemplify the three main alterations: switched narrative perspectives, stories which are set either before or after the canon's story arc, and those which alter the canon's combination of characters, and envision new heterosexual romances. These narrative strategies naturally occur in traditionally published works of appropriative fiction and a section of this chapter is devoted to a contextualization of fan fiction within this longer literary history. We turn here to Abigail Derecho's notion of fan fictions as "archontic [...] texts that [explicitly] build on a previously existing text [and] add to that text's archive" rather than simply imitating it or transgressing its boundaries (65). We show how each analyzed story enlarges the archive with new interpretations and associations, thus illustrating the deeply intertextual process by which the canon affects the fanfic and the fanfic affects the canon.

Chapters four and five are prefaced by an "Interlude" in which we discuss challenges and risks inherent in processes of normalization generally, but with specific emphasis on discourses within queer theory and teratological criticism. These discussions apply to both chapters which follow, concerned with subversions of the canons' norms regarding sexuality and monstrosity, respectively. In "Canon-Transgressive Lemony Goodness," we analyze fan fictions with explicit sexual contents, ranging from a resistance to abstinence (particularly in regards to Twilight), via fanfics which question the canons' heteronorm through depictions of same-sex pairings, to stories which envision the characters' sex with multiple partners or depict the intertwining of pleasure and pain. Our discussions about subversive strategies of various kinds (and to various ends) are combined with considerations of how genre constraints limit authors, particularly noticeable in fanfics which create temporal or imagined spaces in which both hetero- and homosexual encounters play out. The vampire's potentially transgressive sexuality is of special interest in this chapter: binaries such as male or female or categories such as hetero-, bi- or homosexual could theoretically be devoid of meaning. However, the canons' participation in the romance genre and the humanized vampires seem to make these options difficult, and comparisons with other vampire texts, past and contemporary, illustrate the sometimes uncomfortable position between transgression and normativity that the canons occupy.

Comparisons and contrasts with other vampire narratives are central also in the next chapter, "Something Wicked This Way Comes," and the defanged vampire is seen in relation to more menacing instantiations. We analyze fan fictions which deal with metaphysical issues such as the ensouled or soulless state, the boundary between good and evil, and questions about eternal damnation as a potential consequence of the vampire state. As vampires have become more humanized, their metaphysical plights are more applicable to the human state, but increasingly sympathetic vampires also mean a diminished opportunity to investigate what evil means. Fan fiction analyzed in this chapter demonstrates desires to reinforce the human/monster boundary in order to pursue other lines of questioning than the canons. The selected stories reclaim the threat and danger traditionally associated with the vampire, frequently making use of perspectival shifts where the monsters themselves tell the story and ask questions about what it means to be evil or how to find meaning in their unlife. We end this chapter with analyses of fanfics in which the death, destruction, or turning of the female protagonists effectively kill the romance.

In the conclusion, "The Vampire Archived and Re-Fanged," we synthesize findings and discuss what general tendencies we see when it comes to the function the vampire fills in the fan fictions. When literally or metaphorically re-fanging the relatively tamed vampires of the contemporary popular culture canons, and when re-introducing vampiric transgressive sexual identities and practices, fanfic authors draw on instantiations of the trope which in some cases can be located within texts where the vampire is more frightening and more subversive, and which in others build on a general cultural archetype. We also return to the all-pervading interest in the intertextual nature of fan fiction. We are throughout concerned with intertextual relationships between texts rather than looking at canon/fan fiction in terms of influence (exclusively from the former to the latter). In this last chapter we thus revisit the canons and discuss how the analyzed fanfics can produce a new reading of them; how fanfic alterations make us read the canons from new perspectives and how new associations are continuously added to the archives. It is our contention that the added interpretations and the subtly or profoundly altered versions of characters, of agency, of sexuality, of good and evil, make it impossible to read (or re-read) the canons in the same way as before.

1. Single White Females and Sympathetic Vampires: The Canons

Elena Gilbert is powerless against the attraction to Stefan Salvatore, Bella Swan is fated to be with Edward Cullen, and Sookie Stackhouse has waited for a vampire to appear in her personal life for quite some time when Bill Compton enters Merlotte's bar. In the background lurk other suitors, Damon Salvatore, Jacob Black, and Eric Northman, with all that entails of possible jealousies, and once the central couples have confirmed their attachment to each other, members and norms of the depicted societies put spokes in the romantic wheels. All three canons, that is, comply with narrative structures of the romance. This chapter opens with discussions about how these structures are figured, with variations, in the canons, but also how elements in each illustrate points of resistance to the genre's limitations. To give a comprehensive overview of all the twists and turns in the canons' complex plots is impossible (especially where the unfinished TV series *True Blood* and *The Vampire Diaries* are concerned), and our ability to examine in detail the plethora of characters and themes is limited.[1] Still, it is our hope that the genre discussions together with our analyses of the female protagonists and their vampiric love interests will give the reader unfamiliar with the canons enough of a background to the fanfic analyses in the following chapters: the bulk of this book. At the end of this chapter, we return to the domain of fan fiction as we explain which formal features of the canons are particularly prone to sparking fan engagement and creation.

Paranormal Romance

Any discussion about genre is fraught with difficulty since genres change over time or depending on context, and since subgenres have their own structures and conventions. Add to this that many contemporary texts rather than being "monogamous" rather are "promiscuous," as Ken Gelder notes, "invoking an often arbitrary range of affiliations" ("Our Vampires" 29). The selected canons have been labeled fantasy (The Vampire Diaries in particular, see Overstreet), Southern Gothic (True Blood, see Holmgren Troy and Cherry), and as a *Bildungsroman* (especially Twilight, see Taylor). Elements in each given work have further affinities with yet other genres, such as horror and mystery.[2] In discussions about contemporary Gothic texts which similarly display a mix-and-match generic adherence, Cathrine Spooner argues for an understanding based on Jacques Derrida's notion of genre participation rather than belonging. "To participate does not entail complete identification; it merely suggests a relationship with that genre" (26). Promiscuous, then, the closest relationship our canons have is to the genre of romance, and, given the vampire element, more specifically to paranormal romance.

As several critics have noted, the genre as well as readers of romance novels have been derided. The works are seen as trashy, shallow and intensely formulaic and their readers are "criticized, marginalized, and mocked" (Lee 52, see also Regis xi–xiii). At the same time, works in the genre are continuously commercially successful, and theorists such as Janice Radway (*Reading the Romance* 1984) and Tania Modleski (*Loving with a Vengeance* 1982) have shown that readers rather than simply accepting formulaic storytelling can use it as a site of contestation and in some cases emancipation from patriarchal structures. There is further a considerable plasticity within the romance format which in some cases enables a needed revitalization. In discussions about romance and the Gothic, Fred Botting, for example, argues that both genres (or rather a genre and a subgenre) are convention bound and cliché ridden. Romance has been "[p]ushed to the limit of meaninglessness" and therefore aligns with figures and themes from other genres and modes to set up boundaries and create meaning: "romance ... provides a projective screen while gothic furnishes the dark stain around which meaning and affects cluster and collapse" (7, 8).

Migration and generic promiscuity are thus seen as necessities, but Botting also regards the conflation as a loss when romanced Gothic "clean[s] up its darker counterpart, sanitising its depravations" (1). The defanged vampire, to which we will turn shortly, is certainly an effect of a sanitizing project, as is the canons' mainly heteronormative message, but it is perhaps symptomatic that such a regretful statement comes from a Gothic scholar like Botting; it is "his" genre which romance migrates into and makes promiscuous, adding little to the Gothic in the process. The opposite move, whereby romance does not migrate but rather incorporates themes, structure and characters however results in a plethora of subsidiary forms. Among these is the quickly growing subgenre of paranormal romance which Linda J. Lee describes as "a catchall category that includes diverse topics such as time travel, futuristic settings, magic, shape-shifters, supernatural creatures like werewolves and vampires, or other-world settings" (53). These topics and tropes move from their participation in other genres transforming both the romance genre and the conventions attached to, in our case, vampires.

Pamela Regis identifies eight core elements of the traditional mass-market romance which "can appear in any order" but which are nevertheless "essential" (30). A brief outline of canon events and characterizations shows that all are featured in the canons, but also illustrates the canons' heterogeneity. Early in every romance novel, Regis claims, "the society ... is defined" in ways which underscore that it is "in some ways flawed [and] oppresses the heroine and the hero" (31). This formulation suggests rules and norms which will in some way constrict the lovers or circumscribe the romance and is a clear pattern in the canons. The first point we need to make, however, is of a somewhat more prosaic nature and connected to the paranormal element of our canons: we are nowhere concerned with future or alien settings. While Mystic Falls and Fell's Church in the visual and written instantiations of The Vampire Diaries, as well as Bon Temps in True Blood, are fictional constructs, they are figured in relation to other, actual geographical locations, such as Atlanta, Raleigh and New Orleans. In Twilight, protagonists move between Forks and Phoenix in the U.S., and Volterra, Italy. The main canon settings in these recognizable locations — Virginia, Louisiana, and Washington — entail regional cultural differences which at times, and particularly in True Blood, have implications for both plot and characterizations. Temporal markers of different kinds, such as references to Hurricane Katrina in True Blood and a myriad of popular culture quips in the TV series *The Vampire Diaries*, further establish that the settings are contemporary and in this way, a fantastic element is inserted into otherwise realistically depicted fictional worlds. These aspects align the canons with past and contemporary vampire narratives in which the insertion of a paranormal element in a recognizable setting enables the vampire trope to be used in commentary on social and cultural issues.

In Twilight and The Vampire Diaries the paranormal element needs to remain hidden from society at large and its concealment entails particular problems to be negotiated by Bella and Elena in their interaction with other humans. In Twilight, the ruling coven of the Italian Volturi serves as an insurance against vampire detection and the Cullen family, to which Edward belongs, is forced to periodically relocate since their unaltered exteriors otherwise would attract attention. Although Bella is welcomed in the Cullen family, vampires generally regard relationships with humans as unnatural and dangerous. The Cullens, in turn, are sufficiently different from other inhabitants of Forks to make human characters suspicious of liaisons. To Bella and Edward, once committed to each other, both human and vampire societies are thus flawed in that they either cannot embrace or know of their relationship. The situation is similar in The Vampire Diaries where the secret nature of vampires threatens to at all times be exposed, thus oppressing or dissuading intimate human/vampire contact. Vampires as a new minority group in True Blood produces a quite different initial definition of society; it is a world in which humans are getting used to a paranormal presence. This does not mean that all attitudes are accepting, rather that new forms of racism (from both ends) are coming to the fore, with all that entails of disparaging attitudes to "mixed" relationships. The central romances are in this way pitted against societies which either do not recognize or do not fully accept the protagonists' emotions, and their journeys towards happiness represent ways in which societal attitudes are either conquered or altered.

The three core elements of popular romance, "the *meeting* between the heroine and hero; an account of their *attraction* for each other [and] the *barrier* between them," can profitably be discussed together (Regis 14). First, it should be noted that the canon texts differ from traditional romances in that the initial meeting displays "[n]one of the complex negotiations, ambiguities, or misunderstandings of non-paranormal human relationships" (Nakagawa n. pag.). While profound problems arise from the paranormal element, more specifically the female protagonists' struggle to accept that their loved ones are vampires, it seems to do away with the need for traditional types of initial obstacles and the canon narratives move swiftly into accounts of attraction. However, the first meeting between the protagonists often includes a foreshadowing "of the conflict to come" and the barrier between the protagonists which is crucial to the romance (Regis 31). The human/vampire meeting occurs early in all three canons but differences in how these meetings are described, as well as how barriers are depicted, illustrate the different employment of the romance structure in the three canons.

In Twilight, Bella is in a vulnerable position as the new girl at school, and first admires the "devastatingly, inhumanly beautiful" Cullens from a distance (Meyer, *Twilight* 17). Gleaning information from her friends, it is clear that the Cullens are aloof, that Edward does not date, and she is acutely aware of the hostility he directs at her in biology class. Edward's attitude can be read as a sign of the "preliminary dislike" Chiho Nakagawa claims is missing in paranormal romances (n. pag.), but it is significant that Bella's attraction to him is not lessened. The reader is later also informed that Edward's hostility results, precisely, from attraction, specifically the overpowering allure of Bella's scent. Bella, in turn, does not admit to her feelings until Internet research has convinced her of Edward's true nature, but they are nevertheless emphatically stated: "About three things I was absolutely positive. First, Edward was a vampire. Second, there was a part of him ... that thirsted for my blood. And third, I was unconditionally and irrevocably in love with him" (Meyer, *Twilight* 170–71). The revelation of his true nature, which is arguably the central barrier between them, does not work as a romantic deterrent, but enhances Bella's attraction to Edward. External threats acquire far more significance. Rogue vampires target Bella in a vengeance driven plot development and the Volturi are out to put a stop to the romance as it threatens the vampire secret. With a few exceptions, the couple stays in close physical proximity to each other through these events and, individually or together, overcome the obstacles put in their path.

Like Bella, Elena is a high school student, but considerably more self-assured. In fact, the portrayal of her in Smith's novels indicates that she is a small-town bully, convinced and assured of her own attraction. Although Stefan is described as extraordinarily attractive, he becomes an object of Elena's desire because he initially ignores her. Her reputation and self-image are threatened and she thinks: "She'd have him, even if it killed her. If it killed both of them, she'd have him" (Smith, *The Awakening* 22). Elena is well aware that there is a danger about Stefan, but the revelation that he is a vampire does not temper her feelings. Foregrounded is rather a typical romance element: a sense that she can be his salvation since "her gentleness was stronger than all his inhuman strength" (Smith, *The Awakening* 186). Stefan, in turn, is immediately drawn to Elena but hesitates since she is uncomfortably similar to Katherine, the vampire who once turned him. Like Edward, Stefan harbors a fear of hurting his loved one and tells Elena: "The passion is stronger than you can imagine. Don't you understand yet what I am, what I can do?" (Smith, *The Awakening* 184). Obstacles in the way of consummated love in both canons are thus on the one hand connected to the difference in vampire/human nature, on the other to the fact that both Edward and Stefan try to resist the attraction they feel towards the human protagonists. In Smith's novel series, various supernatural creatures and excursions to different realms periodically estrange the couple, but the only specifically romantic impasse is Stefan's brother Damon's interest in Elena (and hers in him). In the TV series, the main threat to the core romance likewise comes in the shape of Damon, but also in changes in Stefan's character which at times disqualify him as romantic hero.

Given the different society portrayed in True Blood, the meeting between the telepathic waitress Sookie and the gentlemanly vampire Bill plays out rather differently. The first sentence in *Dead Until Dark* reads: "I'd been waiting for *the* vampire for years when he walked into the bar" (Harris 1, our italics). Although Bill is portrayed as attractive on an individual level, the sentence draws attention to Sookie's general anticipation, and her preformed notion that vampires are enticing also for what they are. The first encounter revolves around adventure rather than romance but there is no doubt about Sookie's attraction to Bill: "his lips [are] lovely," his voice "cool and clear," the meeting with him is "rare, a prize" (Harris, *Dead Until Dark* 2, 3, 13). Bill, like Edward and Stefan in the other canons, tries to instill a certain sense of fear in Sookie: "Vampires often turn on those who trust them. We don't have human values, you know" (Harris, *Dead Until Dark* 12). However, he does not attempt to enforce a distance between them; it is rather deceit and lies that bring an end to their affair. While monogamy within relationships is important in True Blood, the serial structure shifts romantic attachments and Sookie's next vampire lover is Eric. New hurdles are to be passed, some of them specific to the relationship dynamics, some connected to the depicted society in which distrust and prejudiced ideas about human/vampire relationships guide many characters' reactions.

What Regis calls "the point of ritual death," which is the point of the story at which a union between the hero and the heroine seems impossible, is not always only ritual in our canons (14).[3] In fact, both Elena and Bella actually die but both are brought back to life (or un-life). In a more figurative sense, there are several ritual deaths — points at which the central couples are so far divided by internal strife or external events that no reconciliation seems possible. An example in Twilight is when the Cullens leave Forks in *New Moon* when Edward's brother Jasper's reaction to a paper cut and Bella's blood has re-actualized the danger the vampire presence poses and necessitates distance. Although Edward leaves for Bella's protection, his feigned disinterest in her has its desired effect and the two lovers are alienated for a long time. In Smith's novels, Elena and Stefan are repeatedly estranged, either physically as when Stefan is imprisoned in a well and presumed dead in *The Struggle*, or emotionally, as when Elena returns as a vampire in *The Fury* and believes herself to be in love with Damon instead. In the TV series, there are likewise numerous ritual deaths, for example when Stefan at the end of the second season is turned into a Ripper, the most evil form of a vampire. Any hope of reconciliation at this point seems impossible. In True Blood, as some of Sookie's relationships effectively end, we are faced with more literal versions of the ritual death (albeit not as literal as in the other two canons). Within each relationship, however, there are periods of estrangement, as when it is revealed that Bill's interest in Sookie originally has to do with business rather than pleasure, and as when Eric, memory restored after a bout of amnesia, has no recollection of any intimacy with Sookie. While there are still instances of estrangement reminiscent of the impossibility of the desired resolution in traditional romances, these few examples illustrate that paranormal romances may transform *ritual* death into actual, since characters can die and transform into another existence. The transformation in turn diminishes the power of death to divide the lovers. Further, different realms and supernatural occurrences entail a continuous threat to estrange the couple and to effectively kill the romance.

But threats are to be averted to supply a happy end and the route to it, in Regis' discussion, follows the triadic structure of recognition, declaration of love and (symbolic) betrothal. Depending on when the declaration is made, Regis argues, we are either concerned with "a love-at-first-sight situation" or a narrative in which the protagonists progressively realize and surmount the barrier dividing them (34). The latter scenario often entails an enhanced agency on the part of the female protagonist as she has been through a series of tests (not always in the company of the male) and emerged on the other side as, ideally, more mature and confident. Lee maintains that "[r]omance novels with the 'love at first sight' motif problematize this by suggesting that the heroine is always already loved by the hero, and paranormal romances ... often exacerbate this issue with their common use of destined romantic partners" (58). As is evident from our discussions about the first meetings between the protagonists, the canon texts can to varying degrees be characterized as stories about love at first sight, thus negating the immediate need for or promise of agency. However, feelings are not necessarily verbalized at this stage. At some point, the protagonists declare their feelings for each other, but in contrast to traditional romances, where the barrier has been overcome at the point of the declaration, these verbalizations and realizations do not automatically mean that things progress smoothly thereafter. Instead, the couple is faced with additional barriers in the form of internal or external attitudes to the vampire/human relationships as well as very literal, paranormal threats.

It is also the case that the female protagonists' journey towards self-discovery is foregrounded in the narratives, and the paranormal romance enables other forms of enhanced agency. This is particularly clear in texts such as the canons where the vampire is used to reflect sociocultural issues. The protagonists' reaction to the vampire element — the vampire's potential marginalization — may in this way go hand in hand with the female protagonists' own development. Ananya Mukherjea argues that the vampire state itself can facilitate this process. With particular emphasis on *Twilight* but broadening the scope to the paranormal romance as such, she notes that since "Edward is already frozen in his development [Meyer's novels are] primarily driven by Bella's personal growth and human choices" (6). We will shortly come back to Twilight's limitation of agency, but here note that the situation is similar in the other canons; although riddled with existential queries and relationship problems, Bill's and Stefan's personalities are formed and relatively stable, enabling a stronger focus on the developments of Sookie and Elena.

General developments in the romance genre, attesting to changes in cultural structures and norms, in the characterization of the protagonists, and in the altered desires and foci of contemporary readers, mean that what was once a literal betrothal, the traditional epitome of the happy end, does not necessarily mean marriage but can be figured in the form of a sense of self-recognition on the part of the female protagonist. In Twilight, which has been criticized for Bella's lack of development and agency, we tellingly find a literal betrothal — a wedding Bella has protested against — at the beginning of *Breaking Dawn*, the last installment of the Twilight series. The final point of Bella's internal journey is thus rendered in conservative ways even, as Anthea Taylor argues, as Edward "coerces Bella into an exogamous marriage in an effort to exert control ... over her very self (precarious though it is)" (42). In lieu of a fully formed and stable identity, a literal betrothal creates Bella's sense of self. In True Blood, where human/vampire marriages have only recently been legalized, Sookie is about to accept Bill's proposal, when he suddenly and mysteriously disappears. In the serialized structure of Harris' novels, a literal betrothal is not desired at this point, and even when Sookie later in the series is married to Eric, it is a union which comes about as a result of trickery and does not last. Of greater importance are the symbolic betrothals in True Blood and likewise in The Vampire Diaries which most often coincide with the end of a novel in a series or with a television season. At each such point, the female protagonist has learned something about her desires and needs, and rather than literalized as weddings or engagements, these realizations constitute a temporary happy end, or a cliffhanger for the next installment.

Correlating the canon texts with the core elements identified by Regis establishes that although genres continue to be promiscuous, flirting with other genre structures and elements, Twilight, The Vampire Diaries and True Blood conform to the basic romance structure. At the same time, there are particularities inherent in the paranormal subgenre which cause divergences. In her examination of science fiction romances, which bear only slight differences from paranormal romances, Lynne Pearce argues that they offer "a new romantic love modality that is generated and, indeed, *sustained* by the lovers' exclusion from/opposition to ... affiliative norms," and they remain sources for exploring the "lingering fascination with the *obstacles* that have traditionally precipitated romantic love" (186). Loving a vampire, in other words, cannot be completely equated with loving a human hero and the Otherness — of the vampire but also of the couple — illustrates not only uniqueness and apartness, but a specific set of barriers to surmount. While the vampire's threat is downplayed in the paranormal romances, it is never completely done away with; it exists, rather, as a continuous source of attraction. And while the vampire is humanized, he is still not completely subsumed under the norms and rules that govern human existence. Further, the vampire hero is automatically exceptional, not only in the less attractive aspect of being undead but in that he is "a glamorous outsider" who holds promises of literally changing lives (Williamson 1). Although transformation is a process which the female protagonists resist (with the exception of Bella), it still remains a tentative promise and the vampire hero has the ability to ensure that love will be everlasting. It is also suggested, most clearly in Twilight, that everlasting love does not mean tempered feelings or boredom. The Cullen couples, Esme and Carlisle, Emmett and Rosalie, Alice and Jasper, have been together several decades when the narrative begins, but they are still passionately in love. In *Breaking Dawn*, Edward explains to Bella that they have "rarely changing temperaments" (Meyer 85). Bella's very human parents, on the other hand, have tired of each other a long time ago. The image relayed is thus that even love is paranormally strong, representing a difference from mundane and easily exhausted human feelings, and what more is there to wish for? In the other canons as well, a permanence of emotions is suggested which should arguably be negated by the vampires' long lives, but which is instead represented as the promise they hold.

The Single White Females

While there are several similarities between the single white female protagonists in the canons, there are differences on the formal level which govern what access we have to their individual developments. The omniscient narrative perspective in Smith's novels is interspersed with first-person sections in the form of diary entries by Elena, but she is periodically removed from events (a lengthy removal takes place in *The Reunion*, where she is held captive in the Other world) and other characters, predominantly her friend Bonnie, are used as focalizers or narrators instead. In the novels by Meyer and Harris, a first-person perspective is consistently employed, the only exception being the second part of *Breaking Dawn* which is narrated from Jacob's point of view. Despite this difference, the focal point in all three canons is the protagonists' journey towards self-discovery, precipitated by the meeting with the vampire, with all that entails of a sustained exploration of their emotions, memories and reactions. In discussions about another genre, crime fiction, Gelder argues that the creation of a central "selling" character is crucial to make the audience invested in the story and interested in its outcome. Similar to romance novels, serialized crime fiction is published in stiff competition, and consequently "invests a great deal in the character of the investigator [; the genre] turns on the details, and the idiosyncrasies, of an investigator's personality, history, circumstances" (Gelder, *Popular* 63). The first chapters of the first novel installments make this investment, and the focalization employed in the visual format (often accompanied by voice overs) similarly provides a quick path into the psyches of the protagonists.

What all three female protagonists have in common is their difference from other humans — a very specific idiosyncrasy which attracts attention from the main vampires. In the midst of the clamor of human minds in a busy high school, Stefan notices one that stands "out from the others, [a] personality [which is] powerful" and once he sets eyes on Elena, he notices an "uncanny" likeness with Katherine (Smith, *The Awakening* 18–19). In the TV series, Elena's status as a doppelgänger is emphasized, and both Salvatore brothers are drawn to her because of their past associations with Katherine. Her blood is further a potent ingredient in various vampire-related spells and transformations. Bella's blood is similarly important, not least to Edward who is enchanted by its scent, and she is set apart from other humans because he cannot access her mind. We find the opposite situation in True Blood, where Sookie is the mind reader but closed off from Bill's thoughts, and her clearly pronounced feeling of marginalization is later emphasized by the fact that she is revealed to be part fey. This aspect of her nature in turn renders her blood delicious to vampires. Exceptional minds and exceptional blood: these idiosyncrasies create very particular protagonists and their sense of being marginal to the human world enables them to address questions that can pique readers' and viewers' interest.

When seventeen-year-old Bella moves to the small town of Forks on the American Pacific coast she worries about being the new kid in class, and getting along with her father with whom she has not spent much time. She describes herself in terms of negations, she is not but "*should* be tan, sporty, blond," she is "ivory-skinned ... despite the constant sunshine" in Phoenix from where she has relocated, and has "no color" in the rainy Washington setting (Meyer, *Twilight* 9). This description is aligned with contemporary developments in the romance genre in which female protagonists are "often described as not conventionally beautiful" (Zidle 26). And also similar to this development, Bella's self-disparagement is contradicted by the fact that she does make friends, and that the boys at school are attracted to her: there is a sense of self-deprecation which the reader but not the protagonist can see through. Her self-perception is sustained however, and Bella's insecurity follows her into the relationship with Edward. Even as they discuss marriage, Bella doubts her desirability, characterizing herself as "awkward, self-conscious, and inept" (Meyer, *Eclipse* 394). All the things she is not and the negativity stressed are further equated with her general sense of marginalization: "It wasn't just physically that I'd never fit in" (Meyer, *Twilight* 9). Bella's difference is not contradicted in the same manner as her perception of her looks, but on the contrary continues to be important when the main narrative strand — the romance with Edward — starts to unravel. Edward attempts to maintain a both emotional and physical distance from humans in general and Bella in particular, but her difference from others singles her out and, despite her protestations to the contrary, makes her exceptionally desirable.

As previously noted, Bella is the only one of the canons' human protagonists who does not remain formally single. In *Breaking Dawn*, Bella is not only married and integrated into the Cullen family, but also, and somewhat unexpectedly, considering that vampires are not supposed to be able to procreate, starts a new generation in the form of her daughter Renesmee. The closed format of Twilight in part naturalizes the formalized union, but it is not achieved without protests from Bella. In fact, marriage is figured as a price Bella has to pay to be transformed into a vampire and finally become intimate with Edward. Chastity before marriage and "carnal desire [as] an obstacle that must be overcome," gesture, Lydia Kokkola argues, to the intended young adult Twilight audience, and seemingly conflate genre elements: "although the presence of an obstacle belongs firmly within the adult romance tradition, the nature of the obstacle derives from the tradition of writing for adolescents" (169). It does not fall on Bella to enforce a physical distance, rather, it is Edward who controls the level of intimacy. "Do you get the feeling that everything is backward?" he asks Bella, once they have become engaged, and he has successfully fended off her attempts at seduction, promising to turn her only after the wedding. "Traditionally, shouldn't you be arguing my side, and I yours?" (Meyer, *Eclipse* 400). These representations run contrary to stereotypical cultural notions making young girls and women responsible for setting sexual limits, but they have several counterparts in paranormal romances. Mukherjea argues that it is, precisely, "the vampire boyfriend who enforces restraint ... desiring the woman but also policing that desire" thereby conflating the traditional roles of lover and father (11).

Bella's fervent desire to be turned sets her apart from Elena and Sookie and can be read as a certain form of agency. However, turning simultaneously features into Twilight's general uneven allocation of agency. Taylor characterizes the central relationship in Twilight as "masochistic" and connects Bella's quest for transformation through death to the sustained image she paints of herself as insecure and undesirable (34). Further Taylor argues that the "self-loathing narrative voice serves an important purpose: it works to establish a vulnerable subject for whom a masochistic relationship — and its end point: (un)death — is not only considered viable but desirable" and that the turning itself invests Bella with "certain forms of capital such as an age-defying feminine body and a physical strength that eludes her in life" (35, 32). In this view, Bella's transformation into a vampire, which to boot is enacted as a measure to save her life rather than being a direct consequence of her wishes, is what enables her to transcend her own limitations. On her own, and as a human, she cannot.

Sookie's paranormal mind reading ability renders her unusual at the outset and aligns her with other minority groups. The sense of isolation and marginalization which in Twilight is constructed from the inside, through Bella's sense of self, is in True Blood in place when the narrative opens and has had very real consequences. Other characters fear Sookie and she has kept a distance, particularly to men, since her telepathy provides her with unwelcome glimpses of her partner's thoughts. The resultant sense of insecurity does not translate to a disparagement of her own attractiveness, on the contrary she states, "I am [pretty]. I'm blond and blue-eyed and twenty-five, and my legs are strong and my bosom is substantial, and I have a waspy waistline" (Harris, *Dead Until Dark* 1). The description reads as somewhat mocking, especially given Sookie's penchant for romance novels, but she knows what is considered traditionally beautiful and has no qualms about describing herself as such. Throughout the narrative, Sookie develops into a more confident woman and progressively starts seeing her telepathic skill (which she initially terms her "disability," Harris, *Dead Until Dark* 2) as a gift. Her relationship with Bill, another outsider in the community, and the use she can put her skill to, are instrumental in this process.

Despite what Sookie gains from the romance with Bill, the vampire's function in True Blood is not to represent manifest destiny. Bill and Sookie are not fated to be together forever. In fact, his reasons for approaching Sookie in the first place originate from a business arrangement, and although she forgives him in time, the revelation of his deceit ends their relationship. In Harris' novels, he is superseded by Eric and the weres Alcide and Quinn, and the string of lovers expands Sookie's knowledge and enables her to develop different relationship skills. What emerges from the initial romance, Nakagawa argues, is Sookie's view of the vampire as other than a "safe hero [and t]his realization is crucial to her acquiring a more mature perception of both sexuality and self, one appropriate to an adult woman negotiating the risks of contemporary romance" (n. pag.). In fact, "Sookie moves on to romances where the risk is more clearly visible," succinctly illustrated by Eric who is figured in more traditional ways as flawed, Other, "emotionally inaccessible [and] thus more exotic" (Nakagawa n. pag.). Sookie does not seek safety for safety's sake, rather she learns what excites her, comforts her, and what makes her develop. The intended audience of True Blood arguably requires this perception of adult sexuality and adult, often self-serving, choices.

The insecurity and marginalization prominent in the cases of Bella and Sookie is in Elena's case replaced with confidence, but a precarious one as popularity also needs to be maintained. The narrative perspective in Smith's novels means that Elena is seen from an omniscient point of view and described as "cool and blonde and slender, the fashion trendsetter, the high school senior, the girl every boy wanted and every girl wanted to be" (Smith, *The Awakening* 3). In the remediation process, Elena is the character most altered on a superficial level, but the character's popularity in the TV series is likewise unquestioned. It is rather the development of the female protagonist which follows divergent paths in the two media forms. In the novels, Elena goes through transformations into a vampire and into an angelic being, which both provide her with different sets of abilities and strengths, but she is returned to a human state after each change. Her knowledge of the supernatural world continuously grows as new threats are directed both at her and the community of Fell's Church, in particular her friends Matt, Bonnie and Meredith. However, the last of Smith's novels ends with a status quo of sorts, in which the human community outside the close-knit group has lost all memory of past events. The continuous struggle for Elena's love and affection between Stefan and Damon is also laid to rest as Damon is presumed dead, and with no one suspecting Stefan of being a vampire, the central romance no longer needs to be hidden. While Elena is at this point returned to a human state, she can communicate telepathically with Stefan which strengthens their bond and convinces Elena that she has made the right choices and reached a stage which she is comfortable with. Her soul is "intertwine[d]" with Stefan's, "she was *home*" and "had her bearings now" (Smith, *Midnight* 455, 452, 456).

In the ongoing TV series, Elena's knowledge of the paranormal world is also expanded, but threats are limited to vampires and werewolves, and the fantasy aspects in terms of different realms and dimensions are downplayed.

Stefan and Damon's oscillation between "good" and "bad" vampire is more pronounced, and Elena's shifting emotions play a more central part. Elena's journey towards self-discovery (while not completed) is closely connected to a sense of loneliness, and her romantic attachment to the brothers play a decisive part in this. "If I choose one of you, I lose the other. And I've lost so many people, I can't bear the thought of losing you," she tells them (*The Vampire Diaries*, 3: 21 "Before Sunset"). The realization that choice comes at a price is bound up with Elena's own complicated background and with the fact that one by one her (extended) family members have fallen away. She is the adopted daughter of a vampire, the man she has seen as her uncle is in fact her father, she has lost her guardians because of various vampire-related events and her friends Matt, Bonnie, and Caroline have one by one been revealed to have paranormal powers. The last episode of the third season (the end point for our discussions) sees a dead Elena return to un-life due to a previous ingestion of vampire blood, and involuntarily joining the vampire community.

The particularities of each female protagonist are offset by how they are united by a number of narrative elements emphasizing vulnerability, the first of which is connected to the process by which vampiric presence is established. Stories with fantastic elements entail a "conceptual breakthrough [which] usually involves the challenging and then the overthrowing of an established paradigm, offering in its place an often radically new way of thinking" (Landon 32–33). In Meyer's and Smith's novels it is an ontological shift *within* the narrator's world which is experienced and Bella and Elena are faced with a truth which renders them vulnerable. Unable to communicate their knowledge to anyone but the reader, they are consistently in danger of being perceived as mad by the human surroundings. Sookie, who lives in a society where the ontological shift has already taken place, is still privy to exclusive knowledge (from her vampire acquaintances but also from her telepathic ability), which likewise renders her vulnerable. Instead of going through a process by which "the readers or viewers come to understand the vampire's predicament (and therefore innocence), even if the world at large does not" together with "[t]he reluctant vampire," the canons' audiences reach a stage of recognition and understanding along with the narrator or focalizer (Williamson 44, 43). The expanded knowledge unites the reader with the protagonist against "the world at large" and may be a strongly contributing reason for the popularity of the canons; these promise an inside, privileged view and a space for growth which is not contingent on the outside world and its authorities.

The female protagonists' vulnerability comes to the fore also in connection with familial configurations, or lack thereof. With focus on *Buffy* and

Meyer's novels and on patriarchal structures in both human and vampire communities, Kirsten Stevens argues that there are "dangers which lurk within the domestic spaces" and that "dysfunction and corruption [are] inherent in conservative constructions of family" (§ 10). The nuclear family, once thought to offer protection, is fractured in all three canons and its destruction seems to be a prerequisite for the female protagonists' encounters and relationships with vampires who come to stand in for the protection the family originally provided. Bella's case is seemingly the most problematic. Her parents are divorced and neither of them monitors her actions. On one level, their lack of control makes it easier for her to keep secret her knowledge of vampire presence but, aside from Jacob, she has no one to unburden herself to. Her fate, to a greater degree than Sookie's or Elena's, becomes bound up with the progression of her romantic relationship. Elena has lost her parents in a car accident, and her guardian is seldom restrictive and authoritative, which makes for a relative freedom when battling the paranormal forces which intrude and disrupt.[4] Her friends, however, come to represent a surrogate family, with knowledge of vampires and other paranormal occurrences, much like the Scooby Gang in *Buffy*. Sookie is slightly older than these teens, but her vulnerability comes to the fore when her grandmother early on is murdered and she is left to her brother's erratic attempts at protection. But Sookie lives in a world where vampire presence is no longer a secret, and she forms close bonds with some vampires as well as with other humans. Katarina Rein argues that "*True Blood* depicts neither a crisis of family nor ... individuals who are emotionally broken up or morally depraved due to their difficult familial situations" but rather "elective affinities" in both human and vampire communities (n. pag.). The blood ties established between sire and sired in True Blood, as well as the power of blood to, in the end, determine what group a character belongs to, complicate Rein's notion, but (with a few exceptions), vampires choose who they turn, and humans establish nurturing relations with friends and co-workers, be they supernatural or not.

Questions of vulnerability are indeed accentuated in all three canons, but the teenaged female protagonists in Twilight and The Vampire Diaries underscore this even further. In this, they are somewhat set apart from general developments in contemporary romances, where the heroine is no longer depicted as dependent on the progression of the love relationship and its happy end to acquire freedom and an identity on her own. That is, although the pursuit of romantic love is still central, contemporary romance novels "present portraits of women in command of their lives" (Regis 111). Elena and Bella are not controlling their own lives to quite this extent because of their age and concomitant familial and financial situations. Sookie has a more firm command of her life, but still worries about issues connected to inexperience and there are several references to her lack of financial means. This particular kind of inequality would of course not carry the same implications, had the male protagonists been human and of the same age as Bella, Elena and Sookie, but here we come to a crux inherent in the kinds of canons we are concerned with: the incompatibility stemming from different levels of experience when centuries-old vampires meet teenagers or a woman in her early twenties. A suspension of disbelief is required in this regard, Mukherjea argues: audiences "must accept [the vampire's] appearance of youth as just as valid as [his] actual age; otherwise, his relationship with a young woman loses its romance in becoming perverse" (7). It is not only age difference which presents a problem, but also the fact that the vampires' both lived and undead experience means that they are often well-educated and wealthy. These incompatibilities place the female protagonists in a disadvantaged position already at the outset, which is then coupled with their human frailty and mortality. The paranormal element, therefore, makes it impossible to completely square Bella, Elena and Sookie with general developments of romance heroines.

However, there are other forms of equality which resound with contemporary developments. Among the ideological changes that can be seen in romantic fictions of the late twentieth century, Dawn Heinecken notes that "[r]elationships are no longer based on sexuality and male dominance but on mutuality and equality" (165). The given imbalance between predator and potential victim in our canons is to an extent corrected by the female protagonists' relative equality within the love relationships, enabled in part by the change in the male hero from the emotionally unavailable alpha male to the "Good Provider [...] a source of emotional stability" (Marks 12). While both Edward and Stefan initially resist an intimate relationship, they assure Bella and Elena of their (literally undying) love, and while Sookie and Bill (and later Sookie and Eric) have to overcome obstacles, there is a mutual love often expressed between them. Regis maintains that a crucial change in contemporary romances is that the "courtships ... focus much more on the emotional elements of the ... relationship" (111). The development of a mutual love is central in the canons, rather than what benefits and resolutions the courtship can be expected to produce. The female protagonists and the vampires alike are forthcoming with their emotions and all canon texts, both written and visual, devote substantial time to dialogues in which the characters express their feelings, or to inner reflections on the state of the central relationships.

As in all texts which participate in forms of the romance, the position and agency of the female protagonist is closely related to the function of the hero, the vampire in our case, and vice versa. In an analysis of the altered status of the vampire in Francis Ford Coppola's 1992 film *Bram Stoker's Dracula*, Erik Marshall argues that a crucial part of the vampire's transformation from representing cultural Otherness and threat to romance is affected by how the female characters have been altered in the film version. When Lucy Westenra is attacked by Dracula, Marshall argues, "the endeavor seems nearly consensual" and in the growing relationship with the vampire, Mina Harker seems "a willing participant" rather than a passive victim (295). Instead of being represented as a sexually threatening Other, Dracula becomes approachable though the female characters' increased sexual freedom and agency. Elena, Bella and Sookie continue this development of lessening the emotional and cultural distance between what has traditionally been rendered as hunter and prey. To varying extents, the female protagonists initiate the romantic and sexual relationships and victimization takes on other expressions, removed from its nineteenth-century counterparts.

The Sympathetic Vampires Next Door

If Coppola can be said to powerfully have influenced the contemporary stress on eternal, fated romance and on the depiction of the main vampire as impossible to resist, then Anne Rice's depictions of Louis and Lestat, predominantly in *Interview with the Vampire* (1976) and *The Vampire Lestat* (1985) are the most influential contemporary predecessors for the sympathetic vampire, in turn harkening back to John Polidori's Ruthven in *The Vampyre* (1819) and Lord Byron's Darvell in "A Fragment of a Novel" (1819). Louis' and Lestat's view of themselves as tormented and conflicted makes them both relatable and humanly complex, and the canon vampires similarly share a preoccupation with human life, figured both as memories of who they used to be pre-turning and a respect for human ethics. In the case of Bill, Stefan and Edward, this respect stems not only from the view they hold of themselves as monsters, but from the uncontrollable circumstances surrounding their own transition. Bill falls victim to what can be construed as rape, Edward is made a vampire as a measure to save his life, and Stefan (as well as Damon) is turned as part of a complicated power game controlled by Katherine. Involuntary transformation processes are thus not what they want to perpetuate and all three initially see attacks on humans as unjustifiable. Their own humanity is still close and others' is fiercely protected.

Musings on metaphysical issues and a struggle to live well make the vampires easy to relate to and in many ways they are portrayed as ideal. They have abilities and moral perspectives that are desirable and inspiring and they are depicted as outsiders of a very glamorous kind; as *"slightly* foreign, *slightly* aristocratic"* they are "comfortably Americanized" while still maintaining crucial differences from humans (Nakagawa n. pag.) Their marginalization on both individual and general levels may constitute a source of both fear and attraction not only for the human protagonists but for audiences who recognize more symbolic forms and effects of being an outsider in a given context. But the idealization of the vampire may also present challenges to canon creators, and play into the previously discussed difference between vampires and their human love interests. The inherent power imbalance needs to be negotiated, especially considering that a mutually satisfying relationship is the goal of the romance. The female protagonists' own idiosyncrasies constitute a first step in the leveling out of differences, the second comes in the form of the vampires' very human flaws. Despite their extensive experience, and despite the fact that Bill, Stefan and Edward are clearly different from other men Sookie, Elena and Bella have met, the vampires are portrayed as struggling with the same relationship-related issues as normally aged humans: jealousy, possessiveness, and, at times, doubts about their own desirability.

Questions of imbalance also come to the fore in regards to the vampires' superior financial means and extensive knowledge. Nakagawa notes that the apparent wealth the vampires possess enhances the idea of the vampires as "'immigrants' [who] have succeeded in assimilating to American society and values" (n. pag.). A member of a wealthy and close-knit family, Edward has two medical degrees, expensive cars, and his love for the arts and music suggests well-honed tastes. In True Blood, Bill lives in a large antebellum mansion passed down through generations and is asked to share his extensive knowledge about the Civil War with a church group, which furthers his connection to a specifically American past. Eric's knowledge and wealth have amassed from his vampire birth in the Viking Age and as a business-savvy club owner who wields considerable power in the community, he represents the fulfillment of the American Dream. Wealth is not as pronounced in Smith's novels; although Stefan drives a Porsche, he rents a humble room at a boardinghouse. His and Damon's knowledge and experience, however, date back to the Italian Renaissance. In the TV series, the entire vast boardinghouse is theirs, and Stefan uses both his education and personal experiences of historical events in confrontations with an ignorant teacher. The canon vampires also take part in human society and, for the most part, subscribe to its values.

Developments in the romance genre naturally have implications for how these vampires are portrayed, even if the paranormal element ensures that there will always be a heightened and very literal sense of danger surrounding them. Abby Zidle discusses how contemporary female-authored romance novels combine two tropes: "the playboy and the mythopoetic man [into] The New Hero" (23). The worldly and wealthy playboy is polygamous and often unable (or unwilling) to relate emotionally to women, whereas the mythopoetic man searches for his origins, his "primal, natural self" through close connections with other males, perceiving himself to have become emasculated by contact with women (Zidle 24). In the combined trope in romance novels, consequently, The New Hero retains the playboy's riches and sophisticated view of the world, and "the mythopoetic man's nature-derived strength, power, and ability to express emotion" (Zidle 25). This combination is often figured as a process, in which the hero starts out as a charming version of the playboy, goes through a wildman state and is finally able to reconcile the two. The combination of tropes becomes a narrative element which can parallel the female protagonist's development. However, the vampire's dual nature — the paranormal element — means that the process is seldom figured as smooth and pointing in one clear direction. The vampire's human side (the New Hero) is always figured as at war with his paranormal existence; he is not, indeed cannot be, fully reformed. Much of the plot in the selected canons centers on in which ways these competing aspects are negotiated; by the female protagonist and the couple together. But just like in romances in general, dangerous sides must be at least partly tamed and wounded sides must be healed, processes which hinge on the female protagonist's acceptance of the vampire's monstrous sides. She alone can love both aspects of his nature; prevent him from turning to his darker side and instead cultivate his humanity.

The outwardly teenaged vampire Edward can be read as the boy next door, an archetype which carries associations to wholesomeness, sweetness and shyness, despite the fact that the vampire side to his personality arguably invokes strengths and experiences not traditionally associated with the figure. Edward protects Bella and comes to constitute a seemingly ideal gentlemanly partner. However, this is a process and initially, he has affinities with the hero of twentieth-century novels who in "himself [is] the barrier" to the resolution of the romantic relationship (Regis 113). Bella is made to fight for her love, and even when the two have declared their mutual feelings, he resists physical intimacy as well as her wish to be turned, because he is terrified of hurting Bella in the throes of passion, and because he will not damn her to what he considers a soulless state.

Edward's struggles to resist his bloodlust (and by extension his sexual desires) can, as previously discussed, be seen as signaling a shift in gender roles, by which the male takes increasing responsibility for chastity. However, several critics, Taylor among them, have drawn attention to how "an aggressive masculine sexuality, for which Bella is seen responsible [invokes] the ideologically loaded notion that women should be responsible for (the effects of) men's desire" (Taylor 39). Bella's scent (which she naturally cannot control) triggers Edward's impulses and she repeatedly apologizes for the discomfort physical proximity brings. Somewhat contradictorily, but in line with the romance structure, it is the effects of her scent as well as her human state and frailty (also uncontrollable) which makes Edward a wounded hero. He despises himself for his reactions, for his difference from humans and for past transgressions. Large parts of the narrative are consequently devoted to Bella healing him by being constant. She loves him despite his monstrous side, forgives him his past, and shows him that he is her only path towards happiness.

As in the other canons, the central love story is threatened by jealousy and there is juxtaposition on several levels between Edward and Jacob. They both love Bella, one is a vampire, the other a werewolf, one is cold, the other hot. In fact, Jacob is in a more literal sense the boy next door as he and Bella are childhood friends and as they continue to be close when she returns and when obstacles appear in her and Edward's path. The love triangle is in part used to create new obstacles for the central romance, in part to enable Bella's growing self-awareness. Edward's Otherness is contrasted to Jacob's and the similarities as well as differences between them allow her to figure out what it really is she desires. Although Jacob struggles with his own paranormal issues, he does not appear to need either the healing or the taming that Bella can provide. Rather, he can be likened to other set characters in the romances, emotionally available, trustworthy and supportive, who act as foils to the dark, brooding Byronic hero.

In The Vampire Diaries the boys next door are figured as quite threatening neighbors since their appearance is accompanied by various attacks on humans. Stefan's aim, however, is to find a place to belong; he is "tired of the darkness [and] tired of being alone" (Smith, *The Awakening* 6). There is thus a conscious choice on his part to become a good neighbor and to have a normal life, something he sets out to accomplish by enrolling at the local high school. In the novels, Stefan and Damon hail from Italy and have been drawn to Fell's Church because it is a location where paranormal activities take place. In the TV series they are returning home to Mystic Falls, drawn there by the doppelgänger Elena and they are in close proximity to the human protagonists not only because they metaphorically have become the good neighbor, but because they have returned home, similar to vampires in folkloric traditions. Damon and Stefan are not menacing their descendants as folklore vampires traditionally are thought to do, but there is still a form of haunting in a well-known place — they are recognized in photographs, by townsfolk, and their names are familiar. There is something particularly uncanny about these vampires; they are vaguely recognized, but present in surroundings which they logically cannot inhabit.

Like Edward, Stefan constitutes an initial barrier to the romantic relationship as he tries to avoid closeness with Elena. Initially, it is the resemblance to Katherine which makes him enforce this distance, but as sections of Smith's novels have Stefan as focalizer, the reader knows that he is attracted to the individual, Elena. The reader also knows that this attraction constitutes the same kind of threat underlying Edward's chastity in Twilight; Elena awakens "a specific hunger" in Stefan and "[h]is very feeling for her put[s] her in danger" (Smith, *The Awakening* 20, 107). The shifted narrative perspective in Smith's novels, including relayed memories from the past, means that Stefan's wounded soul is explored to a far greater extent than Edward's in Twilight. It is also damaged in a romantic sense, as his past includes a betrayal by the woman he loved. For a long time, that is, Stefan, like Edward, constitutes a barrier to the central romance. His openness about his vampire nature and his past liaison signal that he can only heal if he is loved for who (what) he is and if Elena's feelings are genuine. It thus falls on the female protagonist to accept his vampire nature and demonstrate that power games are not featured into her affections.

Although Elena does heal Stefan, it is a process hampered and delayed by jealousy and conflicted emotions which come in the shape of Damon. In Smith's novels, when Elena first meets Damon, she comes close to kissing him, but "the worst thing" is not this physical infidelity, rather that "[f]or those few minutes, she had forgotten Stefan" (Smith, *The Awakening* 127). Elena is initially a pawn in the physically stronger brother's power games, and Damon tries to entice her onto his side by playing on her latent strength. Claiming that Stefan sees her as "weak and easily led," he, in contrast, can give her: "Power. Eternal life. And feelings [she has] never felt before" (Smith, *The Struggle* 205–206). Although Elena rejects his advances, the attraction between them is never reduced to a platonic friendship and Elena is depicted as drawn to the paranormal strengths and abilities he offers. In the end, however, she chooses Stefan, although whether this is the logical outcome of the processes of taming and healing or because Damon is removed from events and presumed dead, is left unexplored.

Moments of physical intimacy also occur between Damon and Elena in the TV series and to a greater extent than in the novels the narrative hinges on the brothers alternating roles of good and bad, in fact, the oscillation is required "in order to maintain interest in the complex relationship dynamics" (McMahon-Coleman 177). Elena's attraction to them mirrors these shifts and their display of human emotion is a decisive factor — switching it off turns both brothers into monsters. However, while Stefan flips the off-switch but reluctantly, Damon perceives of feelings as a source of unwanted vulnerability. As Helen T. Bailie notes, this difference manifests itself on existential levels: "the evil vampire makes a deliberate choice to embrace his darker nature, while the vampire hero not only struggles against the temptation but will sacrifice himself rather than succumb to it" (143). The healing required in Damon's case is thus of a different nature than in Stefan's. The prospect of Elena's love is what will enable Damon to get in touch with his own emotions and his human side, eschewing the choice to turn to darkness. However, Stefan and Damon's trading of the roles of good and bad, the different healing processes this entails, indeed Elena's role in relation to them both, means that a resolution is continuously postponed and healing processes remain unfinished.

In True Blood, vampires do not pose as or look like teenagers, and have also escaped the confines of the secret of their nature. Bill, who is the first vampire to appear in the canon, is presented as a confident but protective gentleman. He tries to dissuade Sookie's interest in him, despite their mutual attraction, but his precaution does not stem from the same source that govern Edward's and Stefan's hesitancy. He is not concerned with losing control in Sookie's presence but rather fears sociocultural reactions as human/vampire relationships are not yet accepted and condoned. At the same time, he is careful to make a distinction between himself and humans: "We can sometimes remember what it was like to be among you, one of you. But we are not the same race. We are no longer of the same clay" (Harris, *Living Dead in Dallas* 230). In grouping himself together with other vampires Bill is mistaken, because the canon illustrates repeatedly that there is a difference between "mainstreaming" vampires who live off the synthetic blood substitute which (in part) gives the TV series its name, and partake in the local community, and those who feed off humans and exhibit a will to live apart. The difference establishes ties to other works in the subgenre in which "the vampire hero is often alienated from other vampires and their interaction in the paranormal genre is usually, by necessity, limited to brief and often confrontational encounters" (Bailie 143). Rather than forming lasting ties with others of his kind, Bill longs for a return to a human existence and he remains marginal even in relation to other outsiders. The relationship with Sookie is in many ways healing to him as her marginalized state parallels his.

In contrast to the gentlemanly Bill who strives to mainstream and be accepted by humans, who has tamed himself as it were, Eric represents a more sinister, more primal vampirism. He has lived a long life and has relatively tenuous ties to his past humanity. Although he "enjoy[s] the benefits [of] human laws," he is nevertheless immensely irritated that he also has to abide by them (Harris, *Living Dead in Dallas* 184). Eric, that is, is initially harder to welcome to the metaphorical neighborhood, and he reluctantly lives next door without expressed vulnerabilities or a soul in need of healing. While Sookie and Eric are still compatible, sharing a sense of humor, it is not until Eric loses his memory that the two initiate an intimate relationship. Sookie feels "quite maternal" and like "a large security blanket" to this vulnerable Eric, but there is no sense that she desires the protection or potential healing she can offer to substantially alter him (Harris, *Dead to the World* 54, 43). On the contrary, when he suggests that they could have a life together, Sookie is doubtful: "He would be a false version of Eric, and Eric cheated out of his true life" (Harris, *Dead to the World* 214). This comment reflects how Bill and Eric in many ways function as each other's antithesis. Bill requires healing but not taming, Eric needs to be tamed but not healed. Similar to the deferral in *The Vampire Diaries*, the serial structure of both Harris' novels and *True Blood* postpones resolution, keeping Bill and Eric in character.

Transmedial Storyworlds, Seriality, and Fan Engagement

The delimitations we have made regarding what works we focus on in each canon means that we have disregarded texts which are still closely linked to these, either because written by the canon author or extending the main storyline. Examples of excluded texts are the ghost-authored books in the series *Stefan's Diaries* which outline the vampires' backstory as it is envisaged in *The Vampire Diaries*, Meyer's own continuations in the novella *The Short Second Life of Bree Tanner* and the web-published novel draft *Midnight Sun*, and Charlaine Harris' short stories employing characters from her novel series.[5] The mere mention of these texts, however, calls to mind other products such as computer games, graphic novels, webisodes, interviews and discussion forums which can also contribute narrative meaning. That is, we are acutely aware that we are in all three cases concerned with complex storyworlds. Sharing affinities with fictional worlds, text worlds and narrative universes, "[s]toryworlds can be defined as the worlds evoked by narratives" (Herman vii). A storyworld is evoked by all the events and characters present in a single text (a novel, for example) but also by "the beliefs, wishes, intentions, and imaginations" of the characters as presented in their own background stories and developed by what they encounter and perceive throughout the narrative (Margolin 71). Included in the concept is also everything which follows the properties of events and characters: physical laws, rules for behavior and conduct, and worldviews. All texts thus contribute to the idea of the storyworld. Since we are working with the novels and the adaptations only, we will retain the term canon in the chapters which follow, but here signal our awareness that fanfic authors may have taken inspiration from other texts as well.

We mention storyworlds here also because this mental construct evoked in the minds of audiences often surfaces in discussions about transmediality, our next point of discussion. Transmedial storyworlds generate large fandoms and intense fan activity and weaken the authority traditionally associated with an originator of a work. As the same (or a similar) story appears in print (sometimes in different versions), on the screen or on TV, who is to say where a particular idea originates? Different plot lines in different media give fanfic authors many different ways into the material and constitute various sources of inspiration, and the fanfic author can naturally also create a story which conflates or makes use of different instantiations. Contemporary marketing strategies and the increased access fans may have to information about their favorite texts may be additional reasons why transmedial storyworlds attract and sustain interest well after the first installment, adaptation or season. A succinct example of how fans are encouraged to take part in the emergent storyworld comes in the form of the website www.vampire-diaries.net, which was launched before the airing of the first season of *The Vampire Diaries*. Kimberley McMahon-Coleman notes that the website and other social media used in the launching process created "cyberspace [as an] intermediated location" which complements the fictional locations of Fell's Church and Mystic Falls (170). The possibilities for communication and influence indicate that the producers did not strive to evoke a narratively cohesive storyworld in the minds of the audience, but rather encouraged alternative paths. The creativity of many individuals, not least fans, thus influenced the direction of the TV series.

While a chronology can be determined in regards to the selected canons' first version, its spin-offs and adaptations, fan engagement, and then particularly fan fiction, indicate that audiences have several points of entry. At times, it seems as if the TV series in our canons hold a greater potential for sparking interest and *True Blood* is a case in point. The first fanfics working from Harris' novels were published on FanFiction.net in 2008, despite the fact that the site has been in existence since 1998, and despite the publication of Harris' first novel in 2001. While we do not claim that authors did not write fan fiction connected to the Sookie Stackhouse novels before 2008, the readily accessible information on the large site indicates that a heightened interest coincides with the airing of the first season of *True Blood*. The precise entry points are impossible to conclusively prove, but some authors in all probability came into contact with the storyworld via the TV series and moved on to the novels (for others, the TV series may merely have re-actualized a previous interest in the novels). The same development cannot be seen in relation to The Vampire Diaries, where fan fictions working from Smith's novels started to be published on FanFiction.net in 2001, but further comparisons reveal that the visual format has generated a significantly larger number of fanfics. In October 2012, there were less than a hundred fanfics filed under Smith's novels on Archive of Our Own, and close to 1700 connected to the TV series; on FanFiction.net, the number of fanfics working from the books was at this time about one tenth of the number connected to the show. This is not to say that novels cannot attract a big fan base which the Twilight novels and the global fandom formed around them establish.

The different affordances and limitations of written and visual texts in a transmedial storyworld may also influence fanfic production. A visual text's strength may lie in its emphasis on arresting scenery or action-packed sequences, for example, but it is difficult for visual texts to copy the novel's first-person perspective without resorting to a continuous subjective camera perspective or voice overs. Fan fictions which take the visual instantiations as a starting point mean a remediation (the authors move from film or TV series to the written format), and they can contribute first-person information which is difficult to get at in the specific canon material. The affordances of a TV series also lie in its serialized form. A TV series, Sara Gwenllian Jones argues, presents a "vast, multilayered cultural territory which is only ever partially mapped and partially available at any given moment and yet which constantly presents the promise of fulfillment" ("Starring" 11). It can therefore encourage multiple readings more easily than non-serialized narratives and is well suited for the development of minor plots. It is the "*incompletely* furnished" worlds fans are drawn to, as in these "[t]he invitation to imagine is explicit" (Gwenllian Jones, "Starring" 13). In contrast to films and novels, which often have more definite endings, the future is always a promise to be mined; the everyday, the now, offers unlimited possibilities for creative developments. Gwenllian Jones further stresses the importance of "major characters" as "points of entry" into the imagined archive of meta- and intertextual associations linked to serial narratives ("Sex Lives" 85). The paranormal romance's reliance on the creations of strong characters finds a counterpart here, but is explicitly connected to fan creativity and engagement.

But the serialized form can also be conceived of as inducing fan production because of the possibilities for a repetition of structure. In a discussion about the appeal the extended story arcs in *Buffy the Vampire Slayer* have for fans, Esther Saxey contends that the boundaries between action and closure in a TV series are repeatedly blurred and that there is a "general ... interest in the middle of shows over their closure" (206). While most episodes end with temporary closure where, in the case of *Buffy*, the threat is averted, the vampire slayed or the demon defeated, viewers know that the process and structure will be repeated next week. This structure is of central importance to writers of fanfic, who can add their new threats without upsetting the extended diegesis of the show. The lack of resolution in serialized popular culture texts thus seems to be conducive to fandom activity.

True Blood and The Vampire Diaries are yet unfinished, open canons, but in the case of Twilight, no new written installments have been announced and all film adaptations have been released. This formally closed canon can be perceived as closed also on the plot level since the central romance comes to its conclusion. But each novel in the series and each film adaptation bears resemblances to a serialized narrative in its repetitive structure and its deferral of closure. The reader/viewer is presented with an initial situation, obstacles arise or threats are directed at the protagonists, these are overcome or diverted, and each installment ends with a restored equilibrium and a development of the central romantic relationship. This structure often returns in fan fictions set after the canon's story arc. Authors of these kinds of stories introduce new obstacles and threats (new romantic rivals, for instance, or renewed attacks by the Volturi) or focus on the next generation: Bella and Edward's daughter Renesmee. The latter focus in turn enables continued investigations of new relationships and obstacles, thus leading to a play with new "middles." It is thus not necessarily openness in the sense of a canon's ongoing status that is decisive when it comes to fan production, but the way in which its structure opens for continuous explorations of new storylines.

Fanfic authors who write *in medias res*, inserting their stories in the temporal lag between aired episodes of a TV series, often evince strong reactions to something which has just happened, or simply cannot wait for the next installment but instead offer their own versions. It is often stories of this type that can be, in fanfic vernacular, "Jossed" or "Kripked." The former term, connected to Buffy's creator Joss Whedon, indicates a canon development which contradicts the events in one's own fanfic. As a hypothetical example, we may have a fanfic author who, perturbed by Bill's disappearance at the end of the first episode in the third season of *True Blood*, imagines his death and creates a detailed story about how the other characters handle their loss. This author would be Jossed later in the season, when Bill turns up alive and well. The second term is connected to Eric Kripke, producer of the TV series *Supernatural*, but signals the opposite development: how events in a fanfic are validated by canon developments. If the fanfic author we invented above would instead have written a story in which Bill is kidnapped, is searched for by Sookie and finally escapes, and publishes this story in the weeks between aired episodes, the canon developments would corroborate the fanfic story, and the author would have been Kripked. There is a significant difference between fanfic authors who take written work as their starting point, and those who create stories based on ongoing visual narratives. We have yet to come across a fanfic based on a novel where it is apparent that the author has not finished the canon text (it does not have to be a whole novel series), whereas there is a plethora of examples like the hypothetical ones above in which authors do not wait for a season to end, or a TV series to reach a final point, but instead dive in and become part of a meaning-making process.

2. Vampiric Prosumption: Archives, Genres and Fans' Negotiations of Rules

Scholarship in the first and second wave of fan studies has demonstrated that fans are far from being passive consumers, especially of popular culture narratives such as the selected canons, and the increasingly blurred line between producer and consumer has resulted in what Alvin Toffler terms the "prosumer" (282). Fan fiction is an unusually clear consequence of fan prosumption as texts have first been consumed and then resulted in the fan's own production. There is an intimate relationship between the fan and the canon which is not always one of admiration. But the canon has sparked an interest, the interest has led to a deeper investment, enhanced by the possibility of exchanges with other members of a fandom or a community, and finally to the fan's desire to take an even more active part by offering up for scrutiny her own interpretation of a scene, a character, or an entire narrative. The fanfic's intimacy with the canon takes different forms but even in stories which revise the entire premise of a canon, the latter is there as a reference against which the variation gains additional meaning.

Fan fiction shares a number of characteristics with traditionally printed texts, but collaborative aspects as well as the online, user-generated environments in which stories are published entail specific methodological challenges. In the first section of this chapter, we present our negotiations with some of these, and provide a brief outline of how sites are arranged. Our overview is not exhaustive nor necessarily applicable to fandoms and canons other than the ones at focus but is intended to clarify our processes of selection. Sites in themselves represent one kind of paratextual threshold, as do filing options, genres and categorizations, and fanfic-specific uses of paratextual features such as summaries, author notes and tags further work to provide ways into the material. Paratextual features may also guide the reading of stories and invest the author with power, while rules established on sites and in fandoms in turn guide or control the author.

Our discussions in the section "Playing By or Bending the Rules" evince that there are levels of significance attached to aspects and characterizations in each canon text. Different affordances and limitations give rise to varying kinds of fan engagement, and "'stages' of knowledge and interpretative possibility" influence in what ways fanfic authors engage with the canons (Gwenllian Jones, "Starring" 17). The close readings in the last section of the chapter focus on how authors demonstrate their interpretation of aspects such as temporal settings, characterization and reversals of agency. Of added interest is how questions regarding the paranormal genre are brought to the fore and critiqued, in the selected fanfics as well as in responses from other members of the fandoms.

Method and Material: Archives, Genres, Categories

The circulation of fan fiction on more or less open sites on the Internet, rather than in home-made fanzines, via e-mailing lists or on-line discussion groups requiring membership, makes contemporary fan fiction accessible and potentially widely spread. But there are a number of methodological challenges connected to the dynamic nature of both sites and stories and the number of fanfics published. Sites appear and are closed down, texts are continuously uploaded, some are taken away, chapters are added to stories in progress and some fan fictions are published on several sites. The texts analyzed in this and coming chapters do not necessarily stay online indefinitely and the sites they are taken from may not remain for future readers to peruse. Further, there are thousands of True Blood and The Vampire Diaries fanfics, and hundreds of thousands Twilight stories. Processes of selection are difficult and any study with a scope as wide as ours can only illustrate tendencies in the production.

Even if sites and stories are difficult to pin down, online archives constitute a rich ground for research, with several entrances to the material. Collective sites such as Archive of Our Own and FanFiction.net archive pseudonymously authored stories from many different fandoms. Platforms such as LiveJournal enable the coming together of communities with a joint interest in individual canons or characters. Some sites, for example Twilighted and Truebloodwiki.wetpaint.com, publish fanfic connected to one canon, and there are sites with an even narrower focus on selected characters from the canon texts, such as EricNorthman.net. Fanfic authors also create individual homepages for publication of stories. Many specialized sites are not exclusively dedicated to fan fiction; EricNorthman.net, for example, also contains links to interviews with Charlaine Harris, the astrological profile of actor Alexander Skarsgård, and so on. Activities consequently reflect what concerns and interests the larger fandom. On specialized sites the visitor is presented with a narrowed focus at the outset, whereas the larger sites offer the reader different ways of selecting a text. On Archive of Our Own and FanFiction.net, the first step is to choose a canon of interest, a choice which will bring up all the fanfics filed. Scroll down menus and search fields then enable readers to narrow the search according to individual proclivities. It is also possible to choose to view only completed stories, specify story length, and have the results arranged accordingly.

A site's name and search functions are paired with genre labels and categorizations which tell the reader what type of text each fan fiction is. The genre promiscuity characterizing the canons (discussed in chapter one) becomes even greater when turning to fan fiction as the overarching fanfic-specific genres gen, het and (fem)slash are added to the mix. Stories in the gen genre typically do not focus on romantic or erotic relationships and significantly, genfic based on our three canons is rare, taking a distinct third place in relation to het, depicting heterosexual relationships, and (fem)slash, featuring same-sex relationships. Catherine Driscoll observes that genfic is defined as such through a process of exclusion, it "falls predominantly into no other available genre" (83). That is, as a genre marker, gen is not very efficient, as it often signals what the story is *not* rather than what it is. Driscoll further claims that genfic "is fan fiction that is distributed in opposition to the categorization of stories by pairings" (83–84). The het and slash genres are thus categorized according to what combination of characters the stories feature, and as most fanfic-sites provide the option of limiting searches to the characters one wishes to read about, pairings become a more effective tool.[1]

Matters become even more complex when taking into account more traditional genre labels as well as subgenres specific to the text form. Some genre labels are recognizable also for someone not used to browsing fanfic archives, such as romance, mystery and horror, whereas subgenres such as mpreg (male pregnancy), hurt/comfort (where one character suffers and another consoles) or fluff (an often humorous story depicting a minor event) require a certain level of knowledge on the part of the reader to be decipherable. Genre labels can further differ from site to site and in these user-generated environments, labels and definitions also change over time. What all this suggests, of course, is that while some fanfic genre classifications are vampiric, in the sense that they are based on an existing literary tradition, others are considerably more innovative and spring from the prosumers themselves. Genre and category promiscuity, finally, can be seen in the mix-and-match processes which often occur and which may result, for instance, in a hurt/comfort horror story in the slash and romance genres featuring a Jasper/Edward pairing.

Categorizations and the overall organization of sites have helped us meet many of the methodological challenges inherent in the project. For example, when the aim is to investigate romantic but not overly sexual stories, as in chapter three, we have limited our search to fan fictions rated as suitable for general audiences, and then specified which pairing is of interest. Search options in regards to pairings have further enabled us not only to determine the popularity of certain romantic constellations, but also to find examples which diversify our analyses and offer contesting depictions. When the aim is to explore depictions of sexual encounters and orientations, as in chapter four, we have selected fanfics rated adult or mature, or the equivalent thereof. We have limited ourselves to completed stories in all cases, and have chosen fanfics of different length. As our discussions in the following chapters are thematic we have also conducted specific key word searches (for example typing in "monster" in the search field), and fanfic summaries have guided us to stories which have contributed to the analyses.

As noted in the introduction to this book, we are consumers of the same canons as the studied fanfic authors, but are not active members of fandoms. Our decision to remain "lurkers" at the sites visited is in line with our contention that fanfic can and should be studied alongside canon works (whose creators by the same token have not been aware of our academic interest). From our perspective as literary scholars, the texts are paramount and not their creators. However, there are several ways in which to be active at a fanfic site which leaves traces of our presence. Each story gets "visits" from our computers, and multiple "hits" when we access several chapters. Further, we have created user accounts and verified that we are over eighteen to access stories flagged as adult because of violent or sexual content. We have not, however, posted comments or engaged in debates or discussions, and the reader feedback we have included in our analyses is not prompted by any questions posed by us. Nor have we communicated with any authors (of either fanfic or canon material) regarding interpretations. In addition to retaining a critical distance to the texts studied, these decisions stem from our conviction that readers of this book, provided they are over eighteen, should have access to the same type of information as we have and be able to form opinions about the analyzed texts on these grounds.

Paratexts: Controlling the Reader

Filing options, labels, tags, summaries and chapter notes are paratextual elements which to an extent are specific to the fanfic form, but have affinities with traditionally published works in that they create a threshold for the reader and may influence how the text is approached. Gérard Genette argues that paratextual features such as "a title; a subtitle; ... prefaces; postfaces [and] epigraphs" can determine readers' expectations and importantly, signal both how the text should be read and how it should *not* be read (*Palimpsests* 3). Fanfic titles and epigraphs often fill the same function as in traditionally printed works; the former may signal an intertextual link to a previous work, the latter may set the tone and guide the reader towards interpretations which are preferred by the author and away from readings she has not had in mind. A further division between peritexts and epitexts illustrate the proximity each paratextual feature has to the work they refer to. Peritexts are elements found inside a work or on the cover of a printed book whereas epitexts are situated outside the actual work but still related to it, such as interviews, private diaries, and conversations (Genette, *Paratexts* 4–5). Examples of fanfic peritexts are author's notes commonly introducing stories, along with summaries. Readers' comments or information on authors' profile pages are examples of epitexts.

CavalierQueen's *Paradise Within: Happier Far*, a romantic and fantasy-themed fanfic with the pairing Sookie/Eric, establishes an intertextual relationship with John Milton's *Paradise Lost* through its title referring to the aftermath to the expulsion from paradise, when Adam and Eve are told by the Arch-Angel Michael that living in accordance with God's wishes will grant them happy lives. In the fanfic, Sookie and Eric try to live according to each other's (if not overtly Christian) wishes and readers familiar with *Paradise Lost* can thus expect a returning thematic strand of reaching inner happiness through truthfulness. In the event that readers do not recognize the poem, the author's end notes to the first chapter make the intertextual link clear and she directs readers who "are interested in catching subtle subtexts" to the Wikipedia page for *Paradise Lost*. Songs and poems featured as epigraphs in the fanfic are further connected to emotions or events which will figure prominently in each chapter, the author noting that they "serve the purpose of giving you a head's up." In contrast to traditionally published texts in which peritextual features such as titles and epigraphs commonly go uncommented, the author specifically guides her reader not only to material outside her own text, but also to her preferred interpretation of the True Blood canon.

But fanfic paratexts function in ways which extend these preliminary indications for how the story is intended to be interpreted and draw specific attention to the function of the author. Specifically discussing Author Notes (A/Ns) as occupying a paratextual space, Alexandra Herzog identifies three specific (but often combined) functions they may fill: "to engage in communal writing, declare the original author dead, or resurrect the author in attributing themselves with an authorial grab for authority" (§ 2:11). Performing the first function, A/Ns establish a close bond between fanfic author and the fandom or community she communicates with and prompts and wishes from others are often cited. CavalierQueen writes that she has "had many requests to do another [Eric/Sookie] story," and her fanfic is thus a response to readers who have followed her previous production. But the exchange between fanfic author and fanfic reader goes both ways, and CavalierQueen requests reviews and comments from her own fan base.

Paradoxically, A/Ns figuratively kill the author while simultaneously inserting a disclaimer acknowledging the canon author's work. The example fanfic is prefaced by the short phrase "[c]haracters belong to Charlaine Harris," but it is fleshed out by a description of the author's own readings. Cavalier Queen writes that she has "seen all True Blood episodes to date, and read several of the books, and a lot of fanfiction." With all these possible avenues of inspiration, she acquiesces that she may "have inadvertently borrowed something that is not faithful to the books" and apologizes beforehand. The story is filed in the TV series section on both sites where it is published (Fan Fiction.net and Archive of Our Own), which makes the statement concerning being faithful to the novels somewhat puzzling, but more importantly, the author is aware of possible "contamination" from other sources, among which fan fiction is on par with canon texts. The fact that the story is categorized as an Alternate Universe, along with its characters — the author is "taking them out to play in [her] A/U sandbox"— is an additional insurance against readers reacting negatively to changes, but also determines that the canon author's design is abandoned.

The paratextual information in the form of both peri- and epitexts, illustrates that reading and writing fan fiction is a communal practice. Instead of obscuring author and reader functions, attention is drawn to these, beyond the fanfic text itself. Many of the chapters in *Paradise Within: Happier Far* contain end notes which are not designed to prepare the readers for what will come, but instead express thank you's for epitextual reader comments and positive reviews. At the end of chapter 13, the author changes from signing the end note with her pseudonym into using what is presumably her real name, Renee, and the notes become increasingly personal. Before posting the last chapter, Renee creates a mini-narrative around her bi-polar disorder, a separate chapter which she calls "The Agony and the Ecstasy."[2] She there explains to the reader how she goes through intensively active periods which are then followed by severe depressions. At the end of the chapter, which remains unconnected to the plot of the fanfic but contains an intertextual link to it through the inclusion of a few lines from *Paradise Lost*, she writes that her readers "are really the reason [she] keep[s] going" and that she hopes they "will hang around to finish the ride." In epitextual comments posted on Fan Fiction.net, she is extended sympathy and encouragement from readers and is also lauded for the bravery it takes to expose such a private part of her life. A narrative of personal struggle is in this way made part of a writing process.

While the move from public to private thus fills a complex function in the example fanfic, Herzog notes the commonality of "fan authors [who] voluntarily leave the anonymity of the Internet and constitute themselves as legitimate writers" (§ 4.4). The creation of a legitimate author persona goes hand in hand with specific instructions on how to read and how to not read the text. As Herzog notes, "authors grant themselves the authority to provide lines of interpretation for their audience that they fiercely refuse to accept from the metatext [canon] and its producers" (§ 4:12). A final example from *Paradise Within: Happier Far* illustrates this paradoxical relation between individual interpretation and authorial authority. Through the pairing Eric/Sookie, CavalierQueen signals her preference for a non-canon relationship.[3] In the author's view, Bill is "a sneaky, abusive man/vampire," and as Sookie "deserves better," she has transformed Eric by making him "sweet and gentle" and thereby a more suitable partner (A/Ns chapters 19 and 2). In the author's opinion, Harris has created a romantic mismatch, a flaw which is corrected in the fanfic. But the correction entails that Eric's character is altered as well, and by drawing attention to that he is rendered in Out of Character ways, the A/N's instruct the reader to suspend potential criticism of these changes. In this way, CavalierQueen, like countless other fanfic authors, resists accepting aspects of the canon material, a pre-determined reading of them, and instead focuses on "correcting" them by presenting her own version. At the same time, her own instructions occupy a role which is absent in traditionally printed novels or visual texts and lessen the potential for the same agency on the part of her readers.

Site and Fandom Rules: Controlling the Author

Despite the power an author may wield in the use of paratextual information, fan fiction is surrounded by rules of different kinds, some of which suggest certain limits to fan creativity. A general rule, established firmly enough to not need explicit mentioning on most sites, is to avoid creating a "Mary Sue" character: an Original Character (OC) that can easily be read as an idealized version of the author herself and who interacts with the canon characters (the equivalent male term is "Marty Stu"). To some readers, all OCs are Mary Sues and "dislike[d] ... with varying degrees of passion" because writing oneself into the story is seen as an enactment of private fantasies which do not belong in the public fandom sphere (Fanlore, "Mary Sue" n. pag.). To others, original characters are a logical extension of the creative climate proper to fan productivity and they are evaluated by how well they fit into their respective narrative contexts. Regardless of how they are judged, original characters in the Mary Sue vein signal an intimate relationship with the canon characters. 22wolf makes this intimacy explicit in her A/Ns to *Eric's Gift*, a story revolving around Eric Northman's erotic encounter with an unnamed female character, and also extends it to encompass the readers: "The OC is intentionally not named — pretend its [sic] you and your night with Eric." The author invites the reader to identify with the original character or to Mary Sue-ify herself, as it were.[4]

Other rules and norms are explicitly stated in submission guidelines and the Twilight-specific site Twilighted constitutes a succinct example. First of all, there is a division between story categories and what is considered permissible in each. Stories filed in the Canon category need to demonstrate a high level of intertextual "compliancy" with the canon both when it comes to plot and characters: "it should be evident from your own writing that the scenario you are writing about could grow from established canon." In the story category Alternate Universe, stories "can deviate from canon in any number of ways." However, these deviations have to be motivated, and "characters ... should not act out of character for no discernable [sic] reason." In this category, it is not permissible to remove all issues pertaining to vampirism or lycanthropy, rather "AU Twific must retain some supernatural element, even if not in a canon way." The final category is labeled All Human (also referred to as AU-Human), and authors filing their stories here have a considerable freedom. It is proclaimed that "such stories are generally acceptable in spite of having little relationship to Twilight other than characters sharing the names of those from the books. The characters may act OOC or may be the human counterparts of the Twilight characters." As noted in connection with the fanfic *Paradise Within: Happier Far*, the label OOC stands for Out of Character and refers to a character who does not "behave" according to his or her personality in the canon. Whereas this type of character is permissible in the AU-Human story category, it may in others result in protests from readers. The removal of the vampiric element makes for OOC characters but as the category's name indicates, this is here the desired result.

There are both linguistic and thematic rules for ensuring high-quality content. In the section "Story Standards" it is clear that stories with "more than ten (10) spelling and/or grammar mistakes for every thousand words will be declined" and several quality pit-falls are listed, including "clumsy sentences" and "choppy organization." All stories have to be validated by a beta reader, a critical reader who examines a text for language mistakes and content-related discrepancies or shortcomings, the latter in line with the site's encouragement of stories with an "original plot." Given that fan fiction by definition builds on repetition, most notably of canon characters, originality in this sense pertains to plots within the fandom.[5] Texts can therefore be rejected if there are multiple stories already on the site which delineate a similar plot. As on most fan fiction sites, all stories are labeled with ratings or warnings and despite the open door policy, there are a number of things deemed inappropriate. Incest, pedophilia, necrophilia and bestiality are four issues that should not be featured. However, because of the deadness inherent in the vampire, the animal nature of werewolves, and the difference between centuries-old vampires and high-school humans, the warning are modified a bit. Authors are furthermore discouraged from writing stories in which "a romantic relationship [develops] between characters after non-consensual sex has occurred between them" and are warned that any fanfics depicting racism, or "drug use or other illegal behavior in Real Person Fiction" will be declined.[6]

Prospective authors must consequently relate to site-specific rules about conditions for publication, rating systems, and what is deemed appropriate. Rules established in fanfic communities constitute yet other boundaries as do particular fanfic forms. Louisa Stein and Kristina Busse argue that fan creators are engaged in a "limit play" where "limitations already implicit in the source texts," such as characters, basic plot developments and settings, combine with both "interpretive community expectations and formal impositions" on the fan fictions (198). Firstly, that is, the fanfic author engages with the canon and it is always there as an interpretative grid and as a starting point since the aim commonly is to offer a story which contributes new or alternative developments. Secondly, the fanfic author engages with the readings of the fandom at large or smaller units within it. She may conform to and substantiate majority readings, but also signal a break with them, in the text itself, but commonly also in paratexts such as warnings or tags. Thirdly, formal impositions such as the use of canon characters only, or the choice of a particular kind of story (for example a "drabble" which must be comprised of exactly 100 words) or some form of prompt or challenge given within the community constitute frameworks to work within. An author's success in negotiating these limits may result in increased cultural capital in the Bourdieuan sense; the savvier she is, the more successful she can become. Like communication, interaction and creative processes in other forms of social networks, fanfic production is thus by no means devoid of hierarchies.

Playing By or Bending the Rules

The structure of paratexts and sites, and rules regulating various aspects of the publication process, apply to formal affordances and impositions. But these are paralleled by how the canons' contents and rules are complied with or bent. Canon narratives work "as blueprints for world-creation," that is, as the foundation for the reader's own mental construction, shared by other readers (Herman vii). Although the definition implies a logical consistency within the fictional universe it is simultaneously the case that as large numbers of participants immerse themselves in it, it can grow and change; its rules can become perceived as more elastic. Specific lines of interpretation may also develop in more localized groups within the fan community. Stein and Busse exemplify this by referring to an "interpretive community that has formed around a romantic pairing" of the *X-Files* characters Mulder and Krycek (197). This pairing may remain puzzling to uninitiated readers of fan fiction depicting this romance, while "[m]embers of the community already take the characters' love for each other for granted" (Stein and Busse 198). In this way, smaller groups within a fandom agree on readings which may be completely at odds with the canon, but which in time acquire legitimacy as fanon. Close readings of fan fictions illustrate this play with rules exceedingly clearly, as it is sometimes the intention of fanfic authors to do nothing *but* bend the rules.

Sara Gwenllian Jones' analyses of the "virtual universe" constituted by *Xena: Warrior Princess* help clarify how and in what ways fan fiction either plays by the rules or deviates from them, as her discussions focus on "'stages' of knowledge and interpretat[ion]" at work ("Starring" 17).[7] Gwenllian Jones distinguishes between "*Background Hard Data*" and "*Real-time Hard Data*" which in her discussions pertain to Xena's "background, family, relationships and experiences" illustrated by the extended diegesis of the show, and by the accumulation of information in each episode, respectively ("Starring" 18). We will not enforce this distinction unnecessarily as the two sets of hard data often overlap but instead emphasize that for an author of fan fiction, the story she writes needs to exhibit a certain level of fidelity to the hard data to enable the reader to interpret it. If the aim, for example, is to fill in a narrative gap in an episode of *True Blood*, there needs to be a frame story which correlates with this episode (the real-time hard data) from which the fanfic can start. To be faithful to the extended diegesis, this hypothetical story would also still have Sookie and Jason as orphaned siblings. In cases where there are significant differences between instantiations, the fanfic author commonly specifies what hard data she bases her story on. She can do this by filing her story in either the novel or the TV series section of a site. If an author of The Vampire Diaries fanfic files her story under novels, she tells the prospective fanfic reader to expect a blond Elena who has a baby sister, whereas filing it under the TV series means that Elena is a brunette who has a moody, only slightly younger brother. Although many fan fictions do not demonstrate fidelity to the canon but rather take events in very different directions, it is still vital to retain some elements of the hard data. Even in the category AU-Human, where the vampire element is abandoned altogether, it is not uncommon that Edward, for example, while transformed into a mortal, still has a father named Carlisle and that Bella remains clumsy and insecure. If stories do not have at least a tenuous connection to the canon they cease to be fan fiction and are instead labeled original fiction.

The only instance in which the difference between background and real-time hard data directly impacts on our analysis of fanfic is when authors use the hard data of a particular episode as a starting point or background for their story. This is typically signaled by paratextual markers indicating where in the narrative arc the story is placed, or which real-time hard data the author elaborates on or reacts to. Comments such as psychobabblers' qualification "AU ending for [the episode] Break On Through [*The Vampire Diaries* 3:17]" make it clear that events in the particular episode are crucial to her fanfic *The Haunting*. The author's A/Ns further clarify: "To be honest, I don't particularly like the Alaric is actually a psychotic serial killer subplot." Her story alters the new plot element of Alaric's multiple personality disorder by drawing on his canon competencies as hunter of evil vampires but friend and protector of sympathetic ones. These competencies are used to divert the threat of his evil twin who is obsessed by the idea of destroying vampires indiscriminately, and assure the protection of Damon (the threatened vampire in this case). The author in this way removes the specific real-time hard data she dislikes.

In the fanfic category crossover, authors can intertwine logically connected canons which have elements (such as the vampire) in common, but just as well canons which do not. As an example, among the Twilight-filed stories on Archive of Our Own, there are crossovers combining Stephenie Meyer's canon with Emile Ardolino's film *Dirty Dancing* and J.K. Rowling's Harry Potter series, as well as stories which recast Twilight as regency romance — a crossover in terms of sub-genre and temporality rather than a combination of fictional universes. Even when the author is concerned with two different vampire milieus there may still be considerable differences in both the mythology and "reality" of vampires, to the point where the author may have to expound at some length on how and in what ways the different vampire species can understand each other. Authors of stories in this category combine hard data, or choose one set over another, and may consequently change ensuing interpretation levels.

Gwenllian Jones terms these ensuing levels "*Competencies,*" "*Themes and Motifs,*" "*Behaviour, Ethics, Psychology*" and "*Erotics,*" each with specific affordances for fanfic authors ("Starring" 18–19). Competencies are connected to characters' strengths and weaknesses, their "personalities" if you will, and within the canon denote actions and responses that are expected or possible. Supernatural vampire speed is an example of such a competency, as is Sookie's telepathic gift. By extension, the former would enable fast and effective vampire help in threatening situations, the latter influences Sookie's relationship to people — she is the one in the know who can predict the outcome of a situation. That is, a literal competency has implications for how a character is likely to react. By contrast, the character type OOC indicates that there is a desire on the part of many authors to play with this stage of interpretation as they create, for example, a willful and agile Bella, or an evil and drug-abusing Elena. OOC characters no longer abide by the canon competencies but rather play with the reader's expectations as their range of responses to situations are markedly different.

The canon works' genre participation means that a central theme is romantic love and a majority of fanfics, regardless of their overall level of fidelity, reiterates it. Often it is a question of representing the central romance again, sometimes with a twist, but the romantic theme also appears in stories about characters that are not linked in the canons. That is, a fanfic which depicts a non-canon romantic relationship between Bella and her friend Mike Newton may still be faithful to a canon theme. In the area of behavior, ethics and psychology, Gwenllian Jones notes, "fan engagement and speculation is at its most intense" ("Starring" 18). What can be inferred by background and real-time hard data is seldom enough to answer all questions about the psychological make-up of characters and it is here that fans have an opportunity to fill in perceived gaps by representing missing moments in the main characters' story, switching perspectives, or developing stories about minor characters. The many fanfics which problematize the ethics and behavior of supposedly "good" vampires similarly engage in interpretation at this level. Naturally, alternative versions which play with ethics and psychology may in turn affect other aspects, such as competencies which "determine [the character's] range of possible actions and reactions" (Gwenllian Jones, "Starring" 18). A fanfic in which Edward is depicted as a blood-thirsty monster without regard for human life (a play with his ethics and behavior in the canon) would consequently hold the possibility of influencing his overarching competencies. He would not strive to protect humans and would react with joy rather than restraint to a situation in which Bella offers him her neck.

Finally, the erotics of the storyworld Gwenllian Jones discusses includes a play with characters' sexualities and an intended ambiguity when it comes to their desires. Even though same-sex relationships are featured in True Blood, and even if there are plenty of homosocial moments to be mined for potential in Twilight and The Vampire Diaries, the central relationships are heterosexual in an unquestionably heteronormative society. However, any lack of homoeroticism in the canon does not preclude same-sex relationships in fanfic. On the contrary, same-sex erotic pairings in slash and femslash abound in fanfic connected to all three canons. Importantly, however, it may sometimes also be a question of adding, or expanding, the erotic elements from the canon. Sex between Edward and Bella occurs in the last canon novel but is not elaborated on and the novels in The Vampire Diaries hint to intimacy without making explicit the extent of it. The large numbers of fanfics depicting (not altering) the canons' heterosexual relationships, by inserting detailed descriptions of foreplay and love-making, thus illustrate how authors pick up latent or scantily described elements, and represent them anew.

Fan Fiction Moves in Mysterious Ways

We now turn to analyses of three fan fictions to exemplify different levels of fidelity and illustrate how authors negotiate the rules. The two first fanfics: Lisse's *Moves in Mysterious Ways* and Piper's *The Most Impulsive Thing* re-write canon elements to criticize aspects of Twilight and The Vampire Diaries, respectively. The third story, L'amante di Destino's *True Twilight*, is a crossover combining Twilight and True Blood and is illustrative of the particular challenges inherent in suturing together two canons depicting fairly divergent images of vampirism.

Besides a common critique of the central romance in both canons, *Moves in Mysterious Ways* and *The Most Impulsive Thing* are united by the fact that they have future settings. Lisse's fic is played out several decades after events in Twilight, Piper's seven years after events in L.J. Smith's novels. A third thing they have in common is, actually, Twilight, of which neither of the authors is a fan. Lisse writes in her story notes that her "hatred of the whole premise of Twilight" causes a "problem" for her as she "still want[s] to write fic about it. While attempting to keep the characters ... er, in-character." There is nothing to prevent authors from writing stories about canons they do not admire, of course, even if the label fan fiction becomes a bit misleading (and may be why Lisse has opted to call it just "fic").[8] The reading of the canon material, often in combination with an intertextuality related to genre resulting in a view of the vampire as part of horror rather than romance, may still give rise to a desire to comment, critique and revise, potentially even more so than when the author is an invested fan.

While Lisse is critical of the "whole premise" of the canon, Piper is more specific, stating that her "story is born out of [her] kind of intense hate for something that's running rampant in the Vampire fandom given the rise of the Twilight series: the female who's willing to give up everything for her vampire boyfriend." Piper does not indicate that she is not a fan of The Vampire Diaries, but her story develops thematic similarities between this canon and Twilight by its focus on the perceived unhealthy relationship between Stefan and Elena.[9] Neither author comment suggests that the authors will abandon the hard data of either canon, or create characters that do not conform to their canon competencies. Lisse, on the contrary, indicates that she will attempt to keep her characters in character and Piper will take "Bonnie and Damon along for the ride" without altering their characters too much.

The centrality of the fated love between Elena and Stefan is unquestioned in Smith's novels on which *The Most Impulsive Thing* is based. Even though Elena is not a passive girlfriend but rather takes several crucial initiatives and literally goes to hell and back to save her beloved Stefan, the consistent conundrum is how they can be together given the human/vampire differences. Piper imagines a future for them when "Elena [has] left for Europe with Stefan, bypassing college completely, not to mention life altogether." The reference to bypassing life should arguably be read as Elena consenting to be turned: she has been willing to give everything — life — up for her boyfriend. This is not a choice Bonnie, Piper's central character, is prepared to make to be with the man she loves. The relationship between Bonnie and Damon follows logically from the canon where they are close, albeit not openly romantically linked, and where Damon has given his own life for Bonnie's. At the end of Smith's novel *Midnight* some part of the deceased Damon's soul is stirred by thoughts of her (and Elena). Since Elena has returned from the dead a number of times throughout the novel series, Damon's potential resurrection is hinted at, and in *The Most Impulsive Thing* Piper depicts him as alive and well.

She further re-casts Bonnie as older and more realistic, and her response to Damon's statement that love should conquer all and his insistence that Bonnie herself has nurtured such ideas in the past is her comment: "I was eighteen." The temporal relocation enables the author to let the character stay in character and be true to her canon competencies and ethics, simply by having her reflect on what age and experience do to wishes and desires. It transpires that Bonnie has expressed a will to be turned, to be with Damon forever, but that he has resisted this notion. Within the frame of the story their roles are now reversed, but Bonnie insists on being too attached to her mortality to give in to his present wish. On the meta-level, and in accordance with Piper's story notes, the fanfic comments on a trend prevalent in romances in general and contemporary paranormal vampire romances in particular. Love makes you do "absolutely foolish things," Bonnie reflects, such as putting your life on hold or canceling it altogether but her life is not "some romance novel" where she will go along with what is prescribed.

The protagonist in *Moves in Mysterious Ways*, an Original Character in the form of an unnamed seventeen-year-old boy, is like the adult Bonnie a realist, above all about love, which in itself seems to disqualify the story from participation in the romance genre. Lisse writes:

> He is not the type to believe in happily-ever-after or even 'til-death-do-us-part or the transcendent and all-encompassing power of love, at least not as they apply to his own life. They are well and good, he thinks, for the people who have the time for that sort of thing, but not for him. Never for him. There are no realists in love stories.

As in Piper's story, a difference is made between the central characters and other people. Here, the boy compares himself to "people who have time for that sort of thing" whereas the corresponding phrase in *The Most Impulsive Thing* is "Those girls [in romance novels] apparently don't have anything to do with their lives." The boy and Bonnie are different; they have plans for their own lives and react with distrust to any attempts to change them, especially when this change entails the very drastic transformation into a non-human. The juxtaposition between the stories and romance novels does not mean, however, that love and emotional closeness are discounted. On the contrary, Bonnie professes her love for Damon several times, and the relationship which develops between the boy and the girl in his class, Isabella Swan, is "a friendship or a sort of unstated crush or all the other awkward *normal* things that come with being a teenager." Both Piper and Lisse in this way play with the rules of the paranormal romance paradigm.

At the outset, and used to the "rules" of fan fiction, it is tempting to read *Moves in Mysterious Ways* as a gender-reversed version of Twilight. There are some affinities between the boy and Bella in the canon which initially support such a reading. Like Bella, the boy is the new kid in class, he is insecure and nervous about a host of things, and paired with Isabella (whom he starts calling Izzy) for collaborative work in class. He is also characterized as "ordinary and unremarkable," which seems to further align him with Bella's character in the canon. However, canon–Bella applies this description to herself, whereas the reader soon realizes that others find her very attractive. The characterization of boy in the fic on the other hand is never contested. At this point, the reader of the fic may realize that it is not simply a version of Twilight with new players. Izzy is, in fact, Bella, eighty years after events in Twilight, which negates such a reading. While the story chronicles similar events as Twilight, it has a different starting point and this entails a crucial change to the central theme. As Lisse repeatedly points out by the rhetorical repetition of a key phrase: "This is not a love story."

The removal of the central romantic theme has consequences for each ensuing event and the boy is continuously suspicious of Izzy as "[t]here is something about her that reminds him of danger and dark corners." In contrast to canon–Bella's immediate attraction to Edward, thanks to rather than despite of his Otherness, the boy initially keeps his distance because, it is indicated, that is what humans *do* when confronted with something mysterious and potentially threatening. Ironically, this aligns the story with traditional romances, where there is often a "preliminary dislike" between heroine and hero, rather than with the paranormal romance structure of the canon where the vampire element does away with this type of hurdle to pass (Nakagawa n. pag.). The revelation that Izzy *is* a vampire, starting with her turning the school bus over with one finger and ending with her acknowledgement of the word vampire in the boy's long list of possible explanations, paradoxically continues along the realistic track as it does not shake the boy's worldview completely "even if it goes a little tilty." That is, realism is not connected to the paranormal element (how could it be?) but to how far the boy is willing to be influenced by the changed conditions. Izzy may be a vampire, but that does not entail that the boy changes himself or his outlook on life to accommodate this fact.

Izzy acknowledges the boy's hesitancy, noticing that he does not seem to like her in a "mildly approving [way] as if he has passed some sort of test." In the canon, Edward repeatedly draws attention to the danger he poses to Bella, attempting to dissuade her interest in him. He states, for example, "It would be more ... *prudent* for you not to be my friend" and that Bella "*need*[s] a healthy dose of fear" (Meyer, *Twilight* 72, 189). Instead of worrying about the fact that he is a vampire, however, and could potentially kill her, Bella's main worries in the canon is that she does not measure up and that Edward is an unattainable dream. In the fic, Izzy appreciates the boy's more hesitant reaction to her advances, a representation which suggests the author's view that this is a reaction canon–Bella should have had. The boy sees through the charade of an old vampire posing as a high school student and knows that all is not right with her. He passes the test Izzy (Bella) failed eighty years ago.

Further drawing attention to the division between predatory vampires and human victims, Lisse states in the short summary preceding the fic that "[s]ometimes the prey evolves." The consequences in the story are twofold: the boy *is* suitably frightened of Izzy — repeatedly referring to her as "creepy" — and his blood is "repellent" to her, which reverses the canon element of Bella's blood being intoxicating and irresistible to Edward. Further, it turns out, the boy's blood is also disgusting to other vampires. As in the canon, then, there are both external threats in the form of other vampires and the internal threat of the vampire hurting the human love interest (or as here, friend). Establishing further ties to the canon, there are intertextual links to other works of literature, notably among them Shakespeare's *Romeo and Juliet*. Lisse cleverly combines the two canon elements when rogue vampires appear and the boy saves the day. "[H]e takes a page out of a famous Shakespearean tragedy. The biting-his-thumb page, anyway." Instead of being the equivalent of fighting words as in the play, the literal biting of the thumb ends violence as the boy's blood repels the attackers and drives them away.[10] Predictably, considering the developments so far, Lisse continues: "The dying-for-your-love page will just have to happen to someone else." This may very well be the case, but within the framework of the fic, Izzy realizes that she has put the boy in harm's way simply by trying to be his friend and leaves. The fic ends as follows:

> This is not the way a love story goes: The boy is very nearly eighteen and will live for a long long time — as long as a human being ought to, no more or less. Sometimes he thinks about the girl he never sees again and sometimes he doesn't. He grows up. Life goes on.

In Lisse's version, the central premise of Meyer's novel is completely subverted by suggesting on the one hand that the love story is too unrealistic and unhealthy, on the other that Bella's life did not turn out to be ideal after all. Poignantly, Edward is not part of the story. Izzy wears a ring on her finger, but does not speak of her past or present relationships and on the contrary seems "desperately, terribly sad." The eternal love and happiness promised in the canon have come to naught.

However, the fic does not suggest that events in the following three canon novels do not play out as Meyer envisions them, only that the future beyond the canon story arc can be envisioned in more realistic terms. The hard data is by no means cancelled, rather Izzy's past (as depicted in Meyer's novels) is crucial for who and what she is in the fic and the vampire competencies are retained, albeit put to another use. In the canon, Edward continuously refers to himself as a monster, but Bella remains unwilling to see him as such. In the fic, there is no romance to gloss over monstrosity and both the boy and Izzy conceive of her as an aberration. As the vampire presence produces another emotion than desire, ethics and behavior change as well. Because of her own past experiences, Izzy is responsible to a very different degree and takes the consequences of being a threat to those she cares about. The boy, who goes on to date and have a normal life, continues to be a realist.

Since the story is prefaced by Lisse's statement that she hates the premise of Twilight, it could be assumed that it would attract attention from readers of a similar persuasion. The hundred or so posts published in response to the story illustrate, however, that even readers who like (or at least do not outright hate) Twilight have found the story good on several levels, ranging from the high quality of writing to characterization and the subversion of the central premise. While some posts open with commentators professing to have little knowledge of the canon, others show a careful understanding of it, arguably making them appreciate the plot twists and deconstruction even more. Among these, many focus on what is figured as an improvement of Bella's character. Liradawn writes, "I'm amazed at how you took Bella and made me actually like her and sympathize with her, while keeping her character pretty much the same" whereas Fallowsthorn's view is that Lisse has "given her an actual likeable character, sadly absent in the original." These comments point in different directions regarding Lisse's ability (and stated aim) to keep the character in character, but both stem from a disappointment with Meyer's portrayal of Bella which has resulted in difficulties identifying and sympathizing with her.

In posts that go somewhat further, Riveted voices a wish "that this was canon" and two similar posts by A Mistake and 100TenMillion express the commentators' ideal scenario that *Moves in Mysterious Ways* would be the published version and that Meyer's work is "a fanfic based on this work." The fact that the story itself is tagged as a "Metafic" finds an interesting parallel in these types of comments as they illustrate the readers' awareness not only of the canon, but of the processes involved in creating a work of canon fiction, the ensuing fan production, and textual differences between these. The meta-aspect also gives rise to posts in which the motivations behind creating fanfic are explored, as in the SilverTippedFeather's comment that even intense dislike of the canon material may result in that "you write it out just to try and make it better" and in kosarin's post suggesting that "it does seem to be the flaws that inspire these [fanfic] stories." Among these flaws, the lack of realism in the canon seems to be one of the most serious, along with Bella's underdeveloped and passive character. Paintblot writes of her disappointment with Meyer's novel in which "Bella got all she ever wanted without giving up anything in return" and continues by praising Lisse's fic and its "more realistic conclusion [which] is actually more meaningful and compelling."

Comments of this kind illustrate that prosumers are not necessarily limited to interpretations only on the text level, rather that there are tendencies to juxtapose fiction with aspects of real life. In his early analysis of fan practices and borrowing the term from Ien Ang, Henry Jenkins refers to "'emotional realism' [as] an interpretive fiction fans construct in the process of making meaning of popular narratives" (*Poachers* 107). That is, the emotional realism does not have to be found in the fiction itself. Jenkins' example text is *Star Trek* where emotional rules are markedly different from human norms, especially where Vulcans are concerned. Rather, Jenkins argues, "[w]hat counts as 'plausible' ... is a general conformity to the ideological norms by which the viewer makes sense of everyday life" (*Poachers* 107). Comments on *Moves in Mysterious Ways* by peppermint—"Life is not neatly wrapped and packaged, and it doesn't turn out the way we want it"—and MikitsuSilverquick—"I know only a handful of people who are seeing/still with people they were dating in highschool"—demonstrate that readers of the fanfic move outside the canon's own emotional realism which hinges on fated and eternal love, and instead focus on what they perceive as realistic in their everyday lives.

Even though both Lisse's and Piper's stories illustrate quite radical revisions of canon elements, they are not encumbered by any need to keep several sets of hard data, competencies and ethics in mind. Such is often the case in crossover fanfic where authors combine two (or more) canons and where the relocation of characters into a new setting means consequences for their worldviews. In *True Twilight*, L'amante di Destino crosses True Blood, a canon in which vampires are depicted as a new minority group, and Twilight, where they have to keep their nature hidden. When removed from their original setting and the constraints put on them because of the narrative particularities of "their" canon, the Cullens find other options and a new freedom. *True Twilight* works from the premise that Bella does not wait around in Forks after Edward and the Cullens' departure in *New Moon*. After a falling out with her father she instead moves to Bon Temps, Louisiana, where her mother and stepfather have relocated. She finishes high school there, befriending classmates Sookie and Sam, and is, when the story starts, in the process of becoming a teacher while working extra at Merlotte's bar and coming to terms with the fact that vampires now live openly in society. In contrast to her friends and co-workers, however, the existence of vampires is not recent news to her, given her past with the Cullens.

Although it may seem like a logical choice to combine vampire storyworlds, authors of crossovers are as imbricated in the complexities of sometimes contrasting competencies and worldviews as those who choose to conflate, for example, Twilight with Harry Potter. With the plethora of popular culture vampire narratives in existence it is even the case that each canon establishes its own, unique kind of vampirism, with concomitant weaknesses and strengths, to make an original contribution. Fanfic authors therefore have to explain the existence of very different vampires and find some kind of logic that can account for their diversity. L'amante di Destino includes an early reflection by Bella to come to terms with the differences in the canons she crosses. Despite Bella's experience with the Cullens, who "sparkled like diamonds in the sun" there are "different bloodlines and some vampires were just like the movies and books portrayed them. If they stepped into the sun they could die." She also ponders the notion that her previous vampire acquaintances probably have not been aware of "these other vampires." Explanations like these abound in crossover fan fiction and are necessary when the author wants to retain a level of fidelity to both canons and the logic within her own text. As the setting in this fanfic is Bon Temps, it is the hard data from True Blood which takes precedence, against which the Cullens' unusual abilities and lack of information are pitted.

Or rather, it is the hard data from *True Blood*, the TV series, the fanfic utilizes. In reader comments to the first chapter, IRMFS signals a certain discomfort with the liberties L'amante di Destino is perceived to have taken with the canon material. To start with, the reader is unconvinced that the "straight forward" plot of Twilight can ever be made to gel with the complex world of Harris' novels. This may seem slightly unfair, since L'amante di Destino has nowhere signaled that she is using the Sookie Stackhouse novels as the basis for her story, which is filed under "Twilight and True Blood Crossover" on FanFiction.net. However, IRMFS draws attention to details which do not fit the hard data of either instantiation of the True Blood canon, such as Sam and Sookie being classmates in high school. Then follows the advice: "Do Not Start A Fanfiction About A Siries [sic] You Know Nothing About! Watching TrueBlood doesn't count seeing as it is only uo [sic] to about 20-somthing [sic] eps." Regardless of whether one agrees with these emphatic statements, they draw attention to the need to have a comprehensive knowledge of the canon, not to write a persuasive story as such but to make sure that readers do not start looking for missing or faulty pieces. In the A/Ns for chapter ten, L'amante di Destino answers this criticism and posts from other commentators who are similarly confused about what canon instantiation she has in mind, by stating that she has not read the novels "only begun [and is] far from being able to write fan fiction for them." That is, the author is aware of the necessity for in-depth knowledge in order to enable credible revisions of both plot and character.

As the exchange of criticism and replies indicates, *True Twilight* is a work in progress with chapters published as the author finishes them, finally ending up as a completed, thirteen-chapter long fanfic. L'amante di Destino states in the A/Ns for the first chapter that she does "not know how it will end yet." She does know how she wants to start it, however, by having Bella instead of Sookie taking orders when Bon Temps gets its first vampire, thus bringing Bill a bottle of Tru Blood. There are no references to Sookie's telepathic gift in the story, but it has a corollary in Bella's attitudes, both to the vampire customer and to her shape shifting boss Sam. In contrast to Sookie, it is not an ability to read minds that gives Bella an increased understanding of these supernaturals, but her previous experiences. These experiences should, Bella reflects, prevent her from becoming attracted to another vampire, especially since "this one [could be] even more dangerous than Edward had 'thought' he was to [her]." The question of Bill's potential dangerousness in some ways contradicts L'amante di Destino's initial re-cap of differences where the Bon Temps vampires "are able to drink from humans but not kill them." This ability represents the opposite of what Edward thinks he is able to do in Twilight, but arguably stems from True Blood's generally more threatening depiction of vampires.

At this point in the story, the author has established the idea of a new romantic liaison, and like Edward in Twilight, and thus in Bella's memories in the fanfic, Bill is protective of his love interest. There are differences, however, between him and the Cullens. Bill's protectiveness does not extend to watching over Bella when she sleeps and he also claims, in response to Bella's story about the paper cut that precipitates the Cullens' departure from Forks, that "if you were to cut yourself ... I could put a band aid on your wound, and I could even kiss it and make it better." In contrast to Jasper's real and Edward's suspected lack of control, Bill does not have to battle his instincts as they are not overriding or constitute an ever-present danger to Bella. There are other options in True Blood and a particular individual is not figured as eliciting unusually passionate and uncontrollable responses. So far, then, Bella and Bill seem on the path towards happiness and they become increasingly intimate as the story progresses.

In the third chapter, however, the author changes track by including the first of several sections narrated from Edward's point of view. In her A/Ns, she again reminds the reader that nothing is "cut and dry" and that she is pondering different outcomes. Edward's reappearance and narrative voice are thus added in part "[f]or all the Twilight fans," in part to keep options open for whom Bella will eventually end up with. In chapter four, another Twilight character is awarded a narrative perspective as Alice who, true to her canon competencies, has visions of the future where she sees Bella with Bill and being bitten. Alice's reaction to the vision is regret that she has been forced to spend a long time unnecessarily estranged from her good friend. L'amante di Destino thus plays on the idea in Twilight that Bella has to be protected not only from rogue vampires, but from being turned, a transformation which in that canon entails a loss of soul, or so the Cullens believe. As it seems she will be turned regardless, the Cullens no longer have to keep their distance and it becomes rather an issue of what kind of vampire Bella will become. Here, the author returns to the idea of different bloodlines, used to logically suture the canons together, by which Bella can choose to become a "night creeper" like Bill, or like the Cullens, "sparkling, golden eye[d] and beautiful."

Turning is still not considered to be unproblematic, least of all by Edward who thinks about Bill that "[i]f he truly loved her like I did he would want to save her soul from eternal damnation." Bill does not have a narrative voice in this fanfic, and it remains unclear what his views are on the change from human to vampire, but overarching ideas of evil in the canons hint to a difference in how turning may be approached. The theological framework of traditional vampire narratives is unquestionably overturned in both canons: there is nothing inherently devilish about vampires, nor are they vulnerable to religiously connoted symbolism. In True Blood, vampirism is initially represented as a virus and although this explanation is later abandoned, vampires are figured as a minority group which renders questions of turning social and cultural rather than spiritual. Susannah Clements argues that while the issue of potential damnation crops up intermittently in Twilight, the vampire is presented "as the ideal — as something higher than human, rather than lower" which means that the turning process does not take on a theological significance by which the human would forfeit anything of importance (106). Still, Edward's repeated musings on the loss of his soul are crucial to his resistance to turn Bella.

Rather than gesture to a debate about whether becoming a vampire means having to battle social prejudice or forsaking your soul, L'amante di Destino foregrounds Bella's individual choice in the turning process. As this choice falls on Alice, the threat of a confrontation between Bill and Edward is removed along with any connotations the turning process has to the canon's romantic intimacy. While painful, the transformation leaves Bella with heightened senses (true to vampiric competencies in both canons) and with increased physical beauty (true to Twilight). When a character is transformed into a non-human, and to boot a creature that might constitute a threat to other humans, one challenge may become to render him or her in such a way that any potential identification or sympathy from the reader or viewer is not lost in the process. L'amante di Destino solves this by having the newborn Bella repelled by human blood. In a clever move playing on the Twilight canon idea that vampires bring traits from their human life into the vampire existence, her "distaste for blood" which has her fainting repeatedly in the canon, is heightened to the degree that she will never constitute a threat to humans.[11]

Bella's choice of having Alice as the one to turn her indicates the route the fanfic author has chosen for her ending: Bella has opted to become like the Cullens, and has thus chosen Edward as her eternal partner. The strong grounding in the romance format seems also to induce a desire to create happy endings for the other characters involved. Since Sookie never meets Bill in the first place, her strong canon feelings for Sam have their outlet and they are paired off early in the story. But where does that leave Bill? The last chapter of the fanfic depicts a brief and successful battle with the rogue vampire Victoria and her cohorts, and in the aftermath the Cullens and another vampire clan appear. While not developed further L'amante di Destino has Bill encounter the vampire Tanya and "[t]he smile on her face was soon mirrored in his." This removes any lingering guilt Bella feels about having abandoned Bill and signals a possible future happiness also for him.

The author has throughout the publishing process hinted at different outcomes of the romantic core story and encouraged reader input, and responses to her final solution vary with readers being part of either Team Bill or Team Edward. Aware that she may have disappointed some readers from the former camp, L'amante di Destino writes by way of explanation in her concluding notes, "I just hadn't developed Bill enough in the story to all of a sudden have [Bella] not choose Edward." Bill does remain a somewhat one-dimensional character in the story, acting as a foil to Bella's thoughts and development rather than being awarded a narrative perspective or personal growth of his own. On some level, this takes us full circle to the initial reader comments discussed. The author is clearly invested in Twilight and is able to explain the characters' motivations against the backdrop of her knowledge of this canon, whereas True Blood is a more recent interest. In addition, and in contrast to the two previously discussed stories, *True Twilight* exhibits no desire to criticize and rewrite the central love story, despite the future setting with a more experienced and critical Bella. It is thus not surprising that the fanfic ends like Twilight, with Bella forever in Edward's arms.

Even when authors represent Alternate Universe developments in their stories or as here change either the temporal or geographical setting (or both), fact remains that the stories gain an increased meaning when read with the canon as central intertext. This works on the level of the text itself—a resistance to canon elements is more effective if this element is known by readers—and on the level of reception. Stein and Busse argue that even when fans take some liberties with the canon material "they must ... contend with the fact that many of their readers will read their fan fiction with knowledge of the source text [canon] as a background and a filter" (196). Fan practices such as fan fiction are communal ones: fan fiction is written to be read and reviewed, and canons are discussed and interpreted collectively. Even in fanfics which bend narrative, genre or thematic rules, the intertextual ties to the canon are foregrounded to ensure that readers are on board.

In the three analyzed fanfics, the authors to varying degrees stay true to the canons' hard data, as well as to characters' competencies and ethics. Yet, each story plays with the canon norms attached to these levels of interpretation. Making canon protagonists older and more mature, without necessarily changing their ethics or competencies, enables Lisse and Piper to introduce alternative questions about responsibility and choice, and they both draw attention to how the paranormal romance paradigm does not gel with the emotional realism they look for in texts. While they retain closeness between characters or even romantic love itself, the consequences of these affective bonds play out differently. Izzy leaves the unnamed boy for his own protection and Bonnie does not give up life to be with her vampire forever. Bella in *True Twilight* conforms quite closely to her canon competencies—she is clumsy, has a poor fashion sense and an uncanny ability to attract vampires—and the focus on the successful resolution to the paranormal romance may seem to indicate a higher level of intertextual compliance; less of a play with canon rules than Lisse's and Piper's stories. However, L'Amante di Destino's fanfic hinges on the AU element of having Bella leave Forks instead of waiting for Edward's return. Her canon desolation and passivity (competencies in the specific canon situation) are transformed into an active choice. On the interpretative level of themes, Bella's own choice in the turning process likewise shifts associations to the strong canon link between vampiric transformation and romantic intimacy.

3. The Archive of New Stories

What if Bella is no longer the narrator in Twilight? What kind of life did Eric lead when he was human? And what happens if Elena chooses Damon instead of Stefan? Perspective shifts, prequels and sequels, and new pairings, are forms and narrative strategies which structure fanfic production in general.[1] Alone or combined, they are employed by all fanfic authors in our sample and illustrate different levels of fidelity to canon characterizations and plot lines. In chapters four and five, these forms and narrative strategies are used by fanfic authors to question aspects of the canons when it comes to sexualities and sexual practices, monsterization processes, and issues of good and evil. Our focus in this chapter is on stories which are often overlooked in analyses because they do not seem to offer sites of contestation and resistance. However, they illustrate particular transformative processes in regards to the canon material which are as pertinent as more overtly subversive fanfic.

Shifting perspectives means opportunities to explore the psychology and development of characters other than the canon narrators and focalizers while still staying relatively close to canon portrayals. Prequels analyzed in this chapter delineate how character traits, ethics and behaviors are formed in the past, pointing forwards to the now of the canon. In the selected sequels, fanfic authors envision plot and character developments which follow logically from the canon's narrative arc. Altered pairings commonly fall into the AU category of fan fiction and thus represent authors' desires to explore roads not taken in the canons. The analyzed stories retain the heteronormativity of the canons (slash and femslash are discussed in greater detail in chapter four), but altered pairings have other consequences for both plot and character when authors investigate either the relationships which are implied but not realized in the canons or feature more unusual pairings. The fanfics on the one hand evince particular reader reactions — a dissatisfaction with both realized and implied romances — but also illustrate the curiosity about what happens when characters are combined in rather more unexpected ways.

Intertextuality in the three main types of transformations is in many ways similar to intertextuality in traditionally printed works, but fanfic openly acknowledges the relationship it has with the canon works, and characters, plot lines and themes are dependent on this connection. Rather than veiled references to a previous work, there is a continuous dialogue with it. To situate fan fiction within a longer history of intertextual writing, and draw attention to the transformative potential also of faithful elaborations, we open this chapter with discussions about Abigail Derecho's definition and analyses of archontic writing. Derecho sees texts as archives which can be expanded indefinitely through new additions. Each artifact deposited into a text's archive enlarges it rather than simply imitates it or transgresses its boundaries. Each holds the possibility of influencing future readers' readings of the canon material and in archontic writing, old and new text coexist. Abandoning a hierarchical view on texts stressing lineage, the archontic principle is crucial when thinking critically, ethically and aesthetically about fan prosumption.

Intertextuality and Archontic Texts

Fan fiction is a (relatively) new text form only in that the online environment has increased opportunities for quick publishing, fast and dialogic contact with other members of a fandom, and immediate reader response to the texts. To appropriate narrative elements and story lines is naturally not a new phenomenon, nor is the tendency to create strong, often overt intertextual ties to previous works. When fan fiction is debated today and issues are raised concerning possible plagiarism and "character theft," parallels are often drawn which illustrate the long history of appropriative writing. Lev Grossman, for example, makes a case for approaching fan fiction's use of canon characters in the same manner as one would Virgil's use of Aeneas (originating as a character in Homer's *Odyssey*), Tom Stoppard's use of Shakespeare's characters Rosencrantz and Guildenstern, and Geraldine Brooks' use of the absent Mr. March in Louisa May Alcott's *Little Women* (n. pag.). Similar parallels can of course be drawn to uses of plot elements or narrative arcs — think *Romeo and Juliet* and *West Side Story*— and shifted perspectives, as in Valerie Martin's *Mary Reilly*, which retells events in Robert Louis Stevenson's *The Strange Case of Dr. Jekyll and Mr. Hyde* from the perspective of the doctor's maid. Like fanfic authors, Virgil, Stoppard, Brooks and Martin may admire aspects of the works they appropriate, or they may elaborate on and "correct" aspects of the narratives because they are *not* fans.[2]

Two main tendencies situate fan fiction in this longer historical context, the first being a result of the desire to never let the story die. For authors driven by this desire, sequels are the most readily available form as it enables them to take off *from* a narrative and use ready-made characters. For example, Emma Tennant's *Pemberley* and Susan Hill's *Mrs. de Winter* (sequels to *Pride and Prejudice* and *Rebecca*, respectively), investigate what happens to the characters after a wedding in the first case, after a self-imposed European exile in the second, and while both texts include reflections on the past, these corroborate rather than question information supplied by Jane Austen and Daphne du Maurier. Sequels can affect the perception of, but not alter, events and characterizations in the preexisting narrative, but still represent a certain freedom since characters can develop in unexpected ways. While prequels similarly are results of the desire to have more of the same story, they are comparatively rarer. To an extent circumscribed by the preexisting narrative authors often work *towards* it and explore how characters are formed by past experiences. The threatening presence of Rochester's supposedly mad wife Bertha in Charlotte Brontë's *Jane Eyre* leads Jean Rhys to imagine a backstory in which the madwoman in the attic acquires a different name and a narrative voice in the prequel *Wide Sargasso Sea*. Rhys' novel also aptly illustrates the second main motivation for appropriations: to question aspects of the canon. In addition to expanding Bertha's/Antoinette's agency, it became an important contribution to postcolonial and feminist debates in the 1960s. Parallel narratives such as Alice Randall's *The Wind Done Gone* illustrate a similar critique. Randall's novel tells the same story as Margaret Mitchell's *Gone with the Wind*, but from the perspective of Scarlett O'Hara's illegitimate black half-sister and, like Rhys' novel, it critiques the power structures depicted in the preexisting narrative, in this case connected to gender and race.

Often, fan fictions are a mix between these two tendencies and, as we have argued elsewhere, they "need to be read with an eye to both what they subvert or vary *and* what they endlessly recycle" (Lindgren Leavenworth, "Variations" 70). Every fanfic is a result of the desire to let the story live on. By adding perspectives, altering pairings, or by extending the story to encompass the before and after, the employment of characters, plot strands and narrative details signal, precisely, that the story is intended as a continuation of or complement to the preexisting text. When fanfic authors substantially alter elements, especially when they play with the canon ethics and the characters' behavior and psychology, they effect similar things as Rhys and Randall: they question the heteronormativity of the canon, for example, or engage in a debate about the norms of popular culture through alternative depictions of agency.

Variations as well as recycled elements thus add associations to preexisting narratives, and both past and present transformative activities necessitate a move away from questions of ownership and hierarchies. Based on Jacques Derrida's notion of the open archive in *Archive Fever* (1995), Abigail Derecho suggests the term "archontic literature" to emphasize processes of exchange, whereby each addition to a text's archive enlarges it with new interpretations (65).[3] As a term, archontic replaces words such as *"derivative* or *appropriative"* with connotations to "property, ownership, and hierarchy" signaling that the derivative text is of lesser value because of its indebtedness to the original or source material and dishonest in the sense that it imitates rather than creates (64).[4] Derecho is careful to point out that her definition at first glance has close affinities with other types of intertextuality and that it may therefore be seen as superfluous. However, she makes the precise distinction that new variations "enter the archive of other works by quoting them consciously, by pointedly locating themselves within the world of the archontic text [and] generate variations which explicitly announce themselves as variations" (Derecho 65). Both *Pemberley* and *Mrs. de Winter* openly signal the relationship to the earlier work through their titles, and re-employ characters and central lines. There are, in these novels, no attempts to hide or obscure the relationship with the previous texts; rather, they are contingent on it. Recycled dialogue from the canon texts, the use of canon characters, plot lines, themes and narrative details locate fanfics firmly in the archive on the level of story contents. But the open and explicit intertextual links to a canon are also evidenced by the fact that fanfics are published alongside others on fandom-specific sites and by statements found in paratexts which often situate the story precisely within the canon or acknowledge the source of inspiration through disclaimers.

To further demarcate archontic writing from other forms of intertextuality and to introduce a new way of thinking about the ethics of fan fictions and other types of transformative writing, Derecho uses Edouard Glissant's concept of "relation" in which "changes and shifts are critical. [...] Relation requires humans to take responsibility for keeping objects in play, whether they be stories or racial categories or languages or geographical boundaries" (Derecho 75).[5] The parts are as important as the whole in this line of argument, and relation on the one hand insures against the privileging of one over the other, on the other hand stresses that participation and individual responsibility are crucial to maintain a productive chaos. While reiteration of canon elements is certainly central in fanfic, the idea of the open archive enables a view of the texts as simultaneously creative; authors take part in a process of needed destabilization. In the case of our selection of fan fiction, each interpretation expands the Twilight, True Blood, or The Vampire Diaries archives, ensuring that the canons are "never solidified, calcified, or at rest" (Derecho 77). A canon is the starting point for a fanfic and canon plots and characters lend meaning to the story; when deposited into the archive, the fanfic in turn affects the canon: canon and fanfic "resonate together" (Derecho 73). Aesthetically, that is, both similarities and differences invest the archontic text with significance. Repetition, with a twist, is as crucial to the archontic principle as originality has been in discussions where hierarchies between texts are retained.

Since fans bring influences from other narratives to their readings of canon materials, contemporary vampire archives can extend indefinitely. While some of these readings may go against the grain of the specific canon, they can simultaneously conform to other narratives, associations and conventions. In Milly Williamson's study, fans

> are reading "with the grain," not of a particular text (although often they are), but of an interpretative strategy, a meta-interpretation of the figure of the vampire that is in excess of any single textual construction, although it can be found in many. [...] The popularity of certain conventions, both historically and currently, have produced a way of reading the vampire amongst many vampire fans which is connected to important genre conventions, but partially disconnected from specific texts [69].

As an example, Williamson uses fans' discussions about the vampires in Joel Shumacher's film *The Lost Boys* (1987). There, the vampires are unquestionably "revel[ling] in their fiendish lawlessness, yet the fans read [them] sympathetically because they are reading them through the sympathetic vampire lens that overarches any particular text" (Williamson 70). When fanfic authors re-fang the friendly and civilized main vampires in the canons we analyze, in an opposite move compared to fans' sympathetic readings of the vampires in *The Lost Boys*, it signals their adoption of an interpretative lens which allows the initially sympathetic Bill, Edward and Stefan to be vilified. In the creation of slash and femslash another type of interpretative lens is used, perhaps adopted from the early nineteenth-century homosocial stories by John Polidori, Lord Byron and Sheridan Le Fanu, perhaps adopted from Anne Rice's more overtly homoerotic attachments between vampires, or perhaps from a more general cultural association between vampires and non-heteronormative sexuality (which in turn builds, consciously or unconsciously, on vampire narratives such as the ones mentioned). The canons' genre structure, finally, may supply yet another interpretative lens and fanfics which, for example, focus on the physical consummation of relationships between heterosexual characters can then be considered as reworkings inspired by the romance format, or, in more graphic cases, by erotica and pornography. Evil Bill, Sex-crazed Edward and Gay Stefan are thus added to their respective archive, along with other canon characters, identifiable plots or scenes, or smaller narrative details. In this way, fanfics which read *against* the grain of the canon, but *with* the grain of other genre and culture intertexts, are anchored in the archives of True Blood, Twilight and The Vampire Diaries.

New Perspectives

The canons' foci on the female protagonists' perspectives, reactions and emotions leave fanfic authors with an incentive to give a narrative voice to other characters. Often, stories incorporate several different perspectives, signaled by the abbreviation POV (Point of View), preceded by the name of the character whose narrative voice is featured. Through shifts, fanfic authors elaborate on missing moments or gaps in the canon texts, events which are of no particular significance to the main protagonists, but which can be construed as crucial to minor characters. On the level of character, the altered point of view increases an understanding of minor characters, but may also effect a changed perception of the canons' protagonists. When Bella, Sookie and Elena are no longer narrators, other types of information and description are enabled.

Stories containing switched perspectives are numerous, and several of the fanfics discussed in the following sections and the coming chapters transfer the narrative voice to other characters. In our analysis here, we will focus exclusively on DCWriter16's True Blood fanfic *The Deep*, which contains a series of alternative points-of-views and also illustrates how these indicate how events can be construed differently depending on the temporal position of the narrative subject; that is, new perspectives in both senses of the word. In nine chapters, DCWriter16 alters the narrative style and switches between the POVs of Eric, Pam, Sookie, Sam and Bill.[6] Although we omit references to individual chapters in the other fanfic-analyses in this book, we retain them here since the structure of *The Deep* is of particular interest. Chapters 1 ("In the Evening"), 3 ("Dark Summer") and 7 ("The Long Way Around") are narrated from Eric's perspective; chapters 2 ("The Deep") and 5 ("The Dead") from Pam's; chapters 4 ("Rise") and 9 ("The Fall") from Sookie's; chapter 6 ("Gone Missing") from Bill's; and chapter 8 ("Heart") from Sam's. All chapters revolve around or preface one central plot alteration: Sookie's death and transformation into a vampire, and what that entails of actions and reactions from the other characters. There are temporal relocations between chapters but also within, as characters narrate their stories from a present while including memories from what has previously taken place. Among the myriad of connections between the chapters on the levels of both stylistics and plot, we focus on the idea of burying one's love, depictions of love (be it romantic or familial) and on how very specific imagery connected to water, skies and fire is used to create narrative cohesion. We will, however, start with a discussion about Eric's t-shirt, as it aptly illustrates how seemingly insignificant details are used to trace the characters' development and create connections between the chapters.

The first chapter depicts Sookie and Eric's tender lovemaking, at the start of which Eric removes his t-shirt, throwing it on the grass "which as far as [he is] concerned is another fucking planet." The t-shirt seems to have little significance in the moment, represented only as an obstacle to physical closeness. After making love, however, things between Sookie and Eric take a turn for the worse, culminating in a dramatic breakup. During this breakup, Sookie tries to remain cool and distant, but in chapter four we learn that having collected the items spread across the lawn, she weeps in her bed with the t-shirt pressed to her face. "I wadded it up and buried my face in it. I sobbed and screamed and kicked. Everything he has done for me. There is no one still living who has gone so far" ("Rise"). The t-shirt is thus present (discarded and recovered) in two situations which set the mood for the story and establish the central characters' feelings. Sookie's reaction in the fourth chapter takes the reader back to the first, despite the crucial event of her death depicted in chapters in between.

What also takes place in a chapter in between (chapter three) is that Eric sneaks into Sookie's bedroom, after the funeral following the car accident which ends her human life in the fanfic. Under her pillow he finds his discarded garment, "the one I left here when I stalked away for good. I laid on her bed with my head on her pillow. I crunched the shirt in my hands and pressed my face into it. A salty smell I recognized: her tears" ("Dark Summer"). In a similar position on the bed as Sookie is in the fourth chapter, Eric experiences a similar distress and sadness. Just as Sookie has recognized his scent in the fabric, he is now drawn to the remaining scent of her tears. In the fifth chapter, when Sookie has returned as a vampire, the t-shirt (now flung on the floor) is the first thing Pam packs as the two female characters prepare to leave for Pam's house, and by this point, the smells of Eric and Sookie have mingled in the fabric. The t-shirt becomes emblematic not only of the bond between the estranged lovers, but of Pam's new maternal role — she is the one who has turned Sookie — and it is now her responsibility to ensure that her Child is surrounded with comfort. In her new existence as a vampire, the t-shirt indeed provides comfort for Sookie as it is what she chooses to wear for her first daytime sleep. Eric is also present in this scene and when he reflects on it, in chapter seven, notes that Sookie "is wearing the t-shirt I discarded on the very last night I ever saw her alive" ("The Long Way Around"). His observation connects to a returning theme: how ordinary objects only take on significance when they have featured into moments which in hindsight are life-altering. When Eric flings the t-shirt onto the grass in the first chapter, he does not award this action any particular importance. When Sookie next picks it up, it serves a reminder of hurt and injury, and becomes a receptacle of her tears. But then an event of momentous importance occurs: Sookie's death, and the t-shirt gains significance as a memento of what was. The new narrative perspectives are complemented by new perspectives on the object.

DCWriter16's repeated use of the t-shirt and the different levels of significance it accrues in the chapters are mirrored by the ways in which phrases and imagery are recycled, each time with a slight alteration which invites reinterpretations. The phrase "to love is to bury" provides a succinct example and ties into the fanfic's general theme of self-deception.[7] As in the canon, a relationship between human and vampire is potentially dangerous, and in *The Deep*, Eric has initially persuaded himself that potential threats are enough to terminate the love affair. "To love is to bury. I will let her go," Eric thinks ("In the Evening"). In a conversation with Pam, which Eric recalls, he has claimed that the only thing he can give Sookie is "a shorter lifespan." Pam reacts by calling this bluff and Eric "can't punish her for telling the truth" ("In the Evening"). Even at the outset, Eric knows that he is deceiving himself, and that burying his love might simply be the easy way out.

The figurative burial takes a literal turn with Sookie's death and interment. Following canon vampire lore, a human who is brought back from death through the ingestion of vampire blood needs to be buried for three days before they turn. In the fanfic, Sookie's death is un-dramatic in that it is not connected to anything paranormal — her car is hit by a careless driver. Pam, who has been left in charge of Sookie's protection after Eric's departure, takes the drastic measure to give Sookie some of her own blood, once it becomes apparent that the human life cannot be saved. Waiting by Sookie's grave, Pam thinks:

> I hope Eric will regard my action as a gift to him, in gratitude for my second life and all he has shown me and done for me since my death. I hope their bond will hold through her transformation. [...] Hope springs eternal. To love is to bury. You can't make an omelet without breaking some eggs. Obviously ["The Deep"].

The alternative interpretation of "to love is to bury" is but one of several thematic strands which come together in Pam's reflections. Eric is Pam's Maker and since the fanfic includes references to her backstory, it is clear that her transformation has been a boon to her. She claims that her choices in life were predetermined and that "death had been my salvation, my passage into life" ("The Dead"). By burying her, Eric has shown her his love; by burying Sookie, Pam reciprocates. Pam bases her desire to give Eric a continued existence with

Sookie not only on gratitude, but on the bond, the "soul-deep ... connection" she has perceived exists between them ("The Deep"). But to turn Sookie is potentially dangerous to Pam as Eric may very well punish her for making a decision he has not been able to make, and as Sookie herself may have a thing or two to say about it once back. The broken eggs are thus on the one hand connected to a possible fracture in Pam's relationship with Eric, on the other to that Sookie, indeed, has to die, and then be turned, for the lovers to be reunited.

It is not only Sookie's return to an un-life and their resumed relationship (Pam's successfully executed omelet) which makes Eric completely reconsider his previously held conviction that their happiness is contingent on being apart. Already when he says it the first time, he is starting to question himself, and after her funeral, and when he still believes her to be lost, he thinks: "To love is to bury. Love her enough to let her go, to leave her be. What the fuck was I thinking?" ("Dark Summer"). Towards the end of the fanfic, with Sookie back, he has reformulated his view: "Loving something means keeping it close. Keep one loved thing closest to you. All the rest doesn't matter" ("The Long Way Around"). The reader of the fanfic is taken along Eric's path to self-discovery, depicted in chapters narrated from both his and other characters' perspectives, through the repeated returns to the key phrase and the different meanings (and levels of truthfulness) it accrues in the story's progress.

The theme of self-deception is linked to the reader's growing realization that observation can be fickle indeed. The characters think they know important details which are then, when perspectives are altered, turned on their heads. Among the many realizations of this kind in *The Deep*, an early example comes in the form of stargazing. The very first evening depicted in the fanfic sees Eric and Sookie staring into the sky. Sookie claims that despite the book she is consulting, she has a hard time identifying the constellations and Eric is a willing teacher: "I tell her about the zodiac. I tell her all of the signs and what they mean" ("In the Evening"). At this point, the conveyance of knowledge reads as an endearing gesture. In the first chapter narrated from Sookie's point of view, the reader learns that the book is "an old Southern Living collection of dessert recipes" and that her ignorance of the stars and signs has been a show: "Of course, I already knew all of them. My Gran had taken me and Jason out for many summer nights in our youth, pointing out pictures and telling stories" ("Rise"). Her willingness to let herself be educated is, like the imparted knowledge, a sign of love, and connected to what Sookie believes constitutes a good relationship. "It made [Eric] feel good when he thought he was sharing knowledge I didn't have, when I let him protect me" ("Rise"). What Eric observes — Sookie's lack of knowledge — is challenged by the switched perspective and the expanded knowledge the reader gets, but remains his truth within the actual situation. Yet, in this context, pretense is used to illustrate what lovers are willing to do for each other, rather than creating an obstacle on the road to happiness as the consequences of Eric's self-deception do. Self-deception and pretense which matters and that which does not are juxtaposed and has several parallels in *The Deep*, all illustrating a continuous play with levels of signification.

The character, aside from Eric, whose relationship with Sookie is most profoundly altered, is Pam. Her roles in relation to Sookie, first as friend, then as Maker, is in part explored through imagery connected to ocean creatures and to the theme reflected in the fanfic's title: the deep. In the first chapter from Pam's point of view, Sookie asks her what her daytime sleep is like. Pam, claiming not to remember any dreams, says that "*the day is the absolute darkness and silence I imagine of the deepest parts of the ocean*" ("The Deep").[8] Sookie has read about the ocean depths and the creatures that dwell there. She is particularly fascinated with fish which "*make their own* [light]," or, as Pam reflects, "[f]ireworks" ("The Deep"). Pam acknowledges that the submersion into darkness and the necessity of creating one's own light to see fit well with what little she can recall about vampire dreams. In the second of Pam's chapters, she is able to remember a dream in which she is human and has just become a mother. Her own mother appears in the dream: "*Up from the deep*, she says, and balls her hands into fists and splays her fingers out over and over again. Fireworks" ("The Dead"). The hand movements in the dream correspond to Sookie's when she is first telling Pam about the mysterious sea creatures and the implications of the dream seem to be that Pam can make her own light in the oceanic depth of her days and that she needs to surface because she is now a mother of sorts.

The connection established in the turning process is in the canon rendered in familial terms. As the newly turned, referred to as child, has to forfeit human existence and sever family ties, new bonds appear in their place with concomitant responsibilities. In the fanfic, motherhood has featured into Pam's excessively controlled past since she was expected to procreate but averse to the idea. However, turning Sookie entails the awakening of emotions that are clearly maternal. Pam refers to "the new instinct of a Maker" which can be equated with the alleged natural instincts of a mother and when Sookie returns a vampire she is figured as a child not only in the vampiric sense but in a more traditional conception of an infant: "this new creature leaning heavily on my shoulder, her soft cries filling the deep quiet of the woods" ("The Deep"). Although Pam concedes that Sookie "is not a baby" her vulnerability renders her as one and Pam holds her, comforts her and kisses her "very softly on her temple" ("The Dead"). Although Sookie and Pam have a bond also in the canon, this representation illustrates a significantly different relation, and one Pam cannot resist: her "blood moves now with [the] unexpected love" ("The Dead"). As Pam's dream signals, she has a new purpose in her life after the act of turning Sookie, and the deep no longer represents only the darkness of the oceans but the depth of feelings in their relationship.

A love as deep as the sea is an image which is featured also in relation to Sookie and Eric, coupled with imagery connected to fire and stars. The seemingly fated love between the two is three times connected to gravity and brings with it connotations to both lack of difficulty and inevitability. For example, Sookie says when the relationship is reassumed: "Every broken thing fell back together, with the ease of gravity, of a meteor falling to earth in a gown of flames" ("The Fall"). Her new perspective and identity as a vampire make it easier for her to accept the idea of her and Eric together. They are no longer threatened by characters opposed to human/vampire relationships, and the irresistible pull of the gravitational love no longer needs to be fought. The motif of stargazing connects the end to the beginning, fittingly considering the fanfic's emphasis on complementarity. Sookie thinks: "He said that before me, he had been a forest dry as bone, just waiting for something to light it up. And I, the spark landing deep within and setting us both on fire. Together, he and I are the lights you see, falling through the sky at night" ("The Fall"). The "you" in the final sentence of the fanfic addresses the reader and moves the perspective even further: it is now a question also of what he or she sees.

In addition to providing glimpses into the psyches of characters who do not have narrative perspectives in the canon, *The Deep* adds several new associations to characters to the True Blood archive: Pam-as-mother, Sookie-as-vampire, and a considerably less cynical Eric. More importantly, it also engages in very imaginative ways with the canon themes of observation and knowledge. In both novels and TV series, it is emphasized that perceptions shift and change with expanded (or reduced) knowledge. The Great Revelation of vampire existence is but one of many examples of how some information is made public, influencing views of the new minority, while other aspects remain secret, for longer or shorter periods of time, causing either ease or distrust. The fanfic adds extended ruminations on the nature of observation to the archive, and these underscore that perspectives *on* things are relative also to the perspective *of* the narrative subject. Finally, although some characterizations, Pam's in particular, seem to go against the grain of the canon, they are nevertheless anchored in other central canon ideas, most notably the transformative power of the maker/child bond.

New Beginnings: What Came Before

A majority of prequels in our selection predictably center on the vampire protagonists, as their long lives constitute a pull for fanfic authors. Both brief references to and more developed stories about the characters' past in the canons may be what spark fanfic authors' initial interest, but simultaneously ensure (or demand) a certain level of fidelity to the partially disclosed information. Even when characters in fanfic prequels are represented as very different from their portrayal in the canon, there is often a sense of progression towards their canon state. Stories may start by depicting the vampire characters as wild and evil, for example, but introduce reasons for this and go on to explore precisely how and why they end up as the romantically attractive characters they are in the canon.

In the case of Eric, written and visual texts veer off in different directions when it comes to representations of his turning and his sire, although in both he is of Scandinavian ancestry and made a vampire in the Viking age. In Charlaine Harris' ninth novel, *Dead and Gone*, Eric tells Sookie about his maker Appius Livius Ocella, a Roman fighter who is very strong because of his old age, who commands Eric's obedience and loyalty and also his body (88–90). Ocella makes only a brief appearance in the next novel *Dead in the Family*, and dies shortly afterwards. After his death Eric tells Sookie that his master has taught him "everything about being a vampire. [...] He protected me and loved me. He caused me pain for decades. He gave me life" (Harris, *Dead in the Family*, 309–10). In the second season of *True Blood*, a flashback sequence shows how a fatally wounded Eric is turned by the boy-vampire Godric who asks him: "Could you walk with me through the world? Through the dark?" In exchange for this companionship, Godric promises Eric, "I'll teach you all I know. I'll be your father, your brother, your child" (2:5 "Never Let Me Go"). Godric becomes a recurring character in the TV series, featuring as a ghost after his death. He is a more benevolent character than Ocella, but both are ambivalently regarded. They possess great and sometimes frightening power, they provide their progeny with needed instruction and familial bonds which are supportive as well as commanding absolute obedience. Finally, they are depicted as marginalized and vulnerable because they have lived through long centuries and many changes, and both meet their ends, making Eric an "orphan."

Perhaps because of his temporary appearance and death shortly thereafter, along with the fact that Eric provides scant detail about his past in the novel series, there are very few fanfics which feature Ocella, whereas the TV series' relationship between maker and child has resulted in an abundance of stories.

In the story notes for the fanfic *The Child*, author Roman writes of her fascination with "the show's obviously devoted, but incredibly deferential relationship between Eric and Godric" and how the story is a response to her curiosity about how this relationship has played out and structured their actions and reactions during the thousand years that have passed since Eric's turning. Godric is depicted as creating his child out of curiosity and vanity; he observes the new vampire's birth and initial progress with interest and is content that Eric quickly comes to show him love and submission, "preen[ing] inwardly at the unending chamber of marvels that he was to his child." But the first years of their companionship are marked by continuous tests and Godric's periodic absences. In part, these work as instructions to the rules of vampire existence, but also as ways for Godric "to reassure himself that he wasn't becoming too attached to his child." He claims that the strong bonds will inevitably be broken, and thus wants to insure himself against future grief. Throughout the first sections of the fanfic, Godric remains puzzling and otherworldly; a possessive, complicated and not always likeable character. Eric at first displays attachments to his human life, is unsure of his new place in the world, and mourns what he has been and the deaths of his own people. Only in time does he come to see this as a vulnerability and admire Godric's "disconnect."

Although Godric is interested in some aspects of human development, feelings of ennui periodically surface. The French Revolution, for example, is invigorating because it gives the two vampires something to do, but Godric "could foresee how it would all end already, and to be frank, nothing would ever quite match the fall of the Roman Empire." His boredom is coupled with feelings of marginalization and loneliness, especially when Eric creates Pam, a child of his own. Roman carefully depicts Godric's process of self-Othering, precipitated by jealousy: "He was suddenly so jealous of all those who had ever caught or would ever catch Eric's attention. His human wife, his brothers-in-arms, his petulant child, *his own past self*." Progressively more "disgusted" with himself, the curious and cruel Godric from the fanfic's beginning is replaced with a vampire who ponders the justification of his and his species' existence. This development points forwards to the now of the canon, and the plot strand ending with his suicide. Godric meets the sun also in *The Child* in a scene which adds further associations to the child/maker bond to the archive. Godric has previously denied Eric a release from this bond which reads as puzzling considering that they are drifting apart, no longer entertained or consoled by each other. The refusal to dissolve it, however, ensures Eric's continued deference (the source of Roman's initial fascination with the relationship), and renders the child unable to prevent his maker's suicide.

The Child imaginatively spans several centuries and touches on isolated moments in the characters' time together. *White Nights* by the same author and published six months later is not openly connected to nor described as a continuation of *The Child*, but can be read as a missing-pieces kind of fanfic because it elaborates on one of innumerable missing moments in the first story. Godric spends a night and a morning on an Italian beach, with Eric desperately trying to make him come inside, the rising sun foreshadowing the end Godric will meet. Godric's increasing moodiness, here characterized as "bouts of melancholia," is connected to his insecurities concerning Eric's feelings. *The Child* features one erotically charged encounter between them, which initially reads as another example of instruction and submission. When Godric later in the first fanfic thinks back on it, he characterizes it as an attempt "to curb his boredom by toying with Eric's feelings." In *White Nights*, the temporal setting of which is indeterminable, he reflects on it again, interpreting Eric's "reticence" as "rejection," in line with his increasing uncertainty about his place in the world and his own power. "He was old and alone, an absurd remnant of a world no one wanted to remember in a world that would not welcome him even if it could." The way his and Eric's differences have complemented each other in the past now serve to exacerbate the physical and existential isolation Godric feels. When Eric offers him his body, to lessen Godric's loneliness, the maker refuses, because he will not have Eric's "devotion [...] turn into resentment." Eric accepts this, and also accepts to stay with Godric through the long day, protecting him, comforting him, and reversing the roles they have previously had.

Roman's two fanfics take the reader through the stages of familial relationships Godric promises Eric in *True Blood*. He starts out as a proud but experimental father, becomes a brother in the couple's forays across Europe, and ends a child in need of comfort. Stories like these supply motivation not only for why Godric, an enigmatic character in the TV series, turns Eric in the first place, but for why and how their relationship is maintained during the centuries. *The Child* and *White Nights* render Godric a complex character who at the end of his existence does not *"think like a vampire any more, but ... still think[s] like Eric's maker"* (*The Child*). With turning comes responsibilities, and with being turned comes the need to obey. Roman does not simplify either of these urges, on the contrary, the images of both Godric and Eric, and the expanded associations to them and their relationship added to the archive, hinge on both of them resisting and questioning the strong bond between maker and child, as well as the inevitable final separation between them.

Eric's deference to Godric, and later Pam's to Eric, is rendered as based on love and respect, but is still absolute, in the canon as well as in fanfic such as Roman's. But even fraught relationships, such as the one between Bill and his maker Lorena, entail a reluctant obedience.[9] Katharina Rein argues that the general disintegration of the family depicted in *True Blood* is offset by "elective affinities," by which characters come to choose "alternative concepts of partnership and cohabitation" (n. pag.). While this certainly holds for many of the depicted human relationships, we would argue that the issue of choice in the vampiric familial constellations is problematized. In Twilight, the bonds between maker and children do not result in the same kind of deference, the wishes of the former do not control the latter, and this canon to a greater extent illustrates the elective aspect of belonging to a family. The bonds between the Cullen patriarch, Carlisle, and those he turns, Edward, Esme, Rosalie and Emmett, are strong, based on love but contingent on the progeny's voluntariness. Carlisle himself has no possibility of forming a bond as he is transformed by an anonymous attacker who leaves him to fend for himself, and Alice and Jasper do not exhibit ties to their makers. The latter two elect to become members of Carlisle's family, and their instabilities serve as reminders of the centrality of a maker's responsibility and instruction.

Depictions of how these elective affinities have been made abound in Twilight prequels, often drawing attention to the freedom inherent in the fabrication of the specific family tree. In flute_genevive's *In the Land of One Thousand Years*, Emmett has just been turned, and together with Edward attempts to figure out his position in the new family. "You can be the son of Esme's older sister, who died," Edward suggests at first, but then notes that this identity would create an unwanted uncle/nephew bond between them. He concludes, therefore, "You will be the son of one of Esme's cousins. We can think of a name later." The Cullens' canon lifestyle is restricted by human norms, dictating, for example, that Esme will never be Edward's sister, even though turned after him, because she is married to Carlisle and older than Edward when she was made a vampire. These restrictions are not removed in the fanfic, but stressed are the liberating aspects of being able to choose what family to enter, as well as what position to occupy in it.

Memories of a human life are mentioned in the Twilight canon as important aspects of the characters' present state. In this, Alice stands apart from the others because she "remember[s] nothing of being human" (Meyer, *Twilight* 362) and her "first memory is of seeing Jasper's face in [her] future" (Meyer, *Eclipse* 518). Prequels exploring Alice's past life can contribute pieces to the puzzle without violating fidelity, and point forwards to the now of the canon, while still providing events with a twist. In Lunar Siren's *Alice Smiled*, Alice is Other already as a child because of her visions. These frighten people around her and make her mother see her as a "demon." In contrast to Alice's canon competency of premonitions, however, not all of her visions in the fanfic predict the future. Rather, she often dreams that she shares a body with someone else: "*she watched through his eyes, used his hands.*" These dreams establish an early connection with Jasper, since what Alice experiences is his struggle among the violent newborn vampires, and later his forays with Peter and Charlotte, the nomads who teach him self-control. It is also a dream of Jasper which becomes "the last straw" for her family as Alice's hands have mimicked Jasper's movements and she has "almost strangled her sister." The perceived demon in the family is confined to an asylum, and to a dark "room with distant screams." In dreaming in black and white's *Alice, Interrupted*, Alice is already locked away in her cell at the start of the story and her amnesia is medically induced. The condition which seems to have necessitated the treatment finds a parallel, however, in Alice's sister Cynthia's premonitions. As a frequent but seldom remembered visitor, she at one point has a vision of Alice's cell door opened and a casket carried out. When Alice tells her that "[t]he next time you come back, I'll be dead, you know," all Cynthia can say is "I know."

The fanfics end before the pivotal event of painful vampiric transformation which, it is indicated in the canon, may have contributed to Alice's lack of human memories. Although Alice in Twilight is sprightly and fond of slumber parties and shopping sprees, she is simultaneously sad and struggling with the power of her competency. In both fan fictions, Alice's visions play a complicated part which points forward to the canon depictions. On the one hand, her visions result in prejudiced and frightened surroundings, leading to randomly bestowed and primitive mental care. On the other hand, they offer her hope. In *Alice Smiled*, and in contrast to the dreams about Jasper, Alice has had more traditionally defined premonitions about the dark room she is locked into, and seeing that these have come true enables her to have faith in more hopeful visions. *Alice, Interrupted* has a more ambivalent ending in which Alice is overcome with the effects of drugs, but she still clings on to her conviction that she will meet Jasper "[i]n this world [or] the next." Neither story invests Alice with memories, rather they expound on the reasons why it is impossible for her to cling on to them, and in this way supply pieces to the puzzle of her past.

Seeing that the storyworld of Twilight is by now evoked not only by the canon texts but by several websites dedicated to the Twilight vampires' backstories, as well as Stephenie Meyer's own development of her characters' past in *The Twilight Saga: The Official, Illustrated Guide* (2011), authors who want to contribute pieces to the characters' past have become circumscribed. There simply are not many missing moments left to faithfully fill in if someone else has already done it for you, especially when this someone is the canon author.

An innovative route is taken in Beckylady's *Six Degrees of Separation*, a series consisting of three one-shots, published in 2009.[10] Even though the author has consulted the Twilight Lexicon, a website combining information from the canon texts with interviews with Meyer, she takes things further, by envisioning plotlines which feature characters who even on the quite detailed site are scantily described in the section "Character Bios."

The first story is narrated by a young woman, Helen, who helps her mother out at the family diner and dreams of becoming "the next Great American writer." As inspiration for her would-be masterpiece, she has a frequently returning diner guest, Miss Alice, who comes in on rainy days and never even tastes her coffee. In a recalled conversation, Alice has told Helen that she is waiting for someone special, the *"man of* [her] *dreams"* who will show up, but who is not *"ready yet."* The romance surrounding this expected meeting influences Helen, and when, in the now of the story, the man appears, looking and sounding exactly like Alice has predicted, Helen starts to believe in fate. She sees, already in this first meeting between Alice and Jasper, "that there was a soul deep connection made. Right there in my family's insignificant little diner." That a connection of such consequence can be made in this previously uninspiring place, changes Helen and her view of her own prospects. When a boy from school, Geoffrey Swan, calls to invite her to a dance, she instantly accepts, no longer worrying about the clumsiness her mother teases her about, and finding inspiration to envision fated happiness for herself. The author points it out in the end notes, but the temporal setting, Geoffrey's last name, and Helen's joke to her mother that if "lucky" her clumsiness "would skip a generation or two," indicate that the story recounts the start of the relationship between Bella's paternal grandparents. Further, it suggests that this relationship would not have come about, indeed Bella had not come about, had Alice not diverted Helen's attention away from her literary fantasies.

With less emphasis on fated circumstances surrounding the romance at its center, the second story nevertheless similarly depicts a chain of events necessary for bringing Bella into the world, moving one generation further back and outlining the meeting of Bella's great grandparents. Henry Higginbotham, a medical student, is called into the Chicago hospital where Carlisle Cullen works during an outbreak of the Spanish Influenza.[11] The intertextual links to the canon and even to the material in the Twilight Lexicon are more tenuous in this story, but include Henry overhearing Carlisle make a promise to a dying Elizabeth Masen, and later noting that Carlisle disappears. The reader familiar with the canon knows that Elizabeth is Edward's human mother, imploring Carlisle to save her son, and that Carlisle's disappearance is a result of the need to remove the newborn vampire Edward from the bloody surroundings. The unending deaths at the hospital make Henry gravitate towards a severely injured but recovering female patient. Like her great granddaughter will be, Missy Calloway is "a good listener" and she will also pass on "beautiful brown" eyes and her lack of complaint.

The last story features Liddy Dwyer, a young woman who is pregnant out of wedlock and fascinated by an old diary she has found. The diary is written by a Rosalie Hale and describes her conflicted feelings towards "someone named Carlisle," and her sadness that she will *"never know the joys of motherhood."* Liddy has had torn feelings about her own pregnancy, but her repeated returns to the diary entry convince her that she has made the right decision in keeping her baby. In a later section of the story, Liddy has had an accident and needs emergency surgery, performed by a certain Dr. Carlisle Cullen. There is an obvious parallel to the earlier story in that Liddy asks him to save the baby, but at this point, and without Elizabeth Masen's suspicions about Carlisle's paranormal abilities, Liddy's wish is not of a transformative nature. With both herself and the baby on the mend, however, Liddy starts to suspect that something fantastic is happening. The baby has received a gift from the Cullens, a "plush white baseball" which, a nurse informs Liddy, Carlisle's "daughter Alice insisted he" would have, and it is accompanied by a note signed by names Liddy recognizes from the diary. The baby will grow up to become Bella's baseball-playing stepfather Phil, and while he is divorced from biological ties unlike her ancestors in the previous stories, he too furthers the central canon romance by getting a new job and moving, which lands Bella squarely in Forks.

In contrast to the majority of stories depicting the past of the canon characters, *Six Degrees of Separation* imaginatively envisions fates belonging to characters on the fringe of the action. This kind of addition to the archive is unencumbered by the need to capture a character's voice or characteristics to remain faithful to the canon. It is still, however, an addition which repeats a basic theme in Twilight since the invented or extrapolated characters are no less important than the canon characters for events to be set in motion and for the ensuing, fated, romance to blossom. The vampires' Otherness does not enter into the stories aside from references which the reader familiar with Twilight, but not the fanfic's characters, catch: Alice's aura of danger, Carlisle's promise to Edward's mother and subsequent disappearance, and the puzzling reference in Rosalie's diary to her *"froze[n] ... eternal state."* The fact that the fanfic's central characters, who are in the right place at the right time, are human, thus removes much of the common focus on the paranormal aspect of the universal conspiracy to bring Bella and Edward together.

Like Rosalie's diary entries in Beckylady's fanfic, notes in a book ensure that everything comes together in order for the protagonist in another canon to be born in *The Past is Prologue* by lit_chick08. In this prequel to *The Vampire Diaries*, Isobel Flemming-Saltzman finds "a battered copy of *War and Peace* written in the original Russian." The name Isobel is written in the margin and comparing underlined sentences with an English translation Isobel finds the following sentence: "The whole world is divided for me into two parts: one is she, and there is all happiness, hope, light; the other is where she is not, and there is dejection and darkness...." The book has belonged to Isobel's mother and the sentences make her determined to give birth to her own daughter, Elena. Another similarity between the fanfics is that the vampire element is in the background, in *The Past Is Prologue* featured mainly as a device to bring together members of the Founding Families in *The Vampire Diaries*, and to further Isobel's own change. The story attaches a similar great importance to the past, in the process interrogating the secrets and lies which come with life in a claustrophobic small town.

The fanfic opens with Grayson Gilbert (Elena's father) being told that "it was important that he know his history." This history is not only connected to professions handed down through generations and set positions in the town's hierarchy, but also to information about the paranormal element the Gilberts and the other families need to protect unknowing inhabitants from. In the canon, Elena and her brother (along with the other teenagers, also descending from the Founders) ironically know very little about this aspect of history, thus being quite unprepared for the appearance of vampires. The past envisioned in the fanfic provides an explanation for this. Miranda Sommers does not agree to marry Grayson until he has promised her that their children "will never know about the Gilberts" and the history they protect. Another part of history the young adults in *The Vampire Diaries*, and by extension the audience, are not privy to is related to the friendships, love affairs, and betrayals of the parental generation. Elena's parents are deceased already when the canon narrative starts, and whereas other parents feature, they are mainly depicted as obstructions to the TV series' adolescent relationships. Alternating the omniscient perspective, the fanfic seizes on several of these characters among them Caroline's mother, Elena's uncle John and aunt Jenna and, naturally considering the scant information about them in the canon, Grayson and Miranda Gilbert. The story follows them from their childhood through adolescence and up to the point where the canon narrative starts.

There is no source like the Twilight Lexicon for fanfic authors to consult when imagining The Vampire Diaries prequels which potentially makes for a greater freedom. The point of lit_chick08's fanfic, however, is to establish that history is as always repeating itself. The repetition comes in the form of personality traits as well as behavior. Miranda, for example, has been "extremely popular" before moving to Mystic Falls, with "a certain cache in her social circle," an assessment which squares with how Elena is depicted in the canon. Richard Lockwood is regularly beaten by his father and worries about becoming a father himself; in the canon he often punishes his son Tyler physically. Patterns of infidelity and shifted romantic attachments are also indicated to be passed on from one generation to the next. Liz Forbes (Caroline's mother) sleeps with Grayson, and Jenna is in a string of relationships. But Liz and Jenna are also vehicles for depicting the absolute importance of friendship, which later also characterizes several canon relationships: Grayson is from childhood Liz's best friend, and Jenna's long relationship with Mason Lockwood is "forever love" because not sexual. Through these depictions, the parental generation is revealed as loving, hating, supporting and betraying each other to the same extent that their children later will. Patterns from the canon are thus recycled, adding more of the same, while simultaneously supplying some answers to questions which puzzle the characters in the now of the canon, along with its viewers.

The fanfic prequels discussed thus far do not interfere with subsequent canon events or characterizations, rather the authors are interested in exploring the motivations and circumstances that form the canon characters and lay the foundation for plot lines. But prequels can naturally also overthrow events in the canon and *Adeste Fidelis* by LJ Summers is an interesting example. The Twilight fanfic supplies a contrast to the idea of the right circumstances previously discussed in relation to Beckylady's *Six Degrees of Separation*, and adds yet another take on Alice's premonitions. The fanfic commences as Alice, newly turned and ruled by instinct, is looking for prey on a city street. She is discovered by Charlotte and Peter who react to her lack of instruction which makes her "a danger," both to herself and others, and to the fact that Alice is abandoned by her maker. Like Jasper, they have been sired by Maria and for her purposes of creating an army of newborn violent vampires to increase her feeding territory in the South. To them, perhaps because sired for this purpose, the question of a maker is crucial, whereas to Alice, "the matter [is one] of complete indifference." The two vampires attempt to instruct Alice in how to behave, but she receives even further guidance from premonitions of golden-eyed creatures who live another life, with other dietary choices, than her present companions. Alice desires an alternative because she has visions of her victims' bereaved families. On her own, and vicariously through her visions, she learns the "vegetarian" diet of rabbits, cats and horses. When Alice finally finds the two vampires from her visions: Carlisle and Edward, she notes that they are "entirely different from Charlotte and Peter [...] so *human*," and a more hands-on education starts, by which Alice learns how to blend in and how to become part of the mortals' society.

Finding Carlisle and Edward in 1921 suggests a play with the canon information as there, Alice joins the family later. LJ Summers writes in the chapter notes that her story features an "AU timeline," which reduces the surprise of the meeting, but the temporal setting is not the only alternative development. Peter and Charlotte early on tell Alice about Jasper who, like Alice, has an unusual gift but say: "Our sire had him killed." In the concluding paragraphs of the story, Carlisle further notices something "obvious" when Edward and Alice stare at each other, and sends a congratulatory thought to his son: "*A mate for Christmas is indeed a wonderful gift.*" The seemingly fated alliances between Alice and Jasper, and Edward and Bella, are here eschewed in favor of a new pairing. The story features the idea of right circumstances, but not for the canon's central romance. The focus on Alice and the alternative development of her life envisioned in *Adeste Fidelis* cause rather different consequences for the other characters and the specific future happiness depicted in the canon. While Esme, Rosalie and Emmett may still join the family in this fanfic, Jasper cannot, and even if Bella would later appear, Edward is taken.

New Beginnings: Now What?

Fanfic sequels in our sample range from depicting events taking place immediately after the canon's narrative arc to stories set decades or centuries into the future. *Secrecy* and *Morning*, which we will discuss shortly, begin a few months and a few days, respectively, after the end of the canon texts they work from, while Yodigittyyoyo sets her True Blood fanfic *My Last Sunrise* in a new millennium. In the latter, Sookie remains the first-person narrator and she reflects, as the title suggests, on the last time she saw the sun as a newly turned vampire. In this depiction of the future, Sookie's "human English is now a dead language," the climate has changed and changed again, and together with Eric she "rule[s] the western world." The long vampire existence has given her ample time to reflect on the things she has and those she does not have, but crucial is the sense that she "can finally appreciate [her] Lover's lifespan." While Sookie and Eric will never be perfectly matched in terms of experience (he is still twice her age), "[t]ime has evolved to mean little to" Sookie, which indicates that they are approaching some kind of equilibrium in their life together. Few fanfics we have come across depict this type of extreme future setting, possibly because it entails a kind of imaginative world-building that necessitates a revision of the canon ethics and the introduction of new laws, potentially even shifting the genre into science fiction. Tellingly, Yodigittyyoyo's story is very short and focused on the continued intimacy of the canon romance rather than explicating the future world. In longer stories, set in closer temporal proximity to the canon's story arc, the plot structure of the canon is often repeated: emphasis is on continued obstacles to be overcome, mysteries to be solved, and threats to be averted.

When exploring fanfic sequels, special attention needs to be paid to publishing dates and what instantiation of the canon the author is working from. Published in 2004, Finta's *Secrecy* works from what was then considered to be a closed canon: L.J. Smith's original novel quartet. The fanfic is set after the end of *The Reunion* with Elena and Stefan on an Italian honeymoon and with Bonnie and Meredith away at different colleges. The story stylistically mirrors the canon works as chapters alternate between these three settings and switch between first-person perspectives, in sections written as diary entries by Bonnie and Elena, and an omniscient narrative position. Although the characters are somewhat older than in the canon they retain their canon psychologies: Bonnie is optimistic and emotional, Meredith realistic and careful. Early in the fanfic, Bonnie, who retains her canon paranormal competency, has a vision about being submerged in water, which turns into a large puddle of blood. In addition to introducing the idea of a threat to be averted, her vision works to connect the narrative strands as it ends with her calling out Stefan's name. She is able to summon Damon to her aid; a Damon who is also kept in character as he is surly, sarcastic and sees himself as superior. Bonnie is also joined by the dependable and safe Matt who comes along to protect her, primarily against Damon. Together, the three characters leave for Europe and for Italy, where they have concluded that Stefan and Elena are in danger.

At the end of the canon novel, Elena's competencies and behavior are in a state of flux. She has returned from an angelic state in which she had paranormal powers, and she is confused and childlike. Finta recycles the theme of transition in her fanfic, rendered in the form of marriage, and repeats, with a twist, Elena's naivety and discomfort in a new situation and a new environment. She has had to quickly adjust to married life and although she terms it "a fairy tale," she realizes that the challenges of the relationship are not only connected to the human/vampire relationship but also to their attitude to the arts, culture and language of Italy. In sections narrated in the form of Elena's diary entries, she verbalizes her feeling of Otherness and writes that on his home turf, Stefan "is a stranger to [her]" and small details, such as a different pronunciation of her name cause her to reflect, "I'm not really myself anymore, or not completely." Rather than creating a situation depicting a more mature and confident protagonist — a temptation for many fanfic authors whose stories are set after the canon's story arc — Finta retains a naïve tone in Elena's reflections, and draws attention to her vulnerability. At the same time, she underscores a new set of incompatibilities for the couple to deal with.

Although the fanfic plays with the idea of secrets on several levels, overarching them all is the hidden existence of vampires and it is variously threatened. Meredith's boyfriend Alaric becomes the most manifest incarnation of the threat as his dissertation aims to reveal vampire nature and vulnerabilities. Alaric's plans do not render him an unsympathetic character, out to ruin vampire existence. On the contrary, they stem from his conviction that secrets will be the downfall of mankind and that a researcher's mission should be to spread knowledge, "the most important thing in the world." The secret is also brought up in a conversation between Stefan and the vampire Riccardo Loredan (an Original Character) in Venice. Riccardo's views are the opposite of Alaric's conviction that mankind is ready to know the truth about vampires. When Stefan states that Elena will "never betray us," Riccardo asks: "How can anyone be certain of the future?" To reinforce the impossibility of predictions, he reminds Stefan of their long existence and the changes they have seen, the "strangeness" of humans, and to how the world has shrunk with new inventions. "Tell me," he challenges Stefan, "that you foresaw this when Buonaparte claimed this city as his own. Or when your Medici and my Dogi made the world tremble as they fought one another for supremacy. [...] Tell me you know what the future will bring." In Riccardo's view, the marriage between Stefan and Elena threatens to expose vampire nature, just as Alaric's plans do, and he takes it upon himself to avert this threat by luring Elena outside one night, and transform her into a vampire. The situation reflects Bonnie's initial vision and the fanfic thus repeats the canon structure where ideas and premonitions which are initially difficult to decipher acquire meaning in a later story development. Of course, what Riccardo does not know is that Elena is not unaware of what it means to be a vampire: she has been turned once before in the canon, and this narrative element is retained, again reinforcing the fanfic's close links to Smith's novels.

In the canon, Elena's transformation into a vampire brings with it a shift in emotions and an increased innocence: at the end of *The Struggle* and in the first chapters of *The Fury* she has no inkling of her former attachments to Stefan and instead concludes that it is Damon she loves. There is no corresponding alteration in *Secrecy*, rather, Elena returns with a good grasp of her romantic attachments and with a positive view of her new nature. The vain and popular Elena of the canon is invoked early in the fanfic causing her to worry about growing older (read less attractive) while Stefan remains forever young and beautiful, and her transformation "solves so many problems." Not only can the vampire state ensure eternal togetherness, it can also change the disparaging view that she has had of herself. She has previously thought of herself as "trailing behind" Stefan, whereas now she conceives of herself as "his equal, instead of a weak human." Irreversible vampiric transformation brings with it a host of benefits, at least from Elena's naïve viewpoint.

With Elena as a vampire, there is a renewed urgency for Stefan and Damon, and indeed Bonnie and Matt, to retain the secrets of vampire existence. Word of Alaric's plans thus sets off the second main move of the fanfic and a return to America. During the events played out in Venice, interspersed sections of the fanfic have outlined the problems Meredith and Alaric face. While Meredith is sympathetic to the main drive of Alaric's idea: that humans would be able to protect themselves more effectively if they only know about vampires, her personal attachments — to Elena, Stefan and to some extent Damon — make it impossible for her to condone a plan that will put them in jeopardy. Alaric rightly points out that there is a "price [vampires] pay for their secrecy" in the form of lost or fractured lives, which draws attention to the difficulty inherent in the paranormal romance as such. Vampires may be sympathetic, attractive and depicted as romantic heroes and although the underlying danger may not be overtly directed at the human protagonists, there are other victims along the way. Characters are victimized also in the canon novels, but predominantly by paranormal entities other than vampires, which are dealt with in each installment. Finta's fanfic depicts a much more comprehensive image of vampiric influence and destruction and the consistent narrative strand in the fanfic adds very particular paranormal consequences to the archive.

Although the novels in Smith's series typically end with a dramatic cliffhanger suggesting sinister things to come, there is often also a sense of hope. Finta's story is darker. Alaric is in the end is coerced into terminating his project, but in the aftermath, Meredith sees "a broken man" and she and Alaric move on to an uncertain future. Bonnie is also left considerably frailer. She has periodically been drawn to Damon and, with Stefan and Elena as an example, formed ideas about what a vampire/human relationship can be. When Bonnie tries to convince him that he could make the same kind of diet choices as Stefan, rather than seeing her as one in a long line of "donors," Damon argues that Elena and Stefan have given humans a "sugar-coated version" of vampire reality. "Someone has to have the Powers that they're too virtuous to pay the price for." *Secrecy*'s dark ending draws out the canon implications of a diminished vampire power which comes with too human ways, indicating that this is not just the truth Damon believes in, it is the truth about vampires.

Even Stefan and Elena move on towards a future which is painted in less than ideal terms. Although Elena seems oblivious to the implications, seeing only an eternal and happy life with Stefan, they move on to Venice, California with a somewhat empty goal. "They could compare the two Venices. It was something to do to pass the time." The idea of emptiness in the long vampire existence is in this way Finta's final addition to the archontic text of The Vampire Diaries.

Emptiness due to longevity is less central in Carson Dyle's Twilight sequel *Morning*, where Bella reflects that "[h]aving Edward for eternity hadn't lessened my desire to be with him every moment possible." The prospect of married life stretching indefinitely into the future has done nothing to dull emotions, and family life is blissful, even if Bella initially perceives of herself as slightly outside it. The Cullens relax after their successful stand against the Volturi, engage in their hobbies and, in short, go about their existences in relative peace and quiet. In addition to their support of each other, they possess great material wealth, have a variety of artistic and athletic gifts that occupy their time, and are squarely paired off in stable relationships. Their exaggerated well-being is foregrounded also in the canon, and the family represented as "desirable ... through its categorisation as cohesive and whole" (Stevens § 28). In the fanfic, Bella thinks herself "lucky ... to be part of his extraordinary family" but simultaneously different from them, for example because she does not appear to have any particular artistic gifts. The promise of the cohesive family is thus rendered as attainable but at a slight distance, even if Bella is already an integral part of it.

In the summary of the story, Carson Dyle writes that Bella and Edward's "path to a bright future seems clear, but the darkest nights cast the longest shadows." This paratextual information prepares the reader for some form of danger to intrude on the otherwise peaceful existence and recycles the narrative pattern of the canon novels, in which each installment introduces new threats to the romance. The fanfic author cleverly inserts a number of red herrings which may lead readers down specific interpretative paths. Cullens' extensive basement, for example, intriguingly contains an empty tomb, a mysterious doll house appears in Bella and Edward's cottage, and Bella has visions of red-robed figures. Readers may also be on high alert since Bella has encountered a number of either threatening or mysterious individuals (both known and unknown to her) on her trips to Forks and her walks through the forest. One meeting in the woods gives particular cause for alarm, since the man she encounters has knowledge of vampires. Although their meeting ends with him promising not to tell anyone, there is a strange side effect. As the man looks deeply into her eyes, Bella feels "as though a vortex was whirling around in [her] brain, scattering white downy feathers." After enjoying the sun and the solitude for a little while she returns home, but not to the cottage she shares with Edward, nor to the Cullen house. Instead she is convinced that she is still living in her father's house.

At this point, Edward has been temporarily removed from events and the estrangement is both physical and psychological as Bella has protested against the trip. In his absence, the rest of the Cullens attempt to figure out the reason and cure for Bella's amnesia and patiently let her recollections return at their own pace. Bella's memory loss turns out to be confined to her immediate family, Edward and Renesmee, because she realizes that she has a place in the Cullen family. However, seeing that it exists only of couples she begins to wonder if she too has a mate. When presented with a photograph of the Cullen brothers, the image of the "deep black vortex" returns, "gathering up the fragile pieces of [her] half-constructed memory puzzle." She has an extreme reaction to the picture, tossing it aside and exclaiming, "He tried to kill me — right here in this house! How ... how could anyone survive that many bites?" Alice draws the conclusion that Bella's reaction comes from seeing Jasper in the picture and that the bites refer to the situation in which he attacked Bella (in the canon novel *New Moon*). But here is when *Morning* takes a rather unexpected turn because the monster Bella identifies in the photograph is not Jasper, but Edward.

Since the fanfic starts by depicting Edward and Bella as fated to be together eternally, the reader is unlikely to initially read it as a criticism of Twilight's central romance. However, Bella's reactions, first to the photograph, then to the appearance of Jasper and Edward, introduce precisely such a critique. Terrified by his appearance she can no longer see the love of her life but instead a "demon"; she reads the Cullens' protests as evidence of Edward's manipulation and them as "innocent sheep, unaware of the predator in their midst." This perception of Edward as monstrous rather than romantic turns his relationship with Bella on its head, without altering the hard data of the canon, nor negating Edward's canon competencies. Also in Meyer's novels, he is potentially dangerous and over-protective, but according to romance ethics, any actions and reactions connected to these competencies are interpreted as stemming from underlying love. Carson Dyle's alternative look at things illustrates that the same actions and reactions can be attributed to a monstrous and manipulative stalker. Bella painstakingly goes through the canon events from this reversed perspective, unable to continue seeing them as the acts of love the other Cullens insist on. Rather, she stresses that what she sees is the truth, that "the blinders" have been removed and that she sees "things as they really are." In relation to the canon, examples of this enhanced sight range from the way Bella recalls her first meeting with Edward ("He totally hated me") to how she reflects on the preposterous idea that Edward has taken her to prom ("I'd rather go to the dentist"). The romance in the canon has glossed over Edward's initial reaction to Bella, and represented them going to the dance as proof of their togetherness, but fact remains that these events can be read as disturbing and going against character. Important to note is also that Bella's self-perception in the fanfic is altered in the process, in fact, she comes to see herself as critics of Twilight have seen her. In a conversation with Jacob, for instance, she "shudder[s] to realize how long [Edward] must have had me under his control. When had I become such a push-over? I was like an object lesson for teenage girls in some afterschool special."

Carson Dyle's eventual resolution to the mystery adds to the Twilight archive a view of intense feelings rendering subjects vulnerable, even when these feelings are benevolent. The evil mind behind Bella's change belongs to a manipulative artist, Rupert French, who is the only human (except Bella) that Edward has turned, albeit unwittingly. French has the ability to make humans turn their backs on "the one thing that had been most central to their lives," in Bella's case the love she has harbored for Edward, and react to this one thing with "suspicion and scorn" and he has performed this manipulative act in order to avenge himself on his creator. Bella's emotions have not been lessened by the reversal; on the contrary, they are as passionate as ever, manifesting themselves in the intense hatred for Edward. However, in the hands of the uncharacteristically unmerciful Cullens who bit by bit dismember him, French reverses the amnesia, leaving Bella's mind the way it was before.

The fanfic oscillates between Bella's love and hatred, in the process adding thought-provoking readings of Edward's overprotective and irate canon behavior, but it seemingly comes to echo the contention in the canon that togetherness is the ultimate goal. Even when Bella listens to Edward's confessions regarding his past, she comes to the conclusion that she loves Edward "unconditionally, no matter what," which recycles her contention in Meyer's first novel when Edward's vampiric nature is revealed to her. Further, a sense of cohesion, both within the extended family and in the smaller unit is stressed by the fanfic author's references to W.B. Yeats' poem "The Second Coming." In her amnesiac state, Bella laments the absence of "of a center that could hold," not only because there are pieces of her missing, but because if the center is not filled with love it is filled with danger. In the story's resolution, with criticism and suspicion filed away, Bella no longer sees "horrible blankness, no spinning black hole. At the center was me, clear and whole, and Edward and Renesmee, not three pieces, but one." This reestablished center suggests another recycling of the canon's theme. However, it is possible to interpret the fanfic differently, and as a somewhat sarcastic comment on the canon romance. We have seen that Carson Dyle includes self-reflexive comments on Bella's part which seem to echo critical discussions about Twilight in which Bella certainly *is* presented as "object lesson for teenage girls" in how not to lose agency. Her unconditional love for Edward, which flies in the face of her previous criticism of both Edward's behavior and her own, but which lays the foundation for their continued happiness, can similarly be construed differently by readers because in it, it can be inferred, lies the true danger of romance. Interpreted in this way, the fanfic adds considerably different images of perception and all-consuming love to the Twilight archive.

New Romances: The Clearly Marked Road Not Taken

Pairings are central to the fanfic text form to the extent that specific terms are employed and stories are filed in separate archives. The pairing Damon/Elena, for example, is exclusively explored in fan fiction posted on the blogspot-site "Delena fanfiction," and Teams Edward and Jacob signal which pairing fans root for. One True Pairing (OTP) signals authors' "investment in the romantic relationship of that particular pairing" to the point that this is all they write about and read, and the combination of characters does not have to be the one featured in the canon (Busse and Hellekson 11). The canons' participation in the paranormal romance naturally underscore the centrality of romantic plot strands, leading to relationally oriented and pairing based fan fiction, but important to note is that "[i]n all genres [...], love plots of various kinds are the norm rather than the exception" (Regis 47). Core features of romance find their ways into other genres as well, and by extension into fan fiction based on canons participating in these. A strong friendship in science-fiction, for example, is easily recast as romance, such as in Kirk/Spock slash, arguably the most well-researched early example of relationally oriented fanfic. Thus, we are not arguing that there is an absence of romantic or erotic pairing centered stories connected to canons with a less pronounced focus on romance, but rather that fans are fond of picking up and developing existing relationships in rather more romantic or erotic ways than envisaged in the canons.

The narrative strategy in focus in this section is illustrated by fanfic authors who pair the female protagonist with the beau who draws the short straw in the canon and thus explore relationships that are presented as concrete, albeit un-realized options. Twilight and The Vampire Diaries consistently thematize the eternal love triangle. Bella is drawn to Jacob, and Elena to

Damon, but Edward and Stefan are represented as the right, fated choice. The fanfics analyzed here consequently explore what happens when the other, unsanctioned choice is made. Love triangles feature in True Blood as well, but are less static. In Sookie's initial relationship with Bill, Eric is the potential third, but these roles are later reversed. Bill's and Eric's jealousy and possessiveness then feature into Sookie's romances with Alcide and Quinn. To place Sookie in unexpected, heterosexual relationships in fan fiction can therefore be a somewhat strenuous imaginative exercise, as she already in the canon is portrayed as a rather more modern protagonist with more than one partner in her life, and since the vampire protagonists, similarly, are seldom guided by monogamous ethics.

In The Vampire Diaries there is no doubt that Elena and Damon periodically grow closer, in fact, her shifting feelings and the brothers' trading of the roles good and evil signal the centrality of the triangle theme. Some fanfic authors explore characters' emotions in great detail, especially when teasing out precisely why and how Elena's attachment shifts, whereas others use Damon's conflicted brotherly bond with Stefan as a reason for him to "steal" Elena away. *Saved by Grace* by badboy_fangirl is an example of the former. Published in December 2011, it depicts the aftermath of events played out at the end of the TV series' second season.[12] There are two aspects featured in the canon generally but emphasized in the season which are central to the fanfic. One is the strong bond between the Salvatore brothers which causes Stefan to make an unselfish sacrifice when Damon is dying from a werewolf bite and can only be cured by blood from Klaus, an ancient vampire belonging to the Original family. In exchange for this blood, Stefan has agreed to go on "a decade long bender" in Klaus' company, as a Ripper: the most evil form of a vampire (*The Vampire Diaries*, 2:22 "As I Lay Dying"). The other aspect is that the relationship between Elena and Damon develops in ways which hint to possibilities of an intimate and romantic liaison. The fanfic author plays on these as she spins the story of Elena and Damon's relationship, which eventually sees them married parents of three. When Stefan returns to Mystic Falls in season three of the canon TV series, badboy_fangirl is "Jossed" as she acquiesces in her story notes, since her fanfic depicts a different development. However, although she had no way of knowing at the time, she is also "Kripked" in the last episode of the third season, as one plot development she invents is having Elena turned into a vampire.

Although altering the pairing, the fanfic is true to the monogamous ethics of the canon; despite its implicit possibilities for a three-way love story, Elena's attachment to one of the Salvatore brothers means that her feelings for the other need to be repressed. The brothers' sire Katherine with her long life and less human-governed ethics in fact draws attention to the unnecessary stress on monogamy as she states, "It's OK to love them both. I did" (*The Vampire Diaries*, 2:12 "As I Lay Dying"), lines which are reiterated twice in *Saved by Grace*. In the fanfic, Elena *does* love both brothers, but struggles to maintain an ethical balance. However, to enable a shift of romantic and erotic attachments, badboy_fangirl quickly establishes that Elena's reasons for falling in love with Stefan are romantic but somewhat prosaic. She is looking for a greater purpose in life, having survived the accident that took her parents' lives and at the outset she connects this purpose to Stefan. In a recap of canon events it is said that she "falls for him fast, because there's no reason not to." Orphaned, Elena "wants to have fun, but she wants it to be meaningful. With Stefan, things are meaningful." The author here evinces a reading of the canon romance as stemming from understandable but not fated reasons, and along with this shift in motivations comes a shift in associations to Damon. On the one hand, Elena's feelings for Damon are based on the fact that she knows he is capable of intense love but "has nothing to direct that love to [causing] hate and anger and wrath to spill upon the world." To curb his violent tendencies, all he needs, like the flawed and incomplete hero of traditional romance, is an appropriate object on which to project his intense feelings. On the other hand, Elena is drawn to Damon because "[h]e sees them as equals," something, it is suggested, Stefan was never able to do. Damon's canon encouragement of Elena's agency is played up in the fanfic to create a logical breeding ground for their love.

At the end of *Saved by Grace*, Elena realizes that one of the more crucial decisions she has to make: to become a vampire "is about *her* and the fact that she is a changed person." Her road to self-discovery and independence—following the paranormal romance structure—is clearly illustrated also when she picks up her old habit of diary writing to figure out the motivations behind her romantic choices, or "non-choice[s]" as the case may be. She connects "what she wants from [relationships to] what she wants from *life*," that is, she sees love attachments as part of something bigger. While the relationship with Stefan results from an active choice, she reflects that it "had been about something bigger, something going on with the course of her life." To start something with the older Salvatore brother, in contrast, "would be solely because of Damon. [...] It would be her first adult relationship." With this adult relationship well under way towards the end of the fanfic, the turning process, the thought of which reduced her to tears with Stefan, becomes an easy choice to make with Damon. "I want to be with you forever; and to do that, I have to live forever." Through personal growth and increased self-awareness, Elena is represented as eschewing the fated love, or love as connected to this growth, in favor of what could be construed as a more selfish choice.

So Cold, So Cold, by smc-27, depicts a chain of events which similarly lead Elena to make the choice of being turned; it is "the only way she can ever have [Damon]. *Forever*." Published in October 2009, Stefan is at this point in the canon far from the Ripper state featured in badboy_fangirl's story, still, the fanfic hinges on notions of threat and danger, significantly associated with Stefan rather than Damon. Initially, smc-17 writes, Elena fears Stefan because "she has always trusted him" and because, in contrast to Damon, he "has pieces of her heart." Vulnerability due to trust and intense emotions is thus what causes fear in the first place. Progressively, as the story presents alternative readings of events in the first canon season, Elena comes to reevaluate Stefan's reactions to various things, which by extension shifts her attitudes to and feelings for Damon. Stefan's "calm and peace[ful]" reaction to the reappearance of Katherine, for example, reads as strange, and rather Damon's "anger" connected to the same event seems to reveal "a more human side to [him]." However, Damon's potential humanity is complemented by Elena's musings on his (and Stefan's) true vampire nature. "[S]he realizes that Stefan may have saved her life once, but even though he's had a lot of chances, Damon hasn't ever *taken* her life. She can't decide which of those is more admirable." The sequence of events which alters Elena's perception presents a logical reason for the shift in attachments. "She thinks she may be in love with Stefan, but she's connected to Damon in a way that might be a hell of a lot bigger." Like in badboy_fangirl's fanfic, the as of yet unrealized canon possibility is presented as the only logical one, once Elena has reached self-awareness and maturity.

In *Saved by Grace*, Elena's new view of relationships and choices does not result in an un-bumpy road towards happiness with Damon. On the contrary, there are several obstacles in their way, both internal and external, which mirror how Stefan and Elena are repeatedly pulled together and pushed apart in the canon. One of the external threats is the Originals' interest in their unborn baby. Biological offspring between humans and vampires is an issue fraught with difficulty in our canons, and in vampire texts in general.[13] Vampires are generally represented as unable to procreate (they are undead after all), but since they start out as human, their turned state does not mean that they do not want to. In *Saved by Grace* there is one benevolent version of this desire: Damon's memories of fantasizing about having children when still a human, and a more sinister one: Klaus' wish to create more hybrids to wreak havoc on the world. This threat, one of the fanfic's few instances of using the more adventured-themed aspects of the canon, is later dealt with offstage, whereas Damon's worries about fatherhood becomes more consistent hurdles for the couple to overcome.

These concerns are tied to a theme which runs through the fanfic: Damon's belief that he is not worthy of Elena's love and that he is not good enough (on a moral level) to be anyone's father. Early in the story, Damon files Elena's possible feelings for him "under: Not Possible." His self-image and his perception that she belongs to Stefan produce a hesitancy connected to the same monogamous norm that governs Elena's initial reactions. He sees himself as "a placeholder" until Stefan returns, and fights his emotions since he is convinced that Elena is a "counterfeit version" in his company and that she mistakenly believes herself to be in love with him. Long after the two have become intimate, in fact way into their pregnancy, this attitude persists. "[I]f the truth is told, he's really just waiting for the other shoe to drop with Elena," Damon thinks, and "the scales of justice, good to bad" will never weigh in his favor. While it is clear that Damon has forgotten all about Katherine (a relationship in which he was also number two) and loves Elena deeply, he is used to his and Stefan's polarized roles and so focuses on getting everything back to normal. Even with the baby on the way he thinks that "of the two Salvatore brothers, Stefan is the one who would make a good father. (Well, Stefan pre-blood bender craziness, that is.)"

But Stefan *is* caught up in this craziness, which brings us to the bond and differences between the brothers: the second canon aspect of particular relevance for the fanfic, which enables badboy_fangirl to even further establish Damon as the right choice for Elena. When Damon and Caroline early in the fanfic find Stefan among carnage, Damon thinks that whereas he has "never had the appetite for gluttony, for something that resembled war in the aftermath [...] Stefan was like that once upon a time." Further, Katherine says about Stefan: "I actually think this is *him*, and he's constrained himself for some time." The quotations illustrate two aspects which present Damon as a more logical choice as a partner. Firstly, it is indicated that Stefan in his Ripper state renders Damon good in comparison; the better option of two evils. Secondly, by drawing out the implications of Stefan's oscillation between good and evil, Damon comes to represent a much needed stability in Elena's life.

The story takes Elena's growth to its logical conclusion in ways which, despite presenting an alternate development, are true to the canon. Elena emphatically does not want to be turned in *The Vampire Diaries*. Her canon competencies of practicality, introspection and truthfulness lead her there to protest such a transformation, and when she *is* turned at the end of the third season, it is involuntary. Following the logic established within the fanfic, however, her unwillingness to transform is due to lack of experience and the wrong partner. "It's the wisdom she possesses as the woman she is now," badboy_fangirl writes, "that provided a different answer with a different vampire boyfriend." Elena's maturation is traced throughout the fanfic, and giving up her hesitant nature follows logically from the relationship with Damon and the emotional stability he represents. In this, and other, ways, the story as developed in *Saved by Grace* does not subvert or defy the canon but rather envisions a development which can logically fit in, despite ending with a different pairing and a future for Elena which has not (yet) been realized in the canon. What *is* questioned is the idea of constant miscommunication which underlies not only The Vampire Diaries, but the other canons as well. Elena sums this up nicely in *Saved by Grace*: "*This* is not what she thinks, it's only what *he* thinks she thinks and he couldn't be more wrong, and she doesn't know how he's come to these awful conclusions." Added to the archive are characters who in more mature ways work through these misunderstandings, metatextually commenting on romantic stereotypes.

Certain key scenes in the canons are particularly charged with potential for a favoring of the implied but unrealized pairing. Among them in Twilight are Bella's night with Jacob in a tent and their kiss in *Eclipse*, and her desperate jump from the cliff during Edward's absence in *New Moon*. In her investigation of fan fiction published on Twilighted and connected to the latter canon text, Juli Parrish maintains that "[t]he cliff dive and its aftermath ... comprise the most generative sequence in the novel, as suggested by the number of fanfics that use it as their point of departure" (182). Although not all stories with this starting point champion Jacob as an alternative choice, the fact that Edward is absent and Jacob is there for support and life-saving measures gives ample opportunity for authors to explore the road not taken, and the often minute narrative changes to the canon plot, required for a different outcome.[14] Winter Ashby's appropriately titled story *Cliff Diving* opens with Bella having narrowly escaped death, and being taken to Jacob's house instead of her own. The detail of the changed destination is all it takes for Bella to reevaluate her emotions. "It was like Edward was some kind of disease, and the freezing, churning ocean [...] cured me of him," Bella reflects. This evaluation spills over into a realization of all the things she would have forfeited with Edward: life itself, "feeling the rough stubble of a teenage boy [...] miss[ing] out on what it was like to be an eighteen-year-old." In contrast, of course, she concludes, "Jacob gave me that." The new relationship is not fated, and romantic love not immediate or suited to be put into words — "It was too soon for that" — which suggests that it is not only Bella's object of affection that is new, but also her view on romance. Although the story only takes the reader as far as the next day, Bella's changed mind effectively undoes the projected happy future with Edward, negating developments in the following canon novels.

The romantic triangle in Twilight plays into a highly problematic juxtaposition involving race and class. Brianna Burke describes Edward and Jacob as "contrasting racial hypermasculine stereotypes" and while Bella and Edward are racially "compatible," Jacob "embod[ies] the space of the exoticized Other" (207). Burke's assessment of Meyer's novels is that they are based in a long tradition of racist stereotypes, and that the depiction of the Quileutes confirms it through depictions of the exaggerated connection with nature, poor or nonexistent impulse control, and dismissals of beliefs as magic and superstition. Even more serious, she argues, is that "[b]y imagining her cosmic epic battle between good and evil, between vampires and werewolves/Indians, [Meyer] creates a binary that implies that Native peoples are as equally fantastic, as equally fictional, as vampires" (Burke 216).[15] Natalie Wilson similarly draws attention to a number of value laden binaries in Twilight, such as humans/animals, privileged/unprivileged, body/mind and white/black. In these binaries, even the fact that vampires are considerably less human than werewolves, they still land on the human side of the binary because associated with admirable human traits; reasoning and free will, for example. "Like Bella," Wilson argues, "readers are encouraged to choose between these two different racialized suitors [...] an ultra-white, ultra-privileged vampire and a far less privileged wolf of color" (55, 56).

Readers *do* choose, and many of them, like Winter Ashby, do not make the same choice as Bella, which leads to the by now well established "Team Jacob" and "Team Edward" in the fandom (although fans can and do profess allegiance to both camps and at times consequently refer to themselves as a neutral Team Switzerland).[16] The binaries civilized/savage and culture/nature are not necessarily erased in fan fiction produced by authors who favor the Jacob/Bella pairing, but alternative forms of compatibility more often come to the fore, along with a reevaluation of the supposedly negative side of the binaries. Jacob's both physical and psychological warmth, his emotional consistency and supportiveness, form contrasts in these stories to Edward's literal coldness, his periodic estrangement from Bella, and his overprotectiveness. These aspects are brought up by fanfic authors to enforce the notion that Jacob is the right and logical choice. Still, many authors do not shrink from the fact that Bella in making it forfeits the wealth and privileges which comes with the vampire existence, and rarely create a future for the new couple, rich in anything but love. In *Consolation* by someryn, for example, Bella and Jacob buy "a small house near the reservation," the mortgage paid off by Carlisle and Esme, and they remain there throughout their lives. Bella in time gets an academic degree, but Jacob does not "need a college education" to open the car repair shop he wants.

The issue of concrete choice is moot in *Consolation*— the pairing hinges on Edward's death before the story starts — but does not preclude an exploration of consequences and benefits of the new pairing. The loss of Edward is depicted as a highly traumatic event for Bella, and large parts of the narrative are devoted to her slow process of healing. Only little by little, she comes to see that Jacob is there to offer her the friendship he always has, "the opposite in every way of what [she has] lost." The reevaluation of Jacob finds a contrast when Bella is finally ready to talk about her past. She tries to be as truthful as she can and include "things that were less than ideal about Edward" in the "portrait" she now paints of him. A periodic disregard of Bella's feelings and the lengths he would go to have her and "to save" her are among these shortcomings, the latter aspect romantically glossed over in the canon. Despite the fact that Bella does not have to make a concrete choice in *Consolation*, her reevaluation of Edward and subsequent happiness indicate that she and Jacob are, after all, more compatible. There are material consequences of life with the working class werewolf, but these are never derided, and are far outweighed by emotional stability and happiness.

Edward's death in CatsOnMars' *The Golden Phase of Dying Leaves* features into the story with Bella recalling "the nightmarish sounds of rock-hard limbs getting torn from his body like the brilliant screaming of diamonds." Bella has come "too late" to save Edward in Italy, and the Volturi consequently kill him, which adds a not inconsiderable guilt on Bella's part. The choice in this story, like in someryn's, becomes one between utter despair and deciding that life, in all its horror, is worth living. Bella knows that Jacob is there for her, even during the long time when she is unresponsive, "vacant and catatonic," but initially, this knowledge is "inconsequential." As life continues around her, Bella's thoughts become increasingly occupied with the fragility and progressive corruption of the human body, and the gradual disintegration of love. While an eternity with Edward has seemed to promise unaltered feelings (after all, this is the image of vampiric love in the canon), human emotions "that were once new and passionate [will become] tired and not enough to survive on. [...] Everyone she sees around her is dying." It takes a reappearance of Victoria, fights between her and the werewolves, and specifically the threat to Jacob's life, to make Bella feel again, and the new intimacy between them to an extent reverses her view on the shortcomings of the mortal body. "The body can get infected and its bones broken, it gets tired, it gets hungry, and eventually it just stops and decomposes. It also does this." It is not stated openly in the fanfic, but since it in other aspects follows the canon closely, Bella is a virgin, and her body has not done "this" with Edward, whose body, in turn, was impervious to time's slow destruction.

Both someryn and CatsOnMars can support both Team Jacob and Team

Edward, since the canon rivals never have to face off in the fanfics. Edward can remain a strong influence, and Bella never has to make a concrete choice. In Parrish's study "stories in which Bella actively and deliberately chooses Jacob [are] less common" than those which "accept Meyer's own logic" and rather play with different outcomes due to details being altered — or killing off Edward as the authors just discussed (183). *Patience*, in contrast, opens with precisely such a choice and with Bella claiming that she has made the wrong one. Set immediately after *New Moon*, author sciphile has Bella reevaluate her latest meeting with Jacob which in the canon novel is emotionally fraught and also plays out as a concrete choice. Faced with her plans of being turned, Jacob can no longer promise to be Bella's friend and as Edward pulls Bella back from a last embrace she knows "that last glimpse of [Jacob's] face would haunt" her (Meyer, *New Moon* 496). Also noteworthy in the scene is that Edward is more ambivalently portrayed, "his arms restraining instead of defending," and even though Bella in the final sentence still sees him as her "destiny," his coldness and lack of empathy results in a plethora of fanfic reactions (Meyer, *New Moon* 495, 497). In *Patience*, Bella spends the following night ruminating on how she has hurt Jacob, "choosing the one who was so wrong for her, as she had so many times." Acting on this altered view, she then seeks out Jacob and admits that it is "the idea of Edward" rather than the reality of him she has been drawn to and that she now would choose Jacob "without hesitation."

Just as Bella in the canon is unable to choose because of the love for Edward which once established is famously irrevocable, Jacob in this fanfic is powerless when she apologizes for letting him down. "Like he had a choice. He'd do anything for her," sciphile writes. Interestingly, however, it is not the new relationship which cements Bella's negative feelings for Edward. In an intertextual connection to the canon first novel, Bella's "feelings for him had been irrevocably changed, like a paradigm shift"; the romance has died and even without Jacob, she would not return to Edward's cold arms. This paradigmatic shift also has consequences for Edward who displays a reaction similar to Bella's in the canon when his absence causes her to withdraw: "he just sits around all day, staring out into nothing," Alice tells Bella. The depiction of Edward and the complete shift in emotions represent a drastic departure from the canon, and a contrast to the fanfics previously discussed. Rather than keeping the memory of Edward with her forever, Bella here emphatically asks him to leave, "surprised by how easy it was to say these things." The choice she has made alters not only the relationship, but Bella's competencies and ethics, adding, as the author writes in the notes for the ninth chapter, a "Bella [with] a spine" to the Twilight archive.

When featured in sequels, the pairing carries a particular set of problems to be negotiated because Jacob imprints on Bella's daughter Renesmee. The issue of imprinting, an immediate and involuntary bonding with another individual, is perceived as disturbing by many fanfic authors, and in this case especially since Renesmee is only a child. Critics have further drawn attention to how it not only enforces he canon Quileutes' stereotypical connections to animal instinct and irrationality but also furthers the general notion of racial purity. Burke notes that "miscegenation is a possibility [the canon] novels repeatedly reject," on the one hand because Bella and Jacob do not consummate their relationship, on the other because the Quileutes imprint only on other members of the Nation (213). Jacob imprinting on Renesmee may seem like an exception, but her hybrid status makes her "a fitting companion" (Burke 213). The possible jealousies (indeed, a new love triangle) become logical avenues for fanfic authors to explore, and the instinctual aspect of imprinting is often negatively figured in stories. In someryn's *Consolation*, the fact that Renesmee will never be born defuses issues of incestuous jealousies, but Bella still worries about the possibilities of Jacob imprinting on someone else. He assures her that this will not happen and criticizes the mindless connection to another being: "It's not real love; it's obsession." The comment obviously echoes Jacob's views on Bella's relationship with Edward in the canon, and further introduces the idea that the instinctual drive can be overcome.

In *Masks* and the companion piece *Chains* by light4dawn, the notion of imprinting is problematized further, because the fanfics are set after *Breaking Dawn*, thus featuring the threatening presence of Renesmee. Told from Jacob's and Renesmee's points of view, respectively, *Masks* and *Chains* depict Bella's new vampiric existence as unhappy, because she cannot reconcile the love she harbors for Jacob with her supposedly happy marriage with Edward. The Jacob/Bella pairing is not made explicit in the stories, but foregrounded are their ruminations on both the past and the present, and Bella's inability to completely set him free. She realizes that neither of them are entirely happy, and that she cannot be absolved from the "guilt and wrongdoing" of the past. In response to the pain he still feels, Jacob thinks: "This wasn't the way it was supposed to be. Imprinting was supposed to take all this away, wasn't it?" (*Masks*). Rather than subscribing to the canon logic, according to which the bond with Renesmee immediately and neatly dissolves Jacob's love for Bella, light4dawn is unwilling to advocate such a convenient solution, gesturing instead towards the idea that Jacob and Bella, still the preferred pairing, have an indestructible connection. In the second story, things are taken to their logical conclusion since Renesmee cannot fully have Jacob, and attention is drawn to the eternal triangle drama. As Quileute Leah says to Bella: Renesmee is "in love with Jake and she knows he's supposed to be hers, but he's not. He's still hung up on you, and you *still* can't let him go." In contrast to the have-the-cake-and-eat-it approach Bella is accused of, Renesmee releases Jacob from responsibility and takes off alone, which opens for a continued, emotionally fraught but also rewarding relationship between Bella and Jacob.

We will explore sexual encounters in more detail in the following chapter, and we argue there that fanfic depictions of sexual intimacy in relation to the chaste first three novels (and films) in the Twilight canon and to Smith's novel series, represent a subversion of canon norms. In the Bella/Jacob and Damon/Elena pairings here, however, sex also features into the female protagonists' alternative choices, and their assessment thereof. When Bella in fanfic chooses Jacob instead of Edward or ends up with Jacob because of Edward's death, the canon reason for chastity — Edward's paranormal strength — is removed, and featured is instead an exploration of sexuality by two (almost) human teenagers. In *The Dying Phase of Golden Leaves*, intimacy starts out as a way for Bella to feel again, and in *Patience*, physical proximity to Jacob makes Bella experience a new "languid, swollen feeling" which she connects to the difference between her two suitors. "Sure, Edward was a God, but Jacob was ... a *man*." In both stories, the awakened feelings are used to establish that the altered choice has been the right one to make. The situation is similar even when fanfic works against a less chaste canon text, such as *The Vampire Diaries*. In smc-27's *So Cold, So Cold*, there is no depiction of a fully consummated sexual relationship, yet an "intense" kiss proves to Elena, that "the decision she's made" has been correct. In these fanfics, physical reactions consequently both mirror and underscore a new maturity and a perfect fit.

Even though Sookie has other than only vampiric lovers in True Blood, there is a consistent juxtaposition between Bill and Eric as they vie for her attention, and many fanfic authors explore the road untraveled in the moment.[17] Several key scenes carrying specific potential for alternative pairings come together in the ninth episode of the second season, "I Will Rise Up." The canon episode starts with Sookie taking Eric's blood, sucking pieces of silver shrapnel from his body after an attack by the vampire-hostile organization The Fellowship of the Sun. The blood establishes a bond between them, and Bill cautions her that she may feel an increased sexual attraction to Eric, and it indeed manifests itself is in an erotic dream. The end of the episode features Godric's suicide and an uncharacteristically vulnerable Eric. The days immediately following the aired episode saw the publication of several fanfics on FanFiction.net, which depict the aftermath. TammyDevil666's *Crave* focuses on the element of the dream, and on Sookie accusing Eric of having planted images in her head, while at the same time being sympathetic towards him and his loss. When Sookie later that night wakes up from another dream, mixing eroticism with biting, with "blood coating her fingers," she realizes that she does not want Eric's control over her to end. The implications of this are not drawn out in the story (Bill is comfortably resting beside her), but sows seeds of the development the author has in mind. Queenhaq's *And the Dead Keep on Living* focuses on Sookie chastely comforting Eric after Godric's death, and here as well, there are suggestions of an alternative later development; when Sookie returns to Bill's room she assures him that nothing has changed, but "isn't sure she believes [her words] herself." The same comforting scenarios are depicted in glitter and stardust's *Lullaby* and EricBonesVladCurran's *Aftermath*, and both authors focus on Eric's intense emotions. In *Lullaby*, Eric's grief frightens Sookie since "he had always seemed so strong," and in *Aftermath* he opens his mind to Sookie because his "grief alone is not enough" and he needs "more pain." While the idea of Eric as an alternative to Bill has been established already by this point in the canon, Eric's vulnerability and humanity are consistently stressed in the fanfics to create plausible motivations for Sookie's shift of attachments, and while none of the stories end with Sookie abandoning Bill, the open structure, signaling that something has been set in motion, gestures towards an alternative plot development.

New Romances: How Come No One Else Sees It?

Discussing the unlikeliness of pairings is difficult precisely because fan fiction allows authors to test the limits of the imagination. What is farfetched to one reader may make perfect sense to another, and in all the examples we discuss, there is some form of relationship between the characters involved also in the canon, be this of friendship, antagonism, or just passing acquaintance. Although we cannot conclusively rule out the existence of fanfic pairing characters who have never met each other in the canon (say, Bella's stepfather Phil and the rogue vampire Victoria), we have not come across any such examples in our searches and readings.[18] Rather, there seems to be a need for moments in the canon, however fleeting, in which the characters are in some form of contact, to provide starting points when envisioning a different romance in fan fiction. Unlikely pairings further entail specific forms of inventiveness in order for the author to explain away the relationship established in the canon.

Differences between instantiations in The Vampire Diaries structure which alliances are unexpected in one but not the other. The Stefan/Caroline, or "Steroline," pairing, for example, is not uncommon in fan fiction based on the TV series, since Caroline professes an immediate attraction to Stefan (albeit not reciprocated) and the two are close when he provides guidance and instruction when Caroline is first turned. Smith's novels do not feature similar moments to be mined, and the portrayal of Caroline is very different. A minor character, she does not develop far beyond the initial rivalry with Elena, and hardly features at all in fan fiction connected to the novel series. When she does, the stories often illustrate a conflation of the written and visual instantiation, combining plot elements from the novels with Caroline's TV series character.[19] The character Bonnie more commonly appears in novel-based fanfic, the "Bamon" pairing a favorite with many authors, but pairing her with Stefan is quite rare.

One exception is midnightquiver's *Strong Enough*, set after *Shadow Souls*, the penultimate novel in Smith's series. It thus ignores plot developments in the last novel, and works from the premise that Damon is human and that Elena has changed as well and shifted her romantic interest. "It tore Stefan apart" when Elena chooses Damon over him, midnightquiver writes. As in some of the fanfics discussed in the previous section, the issue of choice on Stefan's part becomes moot; conditions outside of his control have changed, which open for a romance with Bonnie. In this story it is the absence of fated love which lays the foundation for the new pairing. The situation is similar in jazzywazzy08's *Contact*, albeit working from a completely different premise, and being set after the third television season of *The Vampire Diaries*. In this story, the newly turned Elena has withdrawn, spending time with Caroline who likewise has had "immortality thrust upon [her]." Stefan, who is out to apologize for his misdeeds, instead seeks out Bonnie. In this sequel rendition of events, she has turned to dark magic which brings "destruction" and even deaths of "innocent[s]." Her life has taken a turn which aligns her with Stefan, and he thinks that "he is likely the only one that can understand. The only one who has fallen from so high." Physical contact becomes the only cure for Bonnie's state and the only way Stefan can be absolved for his past offences, because with it, human feelings are again awakened. While Elena as Stefan's fated love is removed from this fanfic as well, there is less emphasis on a choice on her part, and the conditions presented in the fanfic, although initially despondent, follow logically from the canon season's rather unexpected ending.

In contrast to canon creators, fanfic authors are not constrained by any need to be consistent in their characterizations from one story to the next, nor do they have to ensure that pairings do not collide with each other. Curiosity about different pairings drives wisedec4u who has a pronounced interest in the character Tara Thornton "not the one from the book, the one from the show," as she writes in her author profile, and in the five stories published on

FanFiction.net, pairs Tara with her canon lovers Sam and Jason, but also with the less expected Eric, Alcide and Bill. *Forget Me Not* is set after the end of *True Blood*'s third season when Tara has been through an ordeal with the vampire Franklin Mott and feels betrayed by everyone including Bill, who has not been able to protect her. The fanfic contains other references to her often tragic past in the canon, along with "her disgust" for vampires in general and Bill in particular. Following canon events, Bill is also in a vulnerable state when the fanfic starts, since Sookie has left him and rescinded her invitation to her house. When Tara seeks him out in *Forget Me Not* he is surprised, and even more so when she reveals her desire to be glamoured and made to forget everything supernatural that has ever happened to her.[20] Grudgingly, he acquiesces and replaces her painful memories with happy ones, in the process shifting Tara's opinion of him. The latter is not accomplished without some soul searching, but Bill decides to "allow himself a few moments of solace." The closeness between them develops into a passionate kiss and a close but chaste night together. Or, rather, chastity is one possible path for the two to take; in an alternative chapter, wisedec4u depicts a consummated and mutually satisfying sexual encounter. Regardless of if the reader chooses the "noble" or the "naughty" storyline, ensuing events are identical and result in the possibility for a happy future for Tara.

While the noble Bill is closer to the character in the canon, the naughty version of him is not divorced from it. He makes love to Tara without losing sight of his love for Sookie or his betrayal, and is driven by a need to pleasure and protect. With Tara, the situation is more complicated. Once her memories have been erased and her attitude "adjusted," Bill thinks, "she was the total opposite of the woman that had showed up on his doorstep just a few hours ago." To enable the meeting between the two characters, regardless of whether the emphasis is on friendship or lust, wisedec4u creates a Tara who is glamoured to forget about all the things that have formed her and, importantly, her hatred of Bill and other vampires. Naturally, the fanfics should be read as freestanding stories, but it is still interesting that *Forget Me Not* is bracketed by two stories (published before and after) in which Tara's views of Bill are very much canon. In *Little Red Riding Hood*, featuring the pairing Tara/Alcide, she thinks of Bill as "Sookie's murdering, two-face, piece of shit vampire boyfriend," and in *Save Me*, which pairs Tara with Jason, "the sight of" Bill makes "her skin crawl." These two stories tellingly hinge on Tara retaining her canon ethics and psychology. Her "personality," if you will, is retained both in the expected (as in faithful to the canon) pairing with Jason, and in the more unexpected relationship with Alcide. Because of Alcide's were nature, the affair is complicated a bit by Tara's firm notion at the beginning of the fanfic, temporally identical to *Forget Me Not*, that she is to start her life over without any further contacts with the paranormal world. However, "Alcide was no bad wolf, he was good, *real good*." His demeanor as well as sexual prowess make up for his nature and Tara can comfortably be left in character, unglamoured and free to make her own choices.

The heteronormative ethos of Twilight and the exclusivity of Bella's and Edward's relationship make virtually all stories featuring Bella with another character, Jacob excepted, unexpected. In MeraNaamJoker's *Holding Sam*, Bella is paired with the minor character Sam Uley, leader of the Quileute werewolves, and their relationship upsets all events which follow in the canon. The author writes in her summary that she has discounted what happens in the following canon novels, especially *Breaking Dawn*: "Everybody was out of character for that book. Forget it, because I did." But discounting later character developments (or lack thereof) does not remove the necessity for inventing plausible reasons for the unexpected pairing, and Bella and Sam are depicted as complementary by the same kind of logic used in fanfic featuring the more common Bella/Jacob romance. In the canon, Sam is a conflicted character, on the one hand because he is the first Quileute to phase into a wolf because of the arrival of the Cullens, on the other because he has hurt the women in his life. In *Eclipse*, Jacob tells Bella that Sam had no one to guide him through the process of transformation and that he consequently "thought he'd gone insane" (Meyer 104). Further, Sam has been engaged to Leah, but then imprinted on her cousin Emily. Emily, in turn, as Jacob informs Bella in *New Moon*, has been permanently scarred when "Sam lost control of his temper for just one second," due to his inner "monster" (Meyer 304). Like Bella, Sam has doubted his sanity and has been torn between love interests, hurting them both. They also complement each other physically which brings Bella a new sense of purpose. They meet because Sam saves her from the rogue vampire Victoria, but is hurt in the process. Bella finds that she can help his healing by closing his wounds, and although she continues to battle the sadness caused by Edward's disappearance she corrects her thought, "I couldn't do *anything*" by realizing "I could save Sam." Together, the couple heal, and hold, each other and understand each other's vulnerabilities in ways which the human/vampire difference precludes in the canon.[21] As in stories pairing Jacob and Bella, attention is generally drawn to incompatibilities between vampire and humans, through Bella's realization of all the "normal" things Sam can give her. And like in many of these stories, Bella is faced with a chance to change her mind, to again choose Edward and a vampire existence, which she declines because of her new experiences.

Unexpected pairings can naturally also involve minor characters and contribute to explorations of their feelings. Megi's fanfic *Empty Sex* is an intensely sexual story featuring the unusual pairing of Esme and Bella's father Charlie. While these characters are on friendly terms in the canon, there are no hints to a more intimate relationship. In the fanfic prequel Bella is still living with her mother, and the Cullen family is new in Forks. Megi immediately establishes Charlie's perception of class difference as he drives up to the impressive new house to help Esme decide what types of alarms she should have installed. The "pointless exhibitionism" of the house only drives home the point that he would never be able to afford it. The attraction to Esme is immediate, as are the incompatibilities between them, and both are used to justify the sexual encounter. Charlie thinks of Esme as a "*sexy trophy wife*," with the underlying meaning that she is trapped in a loveless marriage, and that "*rich people didn't play by the same rules*" as poor, which helps explain why she is flirting with him. Esme also creates justification for their lovemaking. Although she claims that she and Carlisle "have an arrangement," she later concedes that this is a lie. "It would kill Carlisle to know what she was doing, but no more so than her empty life was killing her. If Charlie could fill that void, wasn't it worth it?" Megi thus does not do away with the canon romance, nor does she portray Charlie as unaware of it, rather she establishes that both characters are lonely and can provide each other with comfort.

 The fact that the characters are clearly parental in a canon whose main demographic is young adults results in few indications of sexual conduct, although the love and emotional intimacy between Carlisle and Esme is stressed and although we know that Charlie must have had sex, at least once. To portray Esme and Charlie as vocal about their desires and involved in hot, steamy sex, on kitchen counters and in swimming pools, therefore arguably creates characters that act slightly out of character. However, their actions are naturalized by the temporal relocation which aligns the fanfic with other stories set in the past, such as the previously discussed *The Vampire Diaries* prequel *The Past is Prologue*. Emphasized in both is that the parental generation is as lost and as lonely as the generation portrayed in the canons, but also that passions and an active love life are as desirable to them as to the young adults at the center of the canon texts.

* * *

To see fan fictions as archontic texts turns questions of ownership and hierarchies on their heads, and brings specific aesthetic considerations into play. In terms of the ethics of the text form, the open acknowledgment of co-existence turns issues of poaching into issues of re-planting or, in vampire terms, issues of draining into issues of rebirth. Characters and plot strands, sometimes dialogues and quoted sentences, are openly co-opted, but deposited into the archives the fanfics also give something back, ensuring, as Derecho claims, that "the text is never solidified, calcified, or at rest" (77). The fanfics analyzed in this chapter expand their archives in different, often combined, ways. Perspectival shifts alter perceptions internally of minor characters and externally of the protagonists. Prequels and sequels add to the archives explorations of characters' ethics and behavior: prequels often gesture forward to how the characters are portrayed in the canons, and in sequels attention is paid to how issues can logically be developed. In both cases, fanfic portrayals can accompany readers into (re)readings of the canon materials and affect interpretations.

In relationally oriented, pairing based fanfic, authors move from changing small narrative details to depicting life-altering choices. Whether fanfic authors follow the road marked as a possibility in the canon, or chart new territory in explorations of unexpected pairings, all stories illustrate an intense interest in character. Sara Gwenllian Jones points out that "major characters function as points of entry" into the canon text or the extended fictional universe, and "of primary importance to fans is not how characters move along the narrative but rather what narrative events can reveal about characters" ("Sex Lives" 85, 86). In contrast to plot developments in prequels and sequels in which the narrative trajectory is foregrounded, alternative pairings of both major and minor characters examine their inner workings in great detail. The fanfics add new associations to the ways in which the character has to change in order to accept, embrace, or initiate the alternative relationship, and how this relationship in turn affects the character.

The aesthetics of archontic texts underscores that originality is not the only measuring stock. Fanfics interact in recognizable ways with the canon—the latter an ever-present reference against which the revision gains meaning—and while inventiveness in relation to canon materials is praised, so is fidelity to them. Fanfic authors play with different levels and degrees of both. Stories that are stylistically or formally faithful may include characterizations or plot developments that represent drastic departures from the canon, and vice versa. Authors actively engage with canon elements to laud as well as to critique them, but in both cases, their own readings and their own interpretations are contributed to the ever-expanding archives.

Interlude: The Normal Discussion

In the coming two chapters, the analyzed fanfics subvert *canon* norms, either by circumventing chastity or heteronormativity, or by rendering issues of evil and monstrosity in alternative ways. Important to note at the outset is that we do not argue that there is anything inherently subversive about graphic descriptions of sexuality, same-sex intimacy or kinky sexual practices, nor that issues of monstrosity or darker subject matters are deviant, only that the fanfics represent considerable departures from how canon norms concerning sexuality and sexual orientations, and monstrosity and evil, guide the characters and the narrative. Still, what we through close readings define as the norm in the canon needs to be framed by discussions about the challenges and risks inherent in normalizing processes, and there are points of contact in this respect between the two chapters. This interlude consequently contains arguments and theoretical standpoints which apply both to "Canon-Subversive Lemony Goodness" and "Something Wicked This Way Comes."

Designating some norms, behaviors and characters as normal and others as abnormal and deviant is connected to systems of power. "[P]ower," Michel Foucault claims, "traverses and produces things, it induces pleasure, forms knowledge, produces discourse" (*Power* 119). To control, punish and repress behaviors and identities, these need to be identified (produced) in contrast to the norm. Different kinds of categorizations and classifications, both past and contemporary, are structured similarly to the "multiplicity of discourses [on sex] produced by a whole series of mechanisms operating in different institutions," and they underpin other forms of separations between the normal and the deviant (Foucault, *History* 33). But, as Foucault also points out, transgression becomes part of power, and resistance is always built into discourses. On the one hand, he states there is "[t]he pleasure that comes of exercising a power that questions, monitors, watches, spies, searches out, palpates, brings to light; and on the other hand, [there is] the pleasure that kindles at having to evade this power, flee from it, fool it, or travesty it" (Foucault, *History* 45).

Critique of discourses within teratology (the study of monsters) and discussions within queer theory to an extent overlap in their focus on how the normal is problematically constructed and maintained, and in how questions of Otherness (metaphysical or sexual) are raised. Two longer quotations illustrate this point. In a chapter in *Speaking of Monsters: A Teratological Anthology*, Patricia MacCormack notes:

> Defining, signifying, classifying, and placing certain kinds of subjects into a hierarchy is an act, which is based not on the quality or essence of an entity but by the powers that constitute the capacity to define. The history of teratology has been a history of powers of expression in mechanizing and controlling taxonomical structures. Monster ontology manifests the truth of the aberrant in order to affirm the shift of the "normal" from a cultural, arbitrary category to an idealized natural phenomenon [256].

In the introduction to *The Ashgate Research Companion to Queer Theory*, Noreen Giffney argues,

> Queer is ... often embraced to point to fluidity in identity, recognising identity as a historically-contingent and socially-constructed fiction that prescribes and proscribes against certain feelings and actions. [...] Queer ... denotes a resistance to identity categories or easy categorisation, marking a disidentification from the rigidity with which identity categories continue to be enforced and from beliefs that such categories are immovable [2–3].

The power of the human subject to classify and categorize is the starting point in teratology and this is particularly clear when moving from the original starting point (examining and classifying abnormalities in the human) to considerations of fictional monsters. Teratological discourses fix the monster in a position of Otherness, and the potential for and pleasure in evasive maneuvers (noted by Foucault) is not readily apparent. Conversely, the aberrant Other nails down what it means to be normal and even though represented as the ideal state, normal subjects are likewise likely to remain in fixed positions. The second quotation illustrates that while the power to delineate what is normal still rests with someone or something outside the subject: a "historically-contingent and socially-constructed fiction," subversion is evoked as a potentiality (albeit still difficult). As Eve Kosofsky Sedgwick claims, "'queer' can signify only *when attached to the first person*"; the subjective experience and with it resistance are essential components (*Tendencies* 9). The nailing down of the aberrant pre-exists the resistance; it is against categorizations and classifications that queer readings and queer subjects protest.

The overlaps between analyses of teratology and queer theory find a counterpart in content-based points of contact in the selected canons as well as in fanfic analyzed in the coming chapters. Several fanfics in discussed in chapter four use graphic sexual scenes which represent a subversion of the canons' sexual norms (be this abstinence, heteronormativity or depictions of conventional "non-kinky" practices) while at the same time enhancing the vampires' Otherness in ways which draw attention to potentialities for monstrosity. Conversely, sex is depicted in several fanfics analyzed in chapter five in ways which exacerbate the vampire's monstrosity. By drawing attention to both theoretical and content-based overlaps, we do *not* mean that queer sex and sexualities in any way can be read as connoting monstrosity. However, these similar yet crucially different discourses intersect in the figure of the vampire. Traditionally classified as a monster, the vampire has been, and continues to be identified with a transgression of sexual identity categories and with deviant sexual desires. To unpack challenges inherent in *para*normal fictions, we must firstly establish how the vampires' possible monstrosity collides or coalesces with human norms, and secondly, discuss how vampires are sexually transgressive.

In connection with vampires' possible morals, Gert Magnusson notes three different classifications that can be made by which vampires "can be said to be humans, or demons, or even another species" (§ 1). If a vampire is seen as a human (or ex-human), it follows that he or she would also be invested with some kind of morality aligned with human norms, and actions he or she performs would consequently be judged as "immoral (evil)" (Magnusson § 2). If vampires are seen as demons or another species, on the other hand, the "valuation of their actions" could follow another interpretive path and result in a view of them as "amoral," that is, impossible to judge from the perspective of human morals and ethics (Magnusson § 2). Our selected canons' representations of vampires as humanized, as co-existing with humans and partaking of human life (in True Blood even legislation and human rights) seem to indicate that the vampires' actions, reactions, ethics and behavior should be evaluated on the same grounds as the human characters'. Simultaneously, however, their retained Otherness signals a further need, within the canons, to classify and to name, and some human characters propagate the view that vampires are evil not only because of what they do, but because of what they are. Although the latter essentialist view is refuted as extremist and unproductive, fanfic authors at times recuperate a supposed "natural" vampire state in which the being is in focus. Actions, ethics and behavior are in these types of fanfics linked to an essential identity rather than to actions and choices, thus subverting the canon elements.

In a discussion about vampires' traditional linkage with transgressive sexuality, Judith Halberstam suggests that "the vampire is not lesbian, homosexual, or heterosexual; the vampire represents the productions of sexuality itself"

(344). It is the threat of the vampire's deviant reproductive potential — creating new vampires without the need for biologically differently sexed parties — along with his or her power to seduce and bring out supposedly latent desires in victims that constitute the real transgression, rather than behaving in ways that would go against pre- and proscribed (human) sexual identities. While the canon vampires are certainly transgressive in their reproductive capabilities, their humanization means that their corporeality as well as sexual identities are foregrounded in ways which fix them in sexually coded subject positions. All our canons present heterosexual relationships as central to the human and vampire protagonists, and the few non-straight characters and couples depicted in True Blood are gay, lesbian or bisexual rather than transgressing or exceeding these human-constructed categories. Consequently, processes of normalization within the canons represent vampires as sexually transgressive only in a limited sense. In canon-subversive fanfic, it is not only heterosexuality (or in the case of Twilight abstinence) which is questioned but depictions of conventional sexual desires; authors often using the human/vampire relationships to explore desires conflating pleasure with pain.

The normalization processes noted thus far turn back on themselves when seen in relation to, precisely, the human/vampire coupling. Human/vampire sex, regardless of the fact that it takes place between differently sexed partners, is Other; it is not a condoned practice in any of the canons and may consequently be read as a queering practice in and of itself. "Queering has the job of undoing 'normal' categories," Donna Haraway writes on the topic of the human/nonhuman dichotomy, and the vampires' Otherness remains a powerful injunction against complete normalization (xxiv). The vampire's status as non-human plays a significant role in the fanfic authors' creations. The vampires' long existences are cited, in True Blood for example, as reasons for both their sexual prowess and their willingness to sexually experiment, aspects which are picked up in fan fictions. Vampires' physical strength and their hard-to-destroy bodies are additional non-human characteristics which become significant in stories about sexual torture and pain. Although provocative or even taboo practices are in focus in the analyzed fanfics, they mirror other forms of "deviancy" that the vampire may represent; more symbolic forms of marginalization and the limitations and affordances offered by the outside position.

As is the case with all fan fictions hitherto analyzed, the stories in the coming two chapters are paratextually filed and tagged to prepare the reader for the contents and signal a particular approach. But in contrast to previously discussed fanfics in which this threshold is marked mainly by signaling pairings and general genres, tags signal that the contents may be perceived as subversive, again in relation to canon norms. In chapter four, typical tags are "femslash," "slash," "kink-fic," "vampcest" or "BDSM"; in chapter five, "angst," "horror," "blood play" or "character death." These tags are often followed by exhortations such as "don't like — don't read!" or by straightforward warnings that alert the reader to potentially controversial contents. "Dark," or "darkfic," finally, are tags commonly attached to stories dealing with evil and monstrosity, but which feature in relation to sexually subversive stories as well. Like other forms of revisions, darkfics are "canon-corrective," and specifically aimed at what are considered to be underdeveloped "images of intense violence and broody introspection," which, if dealt with at all in the canons, are "forgotten by the time the next episode or issue comes around" (Fanlore, "Darkfic" n. pag.). Darkfic creates a sense of realism stretching beyond the canons, lingering on the physical effects of traumatic events, and reading characters' reactions from the perspective of human psychology.

In the appropriately named *Dark Fic*, Suki59 provides a humorous take on the category and on a meta-level points to issues often explored in it, conveniently for our purposes conflating issues of trauma with dark physical desires. The story, working from Harris' novel series, starts with Sookie on her way to the vampire bar Fangtasia when a power out affects both streetlights and car headlights, making her crash her car. Feeling her way, and being stepped on and pushed around, Sookie nevertheless makes it to the bar and is greeted by a joyous Pam, who has arranged for Sookie to experience "a dark fic." That is, responsible for the paranormal power out, she has literalized the reading experience and made it into an event, claiming about darkfics that "[p]eople love 'em!" Sookie's sunny disposition in the canon, along with her attempts at normalcy in a world populated by supernaturals (including herself), make her immediately protest that she does not enjoy the literal dark and ensuing confusion in the least, and that it will leave a lasting impression: "My feet are going to be black and blue. Goodness knows what my car will look like tomorrow." The parodying tone of the fanfic displaces the lingering effects of trauma onto something quite mundane but there is nevertheless an insistence that the event will have effects. More importantly, Sookie also stresses that she prefers something "more 'normal.'" Rather than seeing darkfic (and motivations behind writing it) as abnormal or "wrong," however, the author through Pam draws attention to the idea that what is "'normal' is relative [and w]hat's normal for you might not be for other people."

Pam's preparations for the planned darkfic-evening include an Eric in "offensive [...] black face," a "pony [in] the mens [sic] room," one character tied down in the office, and a gender-bending male character in a skirt. Many of the preparations, and in an extended sense familiar depictions in fanfic stories, thus hint to sexual practices which Sookie deems in need of warnings so that she "can make [her] own decision" whether to take part (or read), her main argument being "I might have even liked it had I known what it was." As she has not been adequately prepared, everything is restored to normal. A certain preparation is thus perceived to be needed at the threshold between readers and the fictional texts and paratexts such as warnings and tags are desired. By metatextually commenting on both the fanfic category and the necessity of explicit paratextual warnings, *Dark Fic* offers insights into why some authors are drawn to explorations of dark practices and why these may be potentially disturbing to other readers, but also into ongoing tensions about what constitutes the norm, how this norm can be subverted, and to what ends subversion is employed.

4. Canon-Transgressive Lemony Goodness: Sexual Norms and Undead Desires

Fan fictions with pronounced sexual content abound in True Blood, The Vampire Diaries and Twilight fandoms (and in many others). Sexually charged stories are sometimes referred to in summaries, forum discussions, and metatextual discussions with the terms lemon, lemons or lemony goodness.[1] The origin of the terms can be traced back to the genre-bending anime series *Cream Lemon* (first published in the 1980s) and "an early mailing list for publishing erotic anime fanfic, called 'The Lemon List' in its honor" (Television Tropes and Idioms, "Lemon" n. pag.). Megi's Twilight fanfic *Empty Sex*, which we discuss with emphasis on the unusual pairing Esme/Charlie in chapter three, plays with the idea of lemons in a literal way, contrasting it to "vanilla": conventional sexual practices. In the couple's first meeting, Esme, the sexual initiator, has just made some fresh lemonade and decorates the glasses with lemon wedges. In a later conversation, Charlie recalls a cake his mother used to make, with flavors of "[v]anilla and lemon but not heavy lemon." Then, as they kiss passionately, Charlie says in a metatextual reference to the cake: "That's not what I want right now." Although the sex which follows can hardly be described as kinky it is nevertheless hot and steamy. That is, hardly canon vanilla, and certainly heavy lemon.

In this chapter, we focus on fanfics which deviate from the sexual ethics of the canon and the behavior of the canon characters. The vampire has been (and is, in some contexts) seen as holding queer potential, and although the main revenants in the canon are represented as straight, their ontological Otherness still gestures to possibilities of conflating transgressive practices. In relation to the heteronormativity stressed in the paranormal romance, slash and femslash stand out as obvious examples of subversion, but adding sex scenes in an AU story is similarly indicative of a questioning of norms and proscribed behaviors. Further, even if characters are presented as straight in the canon, they exist in close-knit groups which suggest a homosociality to be mined for potential in same-sex fanfic. Kinkfic: stories about sexual power play such as BDSM, is seen in a variety of fandoms, but the vampire lends itself particularly well to stories about conflations of sex and violence/power, or of fear combined with desire. We consequently analyze how fan fiction authors' depictions of non-canon sexual acts such as pre-marital sex, same-sex relationships, BDSM games, and practices we term undead desires, add important associations to transgression to the archives.

Vampiric Transgression

Vampiric threat and turning processes involve physical intimacy, rendered in ways which conflate desires of various kinds. The vampire's bite targets vital and sexually charged areas such as the neck or the chest, blood exchanges can easily be read as thinly veiled substitutes for other exchanges of bodily fluids, and victims' bedrooms are often the settings for nocturnal invasions. These recurring motifs, along with a lingering threat, make the vampire into an almost automatic "vehicle through which to encode subversive pleasures of sexuality and desire" (Keft-Kennedy 50). Encoded pleasures are then decoded by readers and critics and Robert Mighall notes that the "history of interpretation" of vampire texts has focused on the erotic promises and threats to the point where "vampirism is only the 'ostensible' subject of the text" (210–211). The sexual threat the vampire poses, as well as the latent desires it may evoke, are in this interpretative tradition at the heart of vampire fiction, rather than a monstrous Otherness.

To many critics, the vampire becomes emblematic of alternative sexualities and desires, oftentimes remaining connected to human-constructed categories such as straight, lesbian, gay, or bisexual, rather than making the vampire "immuniz[ed] ... from human erotic norms" (Auerbach 41). Richard Dyer even draws attention to how processes of secrecy and revelation look remarkably similar in discourses about vampires and in discourses about homosexuality. "On the one hand, the point about sexual orientation is that it doesn't 'show'" Dyer notes, "but on the other hand there is also a widespread discourse that there are tell-tale signs that someone 'is.' The vampire myth reproduces this double view in its very structures of suspense" (58). The vampire's similarity to humans here finds a counterpart in the invisibility of sexual orientation and processes of outing are paralleled.

Alternatives to the heteronorm can be read as queer in and of themselves, but critics acknowledge the potential for a further, queer disruption with consequences for both vampires and human characters. Christopher Craft convincingly argues that *Dracula* (as well as Dracula) illustrates the threat of a homosexual Other, but also that "mobile desire," a desire which destabilizes the gendered conduct of both male and female characters, is "imagin[ed] ... as [a] monstrosity" which needs to be corrected (116). Van Helsing's "largest purpose" Craft maintains, "is to reinscribe the dualities that Dracula would muddle and confuse" (117). In Craft's reading, the vampire's sexual Otherness in relation to the Victorian norms of the time period are but one aspect of its threat; more serious is the gendered confusion among the novel's human characters—"a male's desire to be penetrated," for example, and Lucy Westenra's "inversion of sexual identity" (Craft 111, 119). The vampire's blurring of boundaries between life and death is linked to its ability to muddle other distinctions, in Craft's analysis and in many others. Sue-Ellen Case, for example, notes that "queer desire ... breaks with the discourse that claims mimetically to represent [the] 'natural' world" and that the queer "taboo-breaker, the monstrous, the uncanny" has a particular "subversive power" (3). Removing gender and gendered sexual identities from the equation effects, in Case's view, a perception of vampires as "new forms of being, or beings, [which] are imagined through desire" (4). In these discussions, the vampire becomes a figure of fluidity, challenging and transgressing at once both ontological and sexual boundaries.

Disruptive sexual powers in the form of queer "taboo-breakers" and "mobile desires" are few and far between in Twilight and in L.J. Smith's novel series when seen in terms of alternatives to the heteronorm, underscored by the centrality of the heterosexual union. There is sexual tension between human and vampire in both Stephenie Meyer's and Smith's novels, but exclusively between heterosexual males and females. Particularly in Twilight, there is a further stress on abstinence which, somewhat paradoxically, can be seen as a transgression since it resists rather than affirms popular culture representations. The texts are not expressly anti-gay or homophobic, yet the lack of alternative sexualities becomes conspicuous in their absence. If there are closets, in these texts, they are deep. In the TV series *The Vampire Diaries*, the main relationships are similarly heterosexual (but less abstinent) and there is only one character: Caroline's father Bill Forbes, who is described as openly gay. His sexuality does not make him more willing than heterosexual characters to accept other forms of existence which in the canon is marked as deviant. While we do not suggest that his sexual identity should make him more open minded, there are two narrative components which draw attention to a seeming contradiction. Firstly, his open adversity to vampires renders him intolerant and his torture-like treatment to cure his daughter from vampirism alludes to cruel behavioral methods used in the past to correct sexually deviant desires. Echoing Dyer's analogy above, homosexuality is explicitly compared to vampirism by Damon who says that Bill "is threatening to out me. Don't get me started on the irony in that!" (*The Vampire Diaries*, 3:04, "Disturbing Behavior"). Bill Forbes has successfully come out of his closet, but wants to enforce disclosure in Damon's case and revert Caroline back to her "normal" state.

In True Blood, there is a continuous play on the similarities between processes of coming out of closets and of coffins, and discourses of tolerance (or lack thereof) pertain to both ontological and sexual Otherness. Among the non-straight characters, and with slightly different renderings between the media forms, are both vampires, such as Russell Edgington and Pam, and humans, such as Lafayette and Amelia. Some are openly gay or bisexual, others (the vampire character Eddie, featured in the first season of the TV series, is the clearest example) remain in the closet. While the featured resistance to heteronormativity may be perceived as liberating, the conflation of different forms of marginalization combined with the series' stress on assimilation, may paradoxically limit the vampire's queer potential. Accepting that the vampire has traditionally been read as a symbol of repressed or threatening homosexuality, Darren Elliot-Smith argues that "the assimilation of the homosexual (vampire) into mainstream culture demands abstinence from transgressive sexuality and the adoption of a homonormativity where gay masculinity (vampirism) is rendered non-threatening, bland and asexual" (147). Just as vampires are required to de-emphasize their ontological Otherness, alternatives to the heteronorm need to be downplayed and normalized. Susana Loza further notes that "clear lines are drawn between good queers and bad queers" in *True Blood* (104). The non-straight "good" couples are predominantly depicted as monogamous and in relatively stable relationships and the series in the main shies away from visualizing same-sex intercourse. Even if it is suggested that their long existences make them more open to sexual experimentation than human characters, the experiments the True Blood vampires indulge in are about same-sex or kinky sexual practices, that is, transgressions of hetero and vanilla norms.[2]

For our purposes in this chapter, fanfic transgressions of the canons' sexual norms will be of paramount interest, but the authors' conflation between different forms of resistance return us to the vampire's queer potential. In his discussion about "queer vampires," and drawing on Case's article, Ken Gelder notes how queer "gains its effect by continually *collapsing* the conventional polarit[ies] of 'life' and 'death,' normality and the unnatural, regeneration and sterility ... rather than by positioning itself on the negative side of [these]"

(*Reading* 61–62). In his discussion, several vampire practices and competencies come together to denote queerness. Fanfic authors in our sample react to abstinence and heteronormativity by coding different kinds of Otherness in sexual terms and combine the marginalized undead state with particular vampiric competencies (strength, speed, and mind control) to transgress several norms at once. Further, many reclaim the vampire's potential to awaken latent desires of different kinds in the human characters, as well as explore matters such as taking pleasure in being submissive, enjoying pain, humiliation and other forms of domination.

Abstinence Resistance

In Twilight, sex is something that takes place between married and monogamous males and females, regardless of whether they are humans, vampires or shifters. A rule concerning sexual conduct is in this way established and Bella and Edward follow it since their first time takes place on their wedding night. However, obstacles to sexual intimacy remain when they are married, continuously figured as imbalances in physical strength and power which are not resolved until Bella is turned and the two are equal in strength as well as in bed. The insistence on chastity does not, however, mean that eroticism is absent in the canon. In examinations of fan involvement with Twilight, Jennifer Stevens Aubrey, Elizabeth Behm-Morawitz, and Melissa A. Click caution against equating the abstinence theme with a lack of sexuality and argue that "Edward represents a 'safe'" choice because he is "a romantic hero who is both sexually charged and chaste" (§ 2:6). The chaste and romantic love story can be seen as a nice contrast to the (over)sexualization of popular culture, and Edward's responsible attitude towards sex represents a refreshing gender-reversal as it is, for once, the guy and not the girl who says no (Flanagan 117). Read this way, Edward can remain a safe fantasy for young women and girls who may identify with Bella.

The use of Bella as first-person narrator and her female gaze on Edward's body represent a gender reversal in the canon and thematically align Twilight with more overtly erotic stories, in which, Bernadette Lynn Bosky notes, "the vampires ... are quintessentially desirable," and in which the human "become[s] the seducer/predator of the undead, reversing the traditional roles" (224). In the canon, however, Edward as a safe choice and his resistance to intimacy work as an insurance against the sex-before-marriage possibility. In the fan fictions analyzed in this section, the fantasies of Edward move away from the safe realm and allow Bella to express and act on her sexual desires.

In fact, fanfic authors' literalized criticism of the canon mirror critics' reactions to conservative portrayals of Bella and Edward's chaste romance. The critique mainly focuses on the stereotypical gender roles (thinly disguised as vampire/human natures) which entail limitations to Bella's agency, especially regarding the control of her sex life (see for example Seifert, and Isaksson and Lindgren Leavenworth).

The starting point in Taia's story *The Experiment* is a scene from *Eclipse* in which Bella attempts to seduce Edward, because it is "something that [she] want[s] to do before [she is] not human anymore" (Meyer 392). Taia explains in her author notes that she "was ... surprised and disappointed" by the fact that "Bella/Edward's relationship didn't develop further than kissing" in the canon scene and also suggests that it is not logical. Despite "the age-rating," she argues, "[y]ou must admit that any couple passes certain bases in their intimate relationship [before] they have sex." Her story thus grows from her perception of a more realistic view of how relationships develop in real life, rather than in age-rated fiction.[3] To accomplish this development, Taia reduces the threat of Edward losing control of the blood-thirsty vampiric drive by having the couple focus on mutual oral sex, a practice rendered as relatively safe. Oral sex among humans reduces another threat — pregnancy — and arguably constitutes one of the "bases" Taia refers to in her author notes.

Edward is initially portrayed as the (consenting) victim of Bella's experiment. Reflecting their canon dynamics, Bella is the one who wants to take the couple's intimacy further but, in contrast to what happens in Meyers' series, in the fanfic she actually succeeds. Also reflecting the canon, Edward's worries do not completely abate, and vaginal and vascular penetration combine in his mind. Wondering about his girlfriend's possible irresponsibility, Edward thinks: "What if I had stretched Bella on her back, penetrated into her body and sank my teeth into her neck, combining the two ecstasies in one?" Edward's canon worries about loss of control due to irrepressible pleasure thus continue in the fanfic and temporarily threaten to overcome him. Underscoring Edward's dangerous nature, it takes an "impossible effort" to extinguish this "delightful picture, replacing it with reality." It turns out not to be impossible, however, because in contrast to this violent, imagined scenario, Edward is placed lying back in a passive position, gripping the sheets as if to take whatever dangerous reactions out on the bed rather than on Bella, while she performs fellatio.[4]

While Edward's thoughts and fantasies align with his canon worries, they are also vividly sexual, suggesting that Bella is not the only one who has been longing for more than just kisses. "I had been waiting too long to delay it again," Edward thinks as Bella shows signs of hesitation when he starts to undress her. The fanfic in this way emphasizes their equality in this respect. In terms of genre, there are strong links to the canon through the emphasis on romance, mutual feelings of deep love, and the recycling of the star-cross'd lovers trope. Their love surmounts the obstacle to their union and they can safely take the risk inherent in sexual encounters between a vampire and a human. As Bella rhetorically asks: "Were there any real barriers between the two loving hearts?" Using a more general romantic trope than Meyer, who "draws on traditions associated with adolescent problem novels" by posing desire as an obstacle to love (Kokkola 172), Taia makes a union of the couple possible. Further, by placing Bella and Edward's sexual experiments in the doubly secure framework of romance and non-penetrative sex, Taia creates an erotic fanfic that negotiates the sex-within-marriage rules of the canon while remaining true to its ethics.

It is not only specific practices, such as oral sex, which are used to circumvent Twilight's restrictions regarding premarital sex. LaTessitrice's *The Courtyard* is set after the scene in *New Moon* where Edward tries to end his existence in Volterra, believing Bella to be dead.[5] In the fanfic, however, he thinks that both he and Bella have died and that their reunion takes place "in heaven." Bella tries to right the mistake, but soon realizes that Edward's altered view of reality increases opportunities for intimacy: as a ghost (or angel) he is convinced that his paranormal powers can no longer hurt her. After making love, Edward is alerted to the reality of the situation and is shocked by Bella's unhurt body whereas she concludes that the past threat has always been imaginary. In his false belief of their death, she claims, "because you thought you couldn't hurt me, you didn't." In this fanfic, the threat of paranormal powers is thus not only defused by alternative variations of intimacy, but revealed to be always already fictitious.

Daddy's Little Cannibal makes an overt reference to the tag "lemon" already in the title of her story *When Life Gives You Lemons*, thus suggesting contents which are sexually charged. Potential threatening aspects due to power imbalance are not featured or discussed, rather Bella and Edward have seemingly without problems initiated a premarital and pre-turning sexual relationship. The extent of their sexual curiosity is perceived as limiting by Emmett who, to spice things up, gives Bella the challenge to introduce Edward to a new sexual position every night leading up to their wedding. Each chapter of the fanfic is then a "lemon" scene describing the couple trying a new position. In the canon, Emmett is represented as an overtly sexually active character (within his relationship with Rosalie) and he is also continuously teasing Bella (in non-sexual contexts), who often enough rises to the challenge. These canon characteristics are employed in the story, along with characterizations of Edward as resistant and Bella as eager to take their intimacy further. Bella's shyness and both partners' inexperience are also present in this story, as is the romantic and conventional nature of their relationship (the first chapter is, true to Emmett's suspicions, entitled "Missionary"). Convention and romance continue to dictate Bella's actions even after having accepted the challenge; she will not try practices she sees as too kinky, such as anal sex, and dislikes positions in which she and Edward are not face to face. As in the previously discussed fanfics, the centrality of romance ties this story to the Twilight canon and it is the genre's staple of "being meant to be together" that makes sexual experimentation possible. Bella thinks, as she hesitates to try a new position: "I was glad that I was with Edward and not anyone else. He reminds me that no matter what we do, it's for love." Moreover, Daddy's Little Cannibal depicts Bella as more than just a shy and clumsy virgin by having her reflect upon the "naughty" bedroom scenario she is about to stage in the following terms: "good girls didn't do things like this. Of course good girls also didn't date vampires and [they] waited till marriage to have sex, but that was beside the point." The characterization of Bella as adventurous enough to date a vampire, and showing strong desires to move beyond kissing, are thus referred to as background explanations which situate the story in relation to the canon, even as it deviates from one of its "hard limits" by portraying premarital sex.

Setting *When Life Gives You Lemons* within the frame narrative of Emmett's challenge does however mean that it is his and Bella's rather childish game that prompts new sexual practices, not Bella's own initiatives. On the topic of Bella's limited agency in the canon, Susannah Clements argues that it

> taps into a pervasive romantic fantasy of having a powerful, desirable man enter a woman's life and remove all responsibility, make all the difficult choices. Because Edward's hijacking of Bella's choices is all in the service of "her good," Bella can indulge in the pursuit of her desires without actually facing the consequences of achieving them. She can have it both ways [115].

Following this argument, bestowing greater free will and choice upon the (male) vampires makes Bella have less of a choice, but this lack is in the canon represented as positive, even liberating. In a similar way, Bella does not have to accept full responsibility for her sexual initiatives in *When Life Gives You Lemons*, although the author makes it clear that her desires to some extent correspond to Emmett's suggestions. At one point she thinks: "I had actually been kind of hoping to try this position out with Edward for awhile [sic]. Emmett just gave me an excuse to do it." In portraying her as a willing victim of Emmett's naughty plans, the author retains a certain innocence linked to Bella which places her on par with Edward who, true to the canon, is inexperienced like her.[6] As it turns out in the final chapter, Emmett has made a similar bet with Edward, which further reinforces the idea of them as equals (sexually and romantically)—also equally duped by Emmett.

Whether inventing plot developments to circumvent the canon norm of premarital chastity or, like Daddy's Little Cannibal, ignoring it altogether, all stories discussed have Bella and Edward implicitly ask, upon consummating their physical relationship or exploring alternative sexual practices: why on earth have we not done this before? As noted, sexual tension is by no means non-existent in the canon and when resolved in the fanfics, Bella and Edward are revealed as evenly matched when it comes to desires and needs, none of them desiring a return to their previous roles. The elusive equality which in the canon is only reached when Bella is turned is prominently figured as attained in the fanfics. The partners already harbor trust for each other and this develops through the consensual sexual activities. The trope of a fated, true love is recirculated in these fanfics; it is the belief in this love which make the characters willing to have sex in the first place, and to engage in sexual experimentation at later stages of their relationship.

Notable is also that even when fanfics depict a first time between Bella and Edward, it is often represented as intensely pleasurable. In *The Courtyard*, for example, there is a brief moment where Bella is not "entirely sure it was comfortable," but Edward's patience and both parties' prowess guarantee a near simultaneous climax. In fanfics where the paranormal reason for abstinence is removed through the Bella/Jacob pairing, there is at times an interesting distance from *The Courtyard*'s blissful portrayal. In sciphile's *Patience* (which we also discuss in chapter three), the author paints a realistic picture of their intimacy. There are breathless kisses on the porch, awkwardness when things progress, and their first orgasms together are achieved in a fairly innocent way as they rub against each other with their clothes on and with Charlie in the house. With one counterpart who is human and one who is mainly human, in contrast to Bella/Edward pairings, there is a need for mundane forms of protection and comfort, and both Bella and Jacob are in the story responsible enough to wait to have sex until condoms are procured and brought, and fetch towels from the linen cupboard when needed. Both Bella and Jacob are, true to canon, virgins and both worry about the right moves as their intimacy progresses. Concerning cunnilingus, for example, Jacob thinks, "He had no idea if he was doing it right," although Bella's reactions show that he is indeed. The first penetrative sex, which does not end in a satisfying climax, is painful, with Bella exclaiming: "I didn't know it was going to hurt this much." These depictions provide a clear contrast also to traditionally published popular romance where the first time is seldom marked by insecurities, pain and a lack of release.

Imagined or Temporary Homoerotic Spaces

As noted in the introduction, the fanfic genre slash received considerable academic attention in early fan studies, and was often seen as a result of female authors' dissatisfaction with relationships and gendered structures in speculative fictions. The genre, also including stories about female same-sex pairings, has continued to be central to fanfic studies and to more nuanced examinations of resistance (or lack thereof) to popular culture's compulsory heterosexuality. Although slash and femslash are by now tags that can be attached to stories featuring any kind of homoerotic attachments, we use it to denote stories which pair same-sex characters who do *not* have a romantic or sexual canon relationship.

Despite the canons' heteronormativity, there are homosocial tensions between both male and female characters. The three heterosexual and monogamous female protagonists in the canons form close bonds, be these of friendship or antagonism, also with female vampires. Among these are Bella's close friendship with Alice, Sookie's ambivalent relation with Pam, and Elena's fraught relationship with Katherine. The male vampire protagonists similarly have bonds with other members of their sex, particularly with their rivals, most notably Edward with Jacob, Bill with Eric (and vice versa), and Stefan with Damon, the latter relationship made more complex by the fact that they are also biological brothers. Although fanfic authors writing slash and femslash are not limited to these central relationships, a majority is drawn to what these homosocial canon bonds seem to promise; homosociality becomes a subtext, a latent potentiality to be explored. As Virginia Keft-Kennedy notes, there is a "slippage made explicit in slash, between homosociality and homosexuality" (68).

In chapter three we argued that even unexpected non-canon pairings hinge on some form of contact between the characters and the same holds for slash and femslash. Even when placed in antagonistic relationships, the characters paired in same-sex fan fiction have some form of connection which begs to be explored, and characterizations and plot developments exist as a backdrop for ensuing events. In addition to the central couple, humans and vampires form close-knit units in the canon; they are friends, co-workers and family members, and frequently join forces to battle external threats. In what Elizabeth Woledge terms intimatopic texts, "intimacy is normally established before sexual interaction and is always maintained after it," and this intimacy can be engendered by "social closeness" as well as "injury, aggression, or violence" (106, 100, 111). Characters in the three canons paired in (fem)slash have relied on each other and been betrayed by each other, they have offered comforts and deceived. As when differently sexed pairings are imagined, there are often detailed explanations in (fem)slash for the bond between the characters, and inventive changes are made to canon elements to explain why and how the gay or lesbian couple comes out. In most cases, the new couple is also revealed as psychologically and physically matched.

The male participants in the canons' love triangles are often paired in slash, and their union is frequently explained either by what brings them together — their common love interest — or by what separates them, for instance the animosity caused by their rivalry or their contrasting natures and/or personalities. To an extent, slash authors thus partake in the long-standing literary tradition of male homosocial desire in love triangles, explored by Eve Kosofsky Sedgwick in *Between Men*, as the female protagonists are reduced to an alibi, often quickly disposed of. Such is the case in shoefreak37's *The Strange Design of Comfort* in which the death of Bella in childbirth unites Edward and Jacob, forcing them to reevaluate the animosity which has characterized their relationship. But the female protagonist can also be more consistently used as an existing alibi, or a present catalyst that brings the two rivals together. In Sandrine Shaw's *Future Imperfect*, Jacob and Edward tell themselves that "it's always been all about Bella," the love for her is what has brought them together in the first place. In mneiai's *Needful Things* it is the fact that neither of them can have her (Edward because of his strength, Jacob because Bella is with Edward) that brings them together. In both these stories, as well as in shoefreak37's, the same-sex encounters which follow the realizations emphasize the enhanced equality between the parties. Edward cannot physically hurt Jacob and vice versa, and they literally complement each other as one is hot and one is cold. In other slash-fics staging erotic encounters between rivals, Southern Gentleman Bill's ethics are often contrasted to Eric's millennium-old and sinister vampirism, and Stefan's humane and caring attitude is off-set in relation to Damon's ruthlessness both as vampire and womanizer.

Two elements of particular importance to fanfic (fem)slash compete in the paranormal romance: vampirism and the stress on an eventual heterosexual union. Andrew Schopp argues that "[s]ince they are immortal, the vampires can take the time to conquer the barriers, even the fears, that prohibit an enduring male-male relationship" (238). While many slash and femslash authors *do* envision such extended futures for new couples, effectively replacing the heterosexual canon romance with a homosexual one, our focus here is on stories in which same-sex intimacy plays out as dreams or in temporally removed spaces.[7] Analyses of such stories align with our previous discussion about slash connected to J.R. Ward's vampire novels in the Black Dagger Brotherhood series, where we argued that "the genre itself is limited to heterosexual desire, a limitation visible in the use [in fanfic] of erasable moments to create temporary spaces for transgressions of heteronormative rules" (Lindgren Leavenworth, "Lover" 459). That is, we are here interested in exploring tendencies in the fanfic production which may be contingent on genre limitations and consequently in creations of relatively safe spaces in which to explore transgressions of canon norms.

In a fanfic appropriately titled *A Pre-Wedding Day Dream*, MyTwiDreams stages a threesome sex scene between Bella, the "blushing bride," and her bridesmaids Alice and Rosalie whose task it is to help her with wedding make-up and choice of lingerie. The preparations soon become erotic, the two vampires setting out to tangibly prepare Bella for the wedding night, by seducing her and deflowering her with the help of a sex toy. As Alice initiates the sex scene by cupping Bella's breasts from behind, Bella thinks: "This was not something that was supposed to happen between friends, was it?" Although a boundary connected to Bella's own categorization of Alice as a friend is overstepped, she protests no further and quickly comes to enjoy the proceedings. At the end of the graphic sex scene, as Bella is about to climax a second time, she hears Alice moan and call out her name. Only, it turns out that this is Alice trying to awaken Bella who has dozed off while her future sister-in-law is doing her make-up. The story's ending indicates a possible realization of the dream Bella just had: Alice and Rosalie both act in the same way as in the erotic fantasy, hugging and kissing each other in suggestive ways, and as Bella tells them about her dream, which has inspired "thoughts [...] about all the lovely things the three of us could do right now," Alice replies that the future "is always full of possibilities." There is thus an ambiguous return to the "reality" of the characters with a promise of a possible future escape into homoeroticism. Still, the dream does not postpone or cancel Bella's impending wedding and not even the alluring promises seem to constitute an alternative to the heterosexual union. The story thus stays relatively safely within the boundaries of the canon which excludes concrete same-sex relations.

Heteronormativity and its consequences are explicitly addressed in LingeringLuminosity's *Ownership, Apologies and Being Kicked In The Nuts*, which depicts an aftermath of a relationship between Edward and the young werewolf Seth played out on the night of Bella and Edward's wedding. In the canon, tensions are running high between vampires and Quileutes at this point, and Seth is the only werewolf present at the ceremony. He and Edward hug briefly, and the groom appears to be relieved by Seth's congratulatory words (Meyer, *Breaking Dawn* 47–49). The tensions in the fanfic are of another kind as Seth, thinking back on moments of both physical and psychological bonding between himself and Edward, battles feelings of sorrow and jealousy, and reacts strongly to the sense of ownership (Bella owning Edward) which comes with marriage. The author recirculates the short embrace from the canon, but has Edward slip a note into Seth's pocket in which he apologizes for his betrayal, and a short while later, they meet outside in a summerhouse. It immediately becomes clear that Edward is anything but happy with his new status as husband and they kiss passionately. "Seth is fifteen, Edward over a hundred, Seth is a werewolf, Edward a vampire, they're both male and Edward is married and everything is so right" until Edward breaks away from the kiss, apologizing yet again. Monogamy and heteronormativity both hinder Edward, a "closeted bastard" as Seth describes him, from pursuing what is represented as a natural, healthy choice. There are two spaces, one figurative and one literal, used for the depiction of homoerotic desire in this story: the past and the secluded summerhouse. Neither one can provide Edward with enough strength to exit the closet, however.

LingeringLuminosity is not alone in utilizing a temporal space to circumvent the canon's heteronormativity and in many stories, the past is depicted as holding a greater freedom for the characters than it does for Edward in her story. The long existences of *True Blood*'s Eric and Godric have resulted in many homoerotic fanfics which, in contrast to the previously analyzed stories, are not tagged as slash and, in our view, do not fall into the slash category because the characters are in the canon indicated as having been intimate in the past. However, there are few canon scenes which depict their intimacy; it is hinted at rather than visualized, and for fanfic authors focusing on this pairing, the past is often used as a removed space for more detailed and graphic explorations of same-sex desires. Turning to the past also means an opportunity for authors to contrast Eric's self-assured canon character to his vulnerability and inexperience as a new vampire, and the teacher/student relationship, which features in both stories which we turn to now, is mined for erotic potential.

Lenore's *Lessons in Being Inhuman: Two Vignettes* signals a preoccupation with how these roles are established already in its title, and combines lessons about vampire existence with sexual education. In this prequel, Eric and Godric share no affinities with mortals, instead viewing them exclusively as prey, but blood lust and sexual desire continuously intermingle. As Eric drinks from his first human he is aroused as much by the blood as by his victim's "submission," and it is his combination of ruthlessness and desire which makes Godric conclude, "I knew you were the one." The author also suggests that Eric is no stranger to emotionally detached homosexual encounters connoting dominance and power. In his new vampire state, his power is lessened in relation to Godric but a new level of intimacy — affection and love — is reached as they also kiss. Godric "tastes like the beginning and the end and everything in between." The emotion surpasses anything Eric has experienced and establishes Godric as extraordinary. This makes the sexual lesson which ends the second vignette uncomfortable as Godric asks to be penetrated. "To do the fucking is to dominate," Eric thinks, it is "a rule learned early in a warrior's life [and t]his is not what he wants from his maker." Although filled with "frustration," Eric nevertheless carries out the command, the lesson learned being that he has to put his human ways aside and accept vampiric superiority rather than warrior power.

Human Things by linaerys is set one century later and sexual initiation does not feature, on the contrary, Eric "can't remember the first time they were lovers." The teacher/student relationship is still crucial, however, when it comes to blood drinking and killing and Godric determines the extent to and figuration of their intimacy. "Only once since Eric's rebirth has Godric allowed him to taste his blood," linaerys writes, and Eric is careful to not bare fangs when they kiss "or Godric will deprive him of the perfect, hungry bow of his mouth." Eric's deference to Godric is featured in a multitude of ways in the story, even when he, like in Lenore's fanfic, is the penetrating partner. Godric is depicted as on top in this situation, not only physically but psychologically. He is still the one who determines what is to happen: "Open me. I desire you in me." These instructions are coupled with several terms of endearment and, in like the vast majority of Eric/Godric fanfics we have come across, the love between them is depicted as surpassing all others and the bond between the two as extraordinary. In *Lessons in Being Inhuman*, Eric contrasts the memory of his human days — "a dark prison of flesh and bone, empty and limited" — to the promise of eternal togetherness Godric offers. In *Human Things*, Eric thinks back on the "days when Godric was his whole world, when he ... lived only when Godric touched him," a recognition which continues into the temporal setting of the story and, by extension, into the present setting of the canon. While the importance or concreteness of attachments are not denied in any of these stories, the temporal relocation means that the present heterosexual now, guided by genre constraints, is not tampered with. Eric and Godric do not experience erasable moments in the same manner as characters in same-sex encounters featured in dream scenarios or fantasies, but the homosexual experience is still firmly located in the past, creating a relatively safe arena for fanfic authors to explore the characters' intimacy and sexual education.

Even when fanfic authors use the canon's hard data, temporary spaces for sexual transgression are created in ways which do not alter ensuing events and consequently remove the need to sustain homoeroticism into the now. *Cherry-flavoured lip gloss* by pleasebekidding starts off from a scene from *The Vampire Diaries* ("Homecoming" 3:09) which suggests reconciliation between enemies: as a peace offering, Elena returns the Original vampire Rebekah's favorite and centuries-old necklace. The friendly gesture is deceptive and used as a strategy to put the vampire off guard, so that Elena can plant the white oak dagger, which puts the Originals in a coma, in Rebekah's heart. The fanfic author does not alter this ending, but has Elena and Rebekah share a couple of kisses, with a promise of more to follow. Rebekah's impulsive, selfish and fun-seeking nature is in line with her canon characteristics, as is the fact that she represents a real threat to Elena. She possesses none of the ethical vampirism Stefan and Damon (mostly) adhere to and has no reason to protect Elena's life, unlike her otherwise ruthless brother Klaus. In the canon, Rebekah is firmly heterosexual — she is frequently seen flirting, but exclusively with men, while women are compelled into being her "blood bags" or company. In the fanfic, by contrast, Rebekah's idea of "fun" includes "flirting with football players and drinking cheerleaders (or vice versa)." She goes on to suggest that she could "turn" Elena to make her less vulnerable, and clearly alludes to sexual activities, saying: "We could have a lot of fun together." She specifies, "I wouldn't hurt you," before she leans in and "brushes a soft kiss across Elena's lips."

The kissing scene can be read as a successful initiation and Rebekah's promise not to hurt Elena evokes similar lines pronounced by male (romance) characters before deflowering the virgin heroine. In *Cherry-flavoured lip gloss*, the novelty has specifically to do with same-sex erotic experiences, however, and not with initiations to sex or kissing in general. Rebekah's non-aggressive behavior contrasts to what Elena expects from her and, conversely, Elena's eager response to the kiss surprises Rebekah. The latter stops the making out (for selfish reasons: she does not want to miss the homecoming dance), while Elena seems eager to pursue it further. Rebekah's function as the dominant partner is hardly surprising given her superior strength and thousand-year or so sexual experience. Elena's excited response, on the other hand, subverts her canon characteristics as kissing the "wrong" person is depicted as devastating in Smith's novels and is a theme running through the third season of *The Vampire Diaries*. In the fanfic, by contrast, it is made clear that kissing this particular female vampire is extraordinary, and Elena does not care about reactions from others. The author further creates a background explanation for the out of character behavior of welcoming the same-sex kiss by having Elena compare her response to feelings "that she hasn't felt since she and Bonnie practiced."[8] In this version, Elena has previous experiences of kissing a girl before venturing into kissing a boy, however, she is also quick to instruct herself to "let that memory sink below the surface." Just as this memory can be repressed, the consequences of Elena's actions and reactions do not completely follow her into the heterosexual now of the ensuing canon hard data. Instead of distracting Rebekah with the jewelry, Elena has distracted her by kisses. The end result is the same and Rebekah is stabbed in the heart. Although the author indicates that Elena remains aroused by the intimacy, and although Damon is revealed as having witnessed parts of the events, the same-sex kisses can easily be explained away as a devious strategy. The intimacy can thus sink below the surface, much in the same manner as Elena's previous memories of kissing a girl.

To see slash and femslash as subversive text forms holds true when the stories are read against the backdrop of the canon norms. If same-sex couples are not featured, the depiction of such questions a norm. However, as several critics before us have established, the fanfic forms are not inherently subversive, in fact, as Christine Scodari cautions, "broad generalizations about the resistive character and potential" of both slash and femslash run the risk of obscuring elements which can "serve hegemonic ends" (125). The latter elements are not unproductive, nor are they uninteresting to examine; they too reveal specific readings and interpretative limitations, crucial to take into account in sustained analyses of the fanfic forms. While many slash and femslash authors envision relationships which imaginatively extend beyond the ending of the fanfic, the examples analyzed here indicate a certain hesitation to extrapolate the homoerotic love. Various forms of removed spaces are instead figured and these constructions are in many cases clearly influenced by the genre intertext of the romance and by the same norms which the fanfic seemingly sets out to resist. In this sense, the selected stories exemplify a temporary subversion, illustrating the continued challenges in depicting same-sex relationships.

Intimate Strangers and Strange Intimacies

In this section, we examine vampiric transgressions illustrated by the lesbian vampire's threat to patriarchy, and the threat of the vampiric turning process to the centrality of compulsory heterosexuality to reproduction. Men are rendered superfluous when female vampires are sexually and predatorily oriented towards women and turn their prey into creatures with the same sexual orientation. This theme returns in films such as Harry Kumel's *Daughters of Darkness* (1971), various Hammer productions of the 1970s, and in recent productions such as Phil Claydon's *Lesbian Vampire Killers* (2009).[9] Narratives in which the vampire does not automatically turn her victim into a lesbian still mingle the threat to patriarchy with the desire for the intimate stranger. Le Fanu's *Carmilla* is an early example of the lesbian vampire motif, Williamson noting that she is Dracula's "antithesis. She is not remote and solitary, but intimate and connected, and she suggests a sharing and a blending that can occur only outside of patriarchal sexual mores" (35). The lesbian motif and aspects of sharing and blending are echoed in novels such as Jewelle Gomez's *The Gilda Stories* (1991) and Octavia Butler's *Fledgling* (1995). These novels also depict threats to the nuclear family through alternative depictions. Gilda forms various bonds with humans, living off their dreams rather than their blood, in her various existences, and Shori in *Fledgling* is part of a community of vampires on the outskirts of human societies who have nurturing functions in relation to their human sources of sustenance. Butler terms the latter "symbionts," which stresses the closeness and reciprocity of their bond with the vampires, and they gain not only psychological and physical strength from the vampire they feed, but also a place in her/his family-like unit, without being transformed into vampires. More contemporary male vampires also create and represent alternative constructions of the family, such as Anne Rice's Lestat and Louis, who form a unit with the vampire child Claudia. Turning does not feature into Poppy Z. Brite's *Lost Souls* (1992), where male vampires instead can procreate (a process which inevitably kills the human mother), but they constitute an alternative to the human nuclear family through the depiction of an incestuous relationship between the vampire Zillah and his son Nothing. Intimate friendships between vampires and humans are picked up also by fanfic authors, who often retain the double threat of fear and desire, and many authors play on the sexual promises of alternative family constellations. This section situates the contemporary fanfics in a wider context, temporally and metatextually, by reading them in the light of some of the previous "sharing" vampires and showing how fanfic authors recuperate and adapt aspects such as the combination of alluring friendship or intimacy and menacing, potentially erotic sides, in their explorations of same-sex, human-vampire relationships.

Le Fanu's intimate stranger Carmilla is, unlike most female vampires, at the center of the narrative and she initially seems to promise friendship rather than threat. She enters the narrator Laura's life when Laura's father decides to protect and care for what he believes to be a young girl suffering from an unknown illness, and whose mother has had to urgently leave the country. Carmilla is uncannily familiar to Laura, who has had dreams as a child about a young woman entering her bed, soothing Laura by caresses until, suddenly, Laura felt "a sensation as if two needles ran into [her] breast very deep at the same moment" and awakened, terrified (74). The uncanny recognition does not stop Laura from being "drawn towards" Carmilla, and despite the repulsion she also feels, "the sense of attraction immensely prevailed" (87). Carmilla's continued appearances in Laura's bedroom (real or imagined), and the accompanying needle stings, do not end their relationship either. Laura's subsequent illness, however, shifts focus to a revelation of Carmilla's true nature, and the vampire hunter figure of this story, the General, explains that the vampire must be destroyed. After the decapitation, staking and burning of Carmilla — or Millarca, as her real name turns out to be — Laura's health is restored but ambiguous emotions continue to feature. Laura describes thinking about Carmilla as follows, in the very last lines of Le Fanu's tale:

> It was long before the terror of recent events subsided; and to this hour the image of Carmilla returns to memory with ambiguous alternations — sometimes the playful, languid, beautiful girl; sometimes the writhing fiend I saw in the ruined church; and often from a reverie I have started, fancying I heard the light step of Carmilla at the drawing-room door [137].

Laura's final reflections take place ten years after both intimacy and destruction, and as Phyllis Betz argues, "Laura seems unable to recover any interest in or desire for heterosexual love" (68). Although terror, or memory of terror, remains, it combines with a wistful longing for the past intimacy. Passion, in this narrative, is an undying force.

The intimacy between Carmilla and Laura is made possible by the use of the fantasy genre, by the geographical setting in another country which defuses threats to a particular Victorian sexuality, and by gender. Nina Auerbach argues that "[e]verything male vampires seemed to promise, Carmilla performs: she arouses, she pervades, she offers a sharing self. This female vampire is licensed to realize the erotic, interpenetrative friendship male vampires aroused and denied" (38–39). To *Carmilla*'s contemporary audience, a close female friendship was less threatening than a corresponding relation between males, however, the late nineteenth century saw an increased suspicion of the originally noble form of "romantic friendships" result in complex "hesitancies regarding desire between women" (Betz 67). The dangerous promise Carmilla seemed to offer was recast as a threat of another kind, with added connotations to sexuality.

In the canons, the relations between protagonists and female vampires seem to reduce the possibilities for realizing latent erotic tensions and the female vampires are in many cases less erotically charged. In Twilight, Alice takes Bella shopping, for rides in fast cars, or arranges parties for her; their friendship focuses on traditionally feminine activities. Their physical proximity, however, is developed by femslash writers into stories about romantic intimacy and sex, often starting from, precisely, car rides, clothes shopping (what happens in the fitting room?), or slumber parties when Alice is responsible for "babysitting" Bella. In The Vampire Diaries, Elena faces several female vampires, among them her antagonist and double Katherine, and in the TV series the threatening Rebekah and Caroline, who remains Elena's close friend after being turned. Intimatopic femslash in this case thus mines homosociality (in the form of friendship), antagonism and violence for erotic potential. In the case of True Blood, femslash mainly features encounters between the televised incarnations of Sookie and Pam. Arguably this is because Pam in the TV series is a highly sexualized, predatory vampire who also flirts with Sookie on more than one occasion, whereas in Charlaine Harris' novels, she is described as much friendlier and, on the whole, more conventionally feminine (symptomatically, Sookie comes close to calling her a friend in the novel series).

Recuperated by femslash authors, the appeal of vampiric traits make familiar female vampires more than just friends. In *The Edge*, fembuck uses the nocturnal protection of Bella, which in the canon is assured by Edward, to develop a romantic relationship between Bella and Alice. When Bella wakes up in the middle of the night, she expects to find a vampire in her bedroom, but "the delicacy of the arm thrown across her waist, and the petiteness of the body behind her" makes her realize that "it was not Edward that was holding her but Alice; her other dashing protector." The vampire presence in her bedroom is not the expected, but it is still familiar, and it quickly becomes apparent that Bella wants Alice to stay. Bella's reactions present a contrast to the scenario in *Carmilla* since Bella knows that Alice is a vampire, but like the eponymous vampire in Le Fanu's novella, Alice is potentially both a friend and a fiend. Initially, she playfully refers to herself as "a very scary monster," but the consequences of her vampire nature become frighteningly clear as she nearly loses control of her blood lust. Her eyes grow dark from hunger and "the sight of sharp teeth [...] caus[es] a shiver of actual fear to run through" Bella. The revelation of Alice's vampiric nature is not the point of the fanfic, and it therefore produces none of the lingering terror at focus in Le Fanu's novella. However, vampirism in its dangerous form is a part of the attraction and desire Bella feels in this fanfic, echoing the "ambiguous alternations" in *Carmilla* (Le Fanu 177), rather than connecting to Twilight in which the vampire lover's appeal stems from his capability of leading a "human" life by repressing his monstrous instincts.

The intermingling of desire and fear embodied by the vampire is even more pronounced in fanfics which feature vampires figured as antagonistic in the canons. In cyclogenesis' fanfic *Demons*, Rebekah climbs in through Elena's bedroom window, in the same manner as Alice enters Bella's room in *The Edge*.

Her intentions are not as benevolent as Alice's protection, rather her plan is to emotionally tease Elena by bragging about a recent escapade with Damon: "a nice taunting would cap off the evening just right," she thinks. Elena reacts strongly to Rebekah's appearance, and when the vampire pins her to the bed, "Elena's eyes are wide and scared, as they should be." In the canon, fear in this relationship is mutual: Elena is frightened of the vampire's strength, Rebekah of Elena's potential to destroy her (the human's blood is an important ingredient in several spells aimed at the Originals). In the fanfic, however, Elena is not only afraid, she is also embarrassed because Rebekah's appearance has interrupted her masturbating, and the "delicious ... smell of lonely sex" makes the vampire change her plans for the evening. The author indicates that Rebekah is no stranger to same-sex encounters, but it has been a while: the "last time Rebekah slept with a girl it was corsets" rather than bras that needed to be negotiated. Elena on the other hand, or so Rebekah feels certain, is a novice in this context and "this will ... be the first time she's slept with a girl." The danger Rebekah poses is not lessened by the intimacy and it is enhanced by the reader's access to her thoughts. While caressing Elena's breasts, for example, she "knows exactly where she could reach in and pull out Elena's still-beating heart." But the change in focalization also means a stress on a mutual vulnerability. Elena is vulnerable because of her initial embarrassment, her same-sex inexperience, and her human physical inferiority. Rebekah is vulnerable because of jealousy, because she wants to be Elena's friend (or "frienemy" at least), and because the intimacy makes her see that Elena has a number of qualities which explain why everyone around her falls for her.

Attraction to another female is deviant within the canon logic and evokes the Gothic's desire for the monstrous unknown which is often presented as an ambiguous surprise and a form of self-discovery for the protagonist. Anxieties produced by such revelations and processes in older texts are linked to lust itself rather than to any specific expressions of it and the fanfic indicates that the surprise is even greater if the object of desire is of the same sex. In this respect, Elena's early question "[w]hat are you doing?" mirrors those posed by heroines in lesbian romance novels. "When confronting the unknown, all of [the heroine's] behavior and analysis attempts to answer basic questions, one of the most common being 'what is happening to me?'" (Betz 74). Since *Demons* does not provide Elena's narrative perspective, her potential self-discovery is only hinted at through Rebekah's observations, the main one being how much Elena enjoys her seduction. Descriptions of her physical reactions of arousal, or of her willingness to be undressed by Rebekah, make clear that she is a consenting partner. As an explanation for Elena's eagerness to have sex not only with a member of her own sex but with "an enemy," Rebekah reflects that she "had always figured Elena for a thrill seeker, given the company she keeps." This brief reference to background hard data provides a logical basis for her attraction to a dangerous lover and a new form of sexual experience.

Rebekah's vampiric danger is retained in *Demons* and Alice's is played up in *The Edge*. In lil_utterance's *Order Up*, Pam downplays her aggressive sexuality and concomitant potential threat when she approaches Sookie; she acts more like a good friend. Pam takes care of Sookie after an unspecified battle, lends her some clothes — a pastel jumper set, her trademark outfit in Harris' novel series — and cleans her up and does her hair. The setting is the intimacy of Pam's bedroom and although Sookie enjoys being taken care of, she has "to remind herself ... that this was not Bill trying to reassure her before they made love, that this did not constitute foreplay." Being aroused by a woman's touch, according to Sookie, is wrong and she resists the erotic connotations and her own response. Although Pam at the beginning of the fanfic explains to Sookie that "[w]hen I want you, I'll tell you," she does not enforce this conflated promise/threat. Instead, she figuratively seduces Sookie by being a recurring and increasingly tempting presence. In the last chapter it is Sookie who takes things further by challenging Pam to tell her what she *really* wants. What Pam wants, leather clad and ordering Sookie to meet her in the abandoned parking lot behind Merlotte's, is both blood and sex. Both these exchanges are depicted as consensual and driven by a mutual desire. Pam seeks Sookie's approval before biting her ("Are you still offering that drink?") and Sookie signals that she is by "boldly sw[inging] her legs across the vampire's lap," thus granting Pam easy access to her neck and making it easy for the vampire to slide her hand into Sookie's shorts. The depictions of Pam, Alice and Rebekah suggest that sympathetic and dangerous traits taken from romance, erotica and Gothic narratives combine.

Inventive variations on the intimate stranger theme are found in "doppelcest" fics exploring the physical and supernatural match between the vampire Katherine and her doppelgänger Elena. In *Nothing of the Kind* by havocthecat, the two are initially portrayed as very different on a moral level, Katherine having no limits and Elena embodying the good girl ideal. However, they are simultaneously "as much the same person as the five hundred years separating them will let them be," which means that Elena has a profound understanding of Katherine even though she does not think or act like her. This understanding develops into Elena's re-evaluation of her own conduct and the two characters become similar in ways other than the physical. At the end of the fanfic, Elena's guilt regarding Stefan and Damon first "overwhelms her," then she "snaps" and realizes "with perfect clarity" that "[s]he's been using them both this whole time." Under Katherine's seemingly bad influence, Elena "stops hiding from herself," which means she stops "feeling guilty" and instead claims what she wants, like Katherine does in both the canon and the fanfic. In this case, what she wants is for both Salvatore brothers to join her and Katherine in bed, a request encouraged by Katherine and hastily met by Damon, while Stefan, also true to his canon character, joins in only hesitantly. "This is as terrifying as it is exhilarating," Elena thinks, as the foursome is about to take place. The author then realizes Elena's canon desire to have both Stefan and Damon (although in the canon she does not explicitly wish to have them both at the same time), and adds a desire not only to be with Katherine, but also to be like her: free from guilt, ready to act out her wishes, regardless of whether it means transgressing moral or sexual norms.

Femslash authors thus in various ways elaborate specifically on the perceived tension between the female characters, and generally on the homoerotic possibilities linked to the vampire trope. However, even though the vampire characters in the analyzed fan fictions are more open to non-normative sexual practices, there is frequently an emphasis on same-sex practices as extraordinary, which brings attention to the heteronorm and thus precludes any "immunization" from erotic norms and categories. These femslash authors (as well as Le Fanu) use vampirism as an "excuse" for lesbian desires in contrast to, for example, Gomez who "in a move that can be characterized as radical ... has removed bloodsucking from sexual pleasure so that lesbian eroticism is foregrounded in its own right and not elided and normalized by vampirism" (Jones, "Gilda" 162). In contrast to Le Fanu's Laura, however, the fanfic protagonists know of lesbian love as an option, even though it is not their chosen lifestyle; it is not a question of demonized yet erotic mystery.

A retained mystery and a specific vampiric threat is connected and directed to the centrality of compulsory heterosexuality to family structures. As Candace Benefiel notes, "the establishment of a vampire family is a subversive twist on the more normal biological reproduction" even though it can lead to problems similar to the ones found in the ideal human nuclear family and produce tensions particular to the isolation of vampire existence (263). The threat comes to the fore in vampire texts such as *The Gilda Stories* as humans are turned into vampires and choose their families, forming temporary communities. The familial bond between Louis, Lestat and Claudia is another such example, as the need for biologically differently sexed parents is removed. But the most salient example as we are now moving into examinations of the strange intimacies of family comes in the form of Brite's characterizations in *Lost Souls*. In this novel, vampires are born rather than being turned, and as beings half–human, half–Other, they cling on to few norms of human society.[10] They are not, however, completely immunized from gender categorizations. Although "androgynous" in appearance, "Zillah's hands gave away his gender" and the all-male group consisting of Zillah, Twig and Molochai are clearly figured as bisexual rather than as transcending such a category (Brite 3–4). They are further virtually inseparable; they travel, live and love together and "naked and embracing, the three of them [are] as much a family as anyone could be, anywhere, ever" (Brite 83). Of particular interest to us here is Nothing's sexual relationship with his father, Zillah. Thinking back on how the relationship has started, Nothing has tried to convince himself of the wrong inherent in it.

> *For a week now you have been fucking your own father.* [...] But he could not disgust himself. He could not make himself ashamed. He knew these were things he was supposed to feel, things the rational daylight world would expect him to feel. But he could not force himself to feel them. In a world of night, in a world of blood, what did such pallid rules matter? [Brite 227–228].

The consensual and mutually rewarding relationship is incestuous and it is seemingly Nothing's human side that clings on to thoughts of how it is to be judged. His fear of loneliness combined with the freedom from norms his father and the other vampires seem to promise abate his concerns about what is right and wrong, however, and the implied label of incest is abandoned in favor of a stress on love and togetherness.

In the selected canons there are no similar depictions of incestuous relationships, in the sense of sexual relations between biologically related individuals. It remains a taboo which is very difficult to cross in mainstream media. Seen in a wider perspective, there are incestuous relationships between makers and children and bonds between these are described as stronger than human familial attachments. However, relationships between these vampires (between Carlisle and Esme, for example) are not represented as problematic. As Kristina Busse notes in the appropriately entitled article "Crossing the Final Taboo": "The vampire is *both* a highly sexualized and a peculiarly infantlike figure, so that any relationship with and between vampires tends to collapse familial and sexual bounds," yet there is a continuous resistance in the canons to label maker/child relationships as anything but adhering to the norm (212). No taboos are overtly crossed, that is, in the canons.

Many stories deposited into the archive of The Vampire Diaries and categorized as vampcest, *do* break taboos by pairing characters that are related by blood rather than by the turning process, but the relationship may still be rendered as fraught with tension. In Red's *On Our Way to Hell*, to give in to physical desire is presented as a conflicted process and Stefan sees it as a "*sin*" which will damn him. As the fanfic's title suggests, the brothers are destined for hell regardless. Having violated a rule of nature by their mere existence as vampires they have more to atone for than a transgression of sexual mores, and Damon convinces Stefan that the "genetic code" they share means little "in the face of that." In jenny_haniver's *Opus*, on the other hand, it is the brothers' long, shared history which naturalizes and enhances the incestuous love-making. There is "no one else from your childhood who has grown old with you without growing old," Stefan thinks, and no one else who understands exactly what he needs. Although presenting different attitudes to physical intimacy, the two short fanfics establish a connection which is both produced and enhanced by the vampiric state and which is not affected by other characters, or memories of other relationships.

However, female characters (vampire and human) are often used as alibis for the incestuous relationship and Katherine's pronouncement in *The Vampire Diaries* that "[i]t's OK to love [Stefan and Damon] both" presents a natural starting point for fanfic authors interested in exploring a three way relationship (2:22 "As I Lay Dying"). In contrast to the morality which supposedly guides humans, vampires can circumvent norms and rules and in *What Falls Away*, this contrast is used as a backdrop for events. Author some_stars depicts both love and jealousy between the brothers and when Katherine tells them that "there was never any need" for rivalry between them, they accept being turned. Although the process of being transformed into a "monster" is a source of conflict and self-loathing for Stefan, in the fanfic as well as in the canon, the actual event is presented as a possibility for him to grow closer to his brother. "He held on to Damon's face and kissed him, letting him in as deep as he had ever let Katherine." Although it is Katherine's desire for them both that sets off events, the heightened intimacy between the brothers is foregrounded and presented as the true gain of leaving the human state.

Katherine's vampire attitude to human morals makes it relatively easy for both canon producers and fanfic authors to envision scenarios where she can indeed have both brothers, and stories like *What Falls Away* subvert the canon only in making the erotic tension play out in graphic ways and in putting emphasis on the homoerotic vampcest. Fanfic threesomes featuring Elena subvert norms further as she is throughout the canon guided by monogamous ethics which cause feelings of guilt as soon as her double attraction comes to the fore. In CrowX's *Love Is Not Consolation*, which envisions other forms of family than the nuclear, a devastated Damon has just realized that his quest for Katherine, guiding him throughout season one of the TV series, has been in vain, and Stefan is conflicted by three different emotions. He is "livid" that Elena has tried to comfort Damon, eager to comfort his brother like he once has, "[a]nd then there was the small hidden wish to have his brother like in the dreams he used to have." By placing the power to decide in Stefan's hands, the author creates a scenario in which Stefan can accept that Elena is needed to comfort Damon, and Damon's need to be comforted creates a reason for them all to be together. However, Elena is initially represented as a concrete alibi; it is her presence on the couch where they spend their first night that ensures that Stefan and Damon can sleep close together and when Damon wakes up feeling his brother's hand on his leg, Elena's appearance "[l]uckily" saves them from the embarrassment. The second night Elena is in charge of sleeping arrangements and for practical reasons, she preferring the left side of the bed and Stefan the right, Damon is placed "in the middle." Content with this position and with Stefan and Elena "holding hands" Damon feels as if "they were hugging him." Things become progressively more erotically charged between the three characters and, true to form, it is a restored Damon who finally suggests taking things further. Stefan needs persuasion even though "this was a deep buried fantasy coming true," and it is only when Elena says that she will comply with all his wishes that he gives in. The long sex scenes which follow depict a variety of positions and foregrounded throughout are feelings of potential vulnerabilities, both physical and psychological, which need to be assuaged. Damon is vulnerable because of his fear of loneliness and his initially outside status in the relationship, Stefan opens himself up to a continued sense of jealousy, and Elena is vulnerable because of her youth and inexperience. By verbalizing all these emotions and by assuring that all three characters are in control, their desires are completely fulfilled and a new life can start with the three of them constituting a familial unit.

In contrast to Brite's novel that constructs a world in which vampires in time become unencumbered by human morals, the incestuous depictions in the selected fanfics need to contend with the canon portrayals. The human rules which Brite's Nothing perceives of as "pallid," and which he, as Other, can abandon, still hold sway in The Vampire Diaries vampcest because they are always already in place. These norms represent powerful injunctions against breaking of taboos and it is by emphasizing that the only alternative is loneliness and desolation they are contested and finally circumvented. Added to the archive is a continued questioning of the canon norms, signaling the authors' desires to reclaim a transgressive vampire sexuality and family structures which present viable alternatives precisely because the family members are non-human.

Undead Desires: It Hurts So Good

The heading of this section is borrowed from Milly Williamson, who argues that, rather than incarnating our innermost fears, "the vampire today speaks instead to our undead desires" (29). The undead desires reflected by the sympathetic vampires in the selected canons are arguably connected to eternal youth, undying heterosexual and romantic love, high moral standards, self-control, and physical as well as mental strength akin to super-powers. Fanfic authors pick up these as well as other characteristics of the vampire trope and elaborate them into competencies specifically linked to sex. In the fanfics discussed in this section, the undead desires are more specifically of a kinky nature, testing and transgressing the limits of conventional sexual practices and also of sexual ethics regarding consent, albeit in enjoyable ways.

Vampires' contemporary connotations to BDSM, evoked through narratives such as *Buffy the Vampire Slayer* and to an extent *True Blood*, are connected to appearance as well as characteristics. Their leather outfits resemble fetish clothing, many of them live in dungeon-like places, and it is in their blood-drinking nature to derive pleasure from the infliction of pain. The association of vampires to kinky sex has come to stand for the ambiguous appeal of a slightly dangerous, yet thrilling marginality. In analyses of kinkfic related to *Buffy*, for example, Jenny Alexander notes that "the 'permission to play' afforded by the preternatural resilience of vampire and slayer bodies" is particularly well suited to fanfic explorations of limits to pain and that these co-exist "with culturally and historically dominant pornographic imaginations" (§ 5, 27). But even in earlier Gothic novels, George Haggerty notes, "desire is expressed as the exercise of (or resistance to) power" and both power and powerlessness are "charged with a sexual force. [...] This creates an odd sexual mood in most gothic works, closer to what we might crudely label 'sadomasochism' [...] than to any other model of sexual interaction" (*Queer* 2). *True Blood* explicitly plays on this association between vampires and kinky sex with season tag lines such as "[i]t hurts so good," but also through the theme of fang-banging as a morally questionable, physically rough and potentially fatal practice.

The play on power imbalance frequently occurring within BDSM finds a counterpart in generic narrative structures, since partners with unequal agency, one active/masculine, the other passive/feminine, underpin the romance. Discussing the appeal of slash for the heterosexual women who write and read the majority of it, Constance Penley suggests that possible explanations "range from the pleasures of writing explicit same-sex erotica to the fact that writing a story about two men avoids the built-in inequality of the romance formula, in which dominance and submission are invariably the respective roles of male and female" ("Brownian" 153–54). Escaping the formulaic repartition of roles in stories about more equal couples is certainly a plausible explanation for the appeal of same-sex fanfic stories, be they of the male or the female variety, but so is the dominance and submission theme that Penley rightly points out as inherent to romance. Important to note, however, is that the power issues can at times be more complex. The "active" partner is not necessarily the one in power in romance, because "[i]n any portrayal of a plausible romantic relationship, the loved one holds a certain amount of threat to the other one. This threat is usually psychological and emotional—loving makes one vulnerable to being hurt" (Clements 114). In other words, emotional power may very well lie with the otherwise weak and "passive" heroine, just as the ultimate power (of stopping the game) resides with the submissive partner in consensual BDSM scenarios. Drawing on the romance paradigm of the canons means that fanfic authors have but a small step to take in order to create explicit stories with potentially complex depictions of the dynamics of power.

Our studied fanfic authors' explorations of BDSM and similar versions of alternative sexual practices come at a time when, as Monique Mulholland notes in her study of attitudes towards sex, both practices and objects previously linked to "deviant" sexualities have moved towards a more general acceptance (127). The success of E.L. James' *Fifty Shades* trilogy, which we discuss in the introduction to this book, is an example which aptly illustrates the fascination with fictionalized BDSM. Schopp notes that

> [t]he paraxic [a space that exists both inside and outside of our world] world of the vampire product provides a useful space for articulating desires that our culture evokes and yet forbids, desires that challenge current social orders. ... [T]he vampire fan articulates conscious desires that motivate his/her consumption, desires that must be considered alongside the potential unconscious desires [234, square brackets from 233].

When seen in relation to contemporary developments and the increased preponderance of the combined sexiness of pleasure and pain, a question one might ask is if this paraxic vampire space is diminishing. If desires that have previously been seen as transgressive move into the mainstream, what unconscious desires are left to explore?

Our findings show that there is a continued and highly active interest in kinkfic among fanfic authors working from the selected canons (which, in comparison with other cultural expressions, are quite vanilla) and there are also particular tendencies within fandoms which illustrate an interest. Authors responding to challenges such as Twi-Girl Revolution's "we want to see the Twilight ladies take the reins!" thus react to the wishes within the fandom rather than to canon portrayals (FanFiction.net, "Twi-Girl Revolution," n. pag.). While their stories transgress canon norms, they still conform to fandom ones. Fandom movements as well as fanfic categories may in these cases operate as "boxes" to think inside of, which entails a further qualification of purportedly queer kinkfic.

4. Canon-Transgressive Lemony Goodness

The power relations between vampire and human characters are inherently unequal. There are however similarities to elaborate on in homoerotic stories, to create a more equal couple and also to foreground same-sex lovemaking. In urban_folk_girl's *True Blood* fanfic *Human-Girl*, the differences between vampires and human are on a concrete level about coldness/heat, hardness/pliability, strength/weakness, and these differences play a role in an erotic context. For instance, it is a turn-on for Pam to feel the heat and softness of Sookie's body. More exciting still are the similarities between the two, such as Sookie's impetuousness which manifests itself in her talking back to Pam, insisting that she calls her by name rather than referring to her as "human-girl" and contesting her description of Bill as "so boring that he has forgone even the ways of seduction." More specifically, Sookie becomes interesting "for a human" when she takes sexual initiatives rather than just letting herself be seduced by Pam. From Sookie's point of view, the power play is about getting Pam to acknowledge that she, the despised human-girl, can be interesting. Both of them see a challenge in the sex scene; one wanting to prove her sexual/vampiric prowess, the other fighting to make her humanity have an impact. Moreover, Sookie challenges Pam's dominant role, both by biting Pam as she is being bitten, and by questioning her dominant behavior. Even as she is pinned to the wall by Pam, Sookie persists in claiming she is not afraid of Pam, challenging her to go further in their sexy and potentially dangerous game. Despite her initial disregard of human life, including Sookie's, Pam actually respects Sookie's clear "NO," which then functions as a safe word. The story's foregrounding of lesbian practices and its use of biting as a reciprocal and sexually exciting act among others rather than vampiric feeding or draining evokes Gomez's *The Gilda Stories* which similarly divorces the taking of blood from sex. In Gomez's novel, this distinction "desexualizes power and particularly the feminine helplessness that is usually so compellingly present in the vampire mythos" (Jones, "Gilda" 162). In *Human-Girl*, Sookie is indeed presented as anything but helpless, and sex is separated from blood drinking. Portrayed here, then, is a play with and struggle for dominance as well as a negotiation of power roles including the binary related to human and vampire natures.

Power play and role reversals are at the center also of colacherry's *Castration Frustration*, a BDSM story about Edward and Bella, but here through gender rather than human/vampire roles. It is explained that Edward has a "need for dominance," although BDSM games are not specifically mentioned as practices the couple indulges in. In preparing for the game at hand, which is new to both of them, they discuss the relationship between gender and power. Bella maintains that women are treated worse than men in society in general, especially when seen exclusively as sex objects, an argument she exemplifies by the seemingly legitimate practice of "catcalls." Edward instead brings the power dynamics to the personal level and states that "[h]aving a dick has nothing to do with power. [...] In our *relationship* it has nothing to do with power." In the scenario described, roles are to an extent reversed as Bella takes control, penetrating Edward. But as she follows his cues and instructions, she is on another level still in her usual, submissive role. However, Edward moves from being the one giving instructions, telling Bella for instance how and when to use the sex toys, and progressively takes on the role of the submissive partner. As Bella starts to express her wishes and desires she is amazed that Edward fulfills them without questioning. For instance, she asks him to change positions to lie on his back rather than stand on all fours because, she explains, "I want to see you writhing below me. I want to see and feel your facial expressions." Stressed here is the female gaze, rather than the male gaze that Bella criticizes at the beginning of the story. She is now the one gazing at "[t]his beautiful man [...] offering himself" to her, as a willing sex object. Further, along the same gender-reversed lines, Bella takes Edward's virginity in the sense that it is the first time he is penetrated. The canon narrative in which Edward regulates the level of their sexual intimacy until their wedding night is mirrored but subverted by colacherry's portrayal of the couple's dynamics. The BDSM theme in this way opens up for gender reversals, since one of its basic premises involves power exchange. In *Castration Frustration*, the reversal does not only enhance Bella's agency (in comparison with the canon), but it is also explicitly tied to gender politics outside of the bedroom, both in the Twilight universe and in non-fictional contexts.

Another established couple, albeit non-canon, is presented in fembuck's *Damsel*, and while this femslash removes connotations to heterosexual politics, it engages in questions of consent in similar ways as *Castration Frustration*. The beginning of *Damsel*, however, is designed to set the stage for a potentially dangerous situation as Bella, in distress, is tied to a tree in the woods. She is relieved at first that a woman, "and a tiny one at that," comes to her rescue as she cries out for help, but the woman refuses to untie Bella, instead commencing to caress her, and the restraints make Bella unable to physically resist. The threat of this situation, a same-sex unwanted seduction in a vulnerable situation is compounded by clearly vampiric traits in the unknown attacker. Her eyes are "burning" and her teeth are sharp on Bella's neck. When Bella starts to question who, or rather what, the woman is, she is interrupted. "You know the answer already," the woman says: "It's why you're scared." It is unclear what fear is the worst: does it stem from the situation, the same-sex seduction, or the vampiric element? The reader is at this point encouraged to envision the scene from the point of view of a scared victim which arguably makes all fears equally unsettling. Then, in a few short sentences, things are turned on their heads. Firstly, Bella speaks Alice's name, thus revealing that she has all along known the identity of her tormentor. Secondly, "the sight of Alice, eyes dark with lust, lips parted, the tips of her fangs just showing" increases Bella's arousal even further. Thirdly, Alice admonishes her: "You're not supposed to sound like you actually want it, Bella." These sentences make clear that the story is about consensual sex, but that Alice as Other is a powerful aphrodisiac. Bella's expressed pleasure and her unwitting revelation of knowledge interrupt the role play, and in the aftermath of their climax they start pondering new possible scenarios and characters to explore. Sexual roleplay is a recurring thing in Alice and Bella's relationship in this intimatopic fanfic; they are an established couple and have a thorough understanding of each other's desires.

Vampiric competencies are central also in Eternallybills *No Thrill Left in Feeding on the Willing*, in which Eric is cast in the role as Dominant, and the Original Character Laura is his Submissive. The story takes as its inspiration a canon line where Eric complains that "there is no thrill left in feeding on the willing" and in response to a fangbanger's question whether he would prefer it if she fakes not enjoying it, states: "Only if you are really, really good at it" (*True Blood*, 2:6 "Hard-Hearted Hannah). Eternallbills writes that she "couldn't stop thinking: what if Eric met a woman who really, *really was?*" and invents Laura, a successful business woman. Laura's main problem is balancing her quest for an equal relationship "with someone who respected her intelligence and was proud of her achievements" with the desire to be sexually dominated. Eternallybills is not unaware of the contradictions inherent in these conflicting desires, rather she has Laura reflect that she has felt "guilty about betraying her feminist beliefs, but … finally made peace with her sexual tastes." As her friend Andrea can attest to Eric's prowess in bed, and as Laura witnesses how men and women who approach him are characterized as "pathetic fangbangers," sometimes brutally dismissed by an "indifferent" Eric, she feels that he is the ideal partner in the sexual power games she has in mind. However, she quickly realizes that being willing is not attractive to Eric and returning to the bar a few weeks later, she appears "more like one of the more fashionable Fangtasia tourists than a Fangbanger," that is, not as someone who desires a sexual outcome of the visit, but as a woman temporarily slumming it. It is still her desire to attract Eric's attention and to arouse his anger, and this is accomplished through business means as Laura is trying to secure a contract for Tru Blood against Eric's expressed orders. This leads to him marching her back to his private rooms, designed to "intimidate underlings."

There is no question about what will happen and who will be in control in what follows: "She felt at sea, in the midst of the perfect storm, and Captain Bligh was in firm command of the ship." In fact, Captain Bligh seems so much in control of the situation that Laura "regret[s] not establishing a 'safe word' ... a mutually agreed-to code that would end the game if it went too far."[11] On the one hand, this reflection emphasizes the very real threat of the situation; on the other it signals Laura's previous experience of BDSM sex, albeit with human partners.

The difference between Laura's previous human partners and a strong, centuries-old vampire takes center stage in the fourth chapter, where the author also plays with recurring words from *True Blood*, such as "pet" and "master," here recast in clearly sexual terms. Fellatio is substituted by Laura sucking on Eric's fangs, and as Eric approaches his climax he readies to have his fangs put to use in a more traditional vampire fashion, a part of the sexual game which "still frighten[s] her" because this kind of power play and this kind of penetration is something Laura has not experienced before. Despite Eric's vampiric sexual prowess, the sexual games have hitherto played out on a more human level, and, in part, corresponded to Laura's previous experiences and expectations. The bite, the taking of blood, and the unleashing of an untamable beast now emphasize the crucial difference in nature and takes events to another level.

> His inner predator emerged, eyes glowing like red-hot coals, baying for her blood. It drank deeply, howling its desire, and he longed to unleash it, to allow it to drain and devour her, to rip and tear and roar its triumph. [...] Centuries of unbridled passion battled with control developed only recently, but he drove the beast back into its cage. It howled its fury and frustration as he slammed and locked the door.

These reflections are reminiscent of vampire characters' reactions and attempts at control which we discuss in more detail in relation to evil and monstrosity in chapter five. However, there are rules to Eric's power play, not because he is not superior but because he wants to enjoy more of Laura. The victim's pleasure in the taking of blood is possible only when she stops struggling, and there is a pronounced difference in relation to the fanfic's previous dominance/submission games where resistance is crucial to both participants' pleasure.

Eric is the dominant party also in fanfics which draw out the implications of threesomes, hinted at in *True Blood* through Sookie's attraction to both him and Bill which becomes explicit in a dream scenario where Sookie says: "I'm proposing that the two of you ... be mine" (4:9 "Let's Get Out of Here"). Author 4CullensandaBlack takes this scene as a starting point in *There's Always*

Room for More but makes it come true. In the fanfic, Sookie issues a similar proposal, but prefaces it by ordering Eric and Bill to "strip." Their initial reaction, which mirrors the canon scene is one of surprise, since "they assumed they wouldn't have to physically be with her, together" but their hesitation quickly fades as their "nether regions respond." A physical reaction displaces any doubt about what to do and they are clearly not hindered by human morality as in the canon scene. The question of jealousy, which is similarly present in the canon, is briefly touched upon, but as with most other obstacles to the threesome, it is surmounted by the desire experienced. 4CullensandaBlack alters Sookie's canon ethics in ways hinted at in the canon episode both by Sookie's claim that she has been circumscribed by her "self-conscious, good little girl" persona, a "box" which she in the dream is determined to break out of, and also by her exclamation that "you guys are *vampires*, what's with all the morality?" (*True Blood*, 4:9 "Let's Get Out of Here"). Significantly, this dream is represented as disturbing to Sookie and her choice, when awake, is to terminate relationships with both suitors rather than pursuing an erotic three-way experience. The notion of the dream reflecting Sookie's innermost desires is however destabilized by the fact that it is produced by her intake of vampire blood (from both potential partners). In the fanfic, however, group sex is what Sookie desires and initiates, and she has no qualms about it.

The author describes the contents of her fanfic as "Dark themes with Blood play & Domination" and the themes paradoxically feature in ways which draw attention to romantic staples such as first-times and extraordinary emotions. For instance, blood play is related to Bill "taking [Sookie's] virginity again" through anal sex which is facilitated by him using his blood as lubricant. The fact that this act is represented as painful forges links to the dark theme, and is one of the few instances in the story which depict actions which are not pleasurable. The pain reads as an inevitable effect of sodomy but is glossed over by Sookie's arousal. The domination is not surprisingly effectuated by Eric who is the stronger and more experienced partner. Eric's domination manifests itself most clearly in his taking of Bill, the latter enjoying both the domination and the sex: "his eyes blackened from the feeling of submission that Eric invoked in him. This was the first time that Bill truly let his inhibitions go and embraced his true feelings for not just Eric, but men in general." For Bill, the sex consequently also entails a "coming out," an acknowledgement of his true, inner feelings or even nature. While there explicitly is "[n]o love making or words of affection," the author yet shows the emotional and romantic ties between Sookie and her two lovers. Eric is moved by Sookie's manifest desire for him and although his thoughts are hidden from her, the readers learn that "he would never admit it to anyone else now that his memory had returned, but his love for Sookie had only amplified." In addition to literalizing the three-way, the author adds Pam's sudden appearance and participation in the sexual activities. This part is however elliptically described and hinted at in retrospect by Pam saying, as all four characters wake up in the same bed: "Damn, Sookie I knew you were a closeted freak." Her comment alludes to Sookie's canon descriptions of herself as a "freak" but in this context it naturally indicates predilections for kinky variations like group sex and that Sookie turns out to be less heterosexual than she appears.

While there are a number of Twilight fan fictions which, similar to *There's Always Room for More*, create threesomes featuring the rivalry and tension between the male protagonists, Edward and Jacob, an inventive route is taken in prelives' *Practice Run*. Working from the canon premise that Edward and Bella's abstinence is occasioned by his potential loss of control, the author has Alice approach Bella with a suggestion that she and Jasper will divest Bella of her virginity and educate her in the pleasures of sex. Bella's consent is given despite her shyness, and because of the familiarity she feels: "it's just *Alice*," she thinks as the vampire starts to undress her. The same-sex encounter, which is just as pleasurable as Alice has promised (and predicted, given her retained canon competency), is followed by heterosexual, penetrative intercourse with Jasper. Bella is worried at first that Jasper will suffer from a lack of control when overpowered by blood and sexual lust, but the bond between Alice and Jasper is strong and the female vampire promises Bella that she will "keep him in line." Although painful at first, Bella quickly starts to respond to Jasper inside of her, all the while comforted by Alice's presence. The power to decide rests in the hand of the vulnerable partner and in this way, the potential transgression constituted by the threesome gives way to a depiction which stresses agency and responsibility; the three-way is seen as a healthy choice, be this for reasons of comfort or curiosity.

Mighty Wangs and HooHas, and Dubious Mind Games

In popular romance novels, the hero's social and financial skills and success are commonly combined with forms of sexual prowess; he is uniquely talented in bed, potent and well-endowed. Using a term coined by Sarah Wendell and Candy Tan in *Beyond Heaving Bosoms* (2009), Laura Vivanco and Kyra Kramer call the romantic hero's combination of attractive characteristics and competencies "the Mighty Wang," which functions as a phallic "symbol of the ideal masculine sociosexual body" (n. pag.). But this body is not only ideal; the functions it performs are exaggerated and hyperbolic. Vampiric sexual extraordinariness in fanfic exaggerates prowess and competencies even further. Their Wangs, if you will, are paranormally Mighty and the exaggeration is naturalized, to an extent, since they are, after all, not human and at least theoretically have extensive sexual experience from their long existences. Vivanco and Kramer see the Mighty Wang in relation to the "Glittery HooHa," symbolizing the heroine's "sociosexual body and [her] sexual allure" (n. pag.). This term, connected to female genitals just as the Wang is connected to male, suggests other competencies, specifically the heroine's power to make the male abandon all other HooHas in exclusive favor of hers. As vampiric sexual initiators and aggressors in fan fiction are as often female as male, we appropriate the term here intending it to indicate the exaggerated prowess also of female lovers. In our discussions, that is, the HooHa no longer just glitters, it is as mighty as the Wang.

The vampiric Mighty Wang results, in EternallyBill's *No Thrill Left in Feeding on the Willing*, in no less than eighteen orgasms for Laura. In 4Cullens andaBlack's *There's Always Room for More*, Eric's prowess results in Bill's changed outlook on sex and his own sexual identity. Pam's Mighty HooHa, her sexual allure combined with paranormal speed and strength, results in "Tara [finding] herself nude from the waist down in a supernaturally quick amount of time" in fembuck's *A Girl Like You, A Place Like This*. It also brings cunnilingus to new heights and results in "multiple somethings" and a Tara nearly passed out from fatigue. In both hetero- and homosexual encounters, that is, the vampires' stamina, inventiveness and unique sexual competencies ensure a paranormal pleasure for their partners, in transitory encounters as well as in lasting relationships.

Fanfic initiation scenarios, and then particularly of a same-sex nature, often underscore the mightiness of the vampires' Wangs and HooHas, and the human counterparts are powerless against it. In Lady Dragoncrow's *The Vampire Diaries* fanfic *The Beauty of the Dark*, the otherwise straight Jeremy (Elena's younger brother) is instantly drawn to Damon and a contrast is established to previous relationships. A few seductive words whispered into his ear "ignited Jeremy's arousal, more so than any girl had done before. He began to wonder what real sex with Damon would feel like when just this was so incredible." It takes very little for Jeremy to want to pursue the same-sex encounter since Damon seems to promise experiences beyond what any girl — in Jeremy's case his girlfriend Vicki — has given him. The comparison is made explicit, as Jeremy thinks Damon's "fingers had to be magic; Vicki's have never been that good." Sex with a vampire further includes specific acts hardly included in intercourse with humans, such as blood drinking. The bite is a bit painful, but "Damon's mouth on him was fantastic. [...] Moreover the pain increased the arousal" and it blends into the sex act. Damon's Mighty Wang skills bring Jeremy to levels of intense pleasure which end in a simultaneous climax and leave Jeremy "[d]eeply sated as never before." Combined with the vampire lover's paranormal ability for increasing speed and heightening senses is also the lack of need for recovery time after orgasm. The fanfic ends by Damon regretting, even as he pulls his trousers back up, that his partner is "already done" since he would happily go another round.

Added to paranormal stamina and experience are vampiric competencies which in the canon are used mainly for purposes of feeding and control, but which in fanfic is used to sexual ends, often resulting in relations based on somewhat dubious consent (dub-con). The initiation scenario in *The Beauty of the Dark* contains dub-con issues related to mind manipulation, or compelling as it is referred to in The Vampire Diaries. Damon's explicit project in this fanfic is, like in the canon, to bring his love Katherine back from the tomb and Jeremy starts out as a pawn in this game. The canon hard data referred to by the author ("sometime between 1:09 and 1:10") means that events play out before Jeremy finds out about vampires, and he is innocent in more ways than one. When Damon climbs through Jeremy's bedroom window, the human is "already under his thrall." Damon's vampiric gaze is "mesmerizing" and impossible for Jeremy to "look away from." Presented here are consequently images that in part seem to go against the depiction of Jeremy as immediately and voluntarily drawn to Damon, but both pleasure and manipulation are part of the power of Damon's Mighty Wang.

Both in True Blood and The Vampire Diaries, vampires can also create emotional bonds with humans by having them drink of their blood, and, referred to as "V," in *True Blood* it is also a powerful and addictive aphrodisiac. Blood bonds in fanfic can be used to pair characters who are estranged in the canon, as it removes the need for accounts of attraction. The *True Blood* character Lafayette, the gay cook working at Merlotte's bar, harbors a deep fear of vampires and Eric in particular, and is deeply suspicious of human/vampire relationships. In oliviacirce *Show Me Your Teeth* the fact that he has had the vampire's blood is used to circumvent the distance Lafayette enforces in the canon, without him having to reformulate his strongly held views. The fanfic depictions in this way hinge on the notion of dub-con but simultaneously stress the pleasure Lafayette feels despite the fear. In the story, the previous intake of vampire blood causes Lafayette to have erotic dreams about Eric. The vampire's Mighty Wang — "maybe there's something to be *said* for a thousand fucking years" — combine with the inevitability of the blood bond, and Lafayette's terror mingles with desire. Even afterwards, awake and shaken, he cannot fool himself, and "doesn't stop wanting it." Indicated here is that the intake of blood works similarly as invitations into houses. Once the vampire or his blood has crossed the threshold, to the home or to the body, processes of change are set in motion and the human is powerless against them.

Drawing on vampiric sexual amorality, fanfic authors can explore transgressions of sexual ethics and limits which are nevertheless experienced as thrilling and pleasing by the human partner. This is the case in pleasebekidding's *Lessons*, a BDSM story pairing Katherine with her doppelgänger Elena. Working from the TV series and published on Archive of Our Own, the story has the warning label "Rape/Non-con [non-consensual]" attached to it. At the site, this warning is one of a few authors have to choose from and the author stresses in her summary that it is in fact "Not non-con — dub-con [dubious consent] at worst." Already in the first sentence of the story, it is hinted that Elena, the submissive partner, is in fact a willing victim of Katherine's cruel and humiliating treatment: "The fact that Katherine is so much stronger makes it easier, in a way. Elena tells herself resistance is futile." The inherent inequalities are used as an excuse to step into the role of the defenseless victim and "resistance is futile" is repeated like a mantra throughout the story. As Elena is the focalizer in this third-person narrative, her thoughts and feelings are conveyed throughout the long sex scene that constitutes the fanfic. When Katherine states, "You love to be humiliated," this is confirmed by Elena's ensuing thoughts, "If this was not so fucking true, Elena would start locking her window," thus barring Katherine's entrance into her bedroom.

Elena is not just consenting to but also enjoying the hard and specifically vampiric treatment Katherine puts her through, as well as the power imbalance. As Elena answers one of her questions in a way that displeases her, Katherine wraps her hand "around Elena's throat, one finger on her pulse point, just starting to threaten Elena's blood supply," simultaneously threatening to never give her oral sex again if she refuses to answer in a satisfying way. Katherine's paranormal strength makes the strangling act particularly dangerous, but it is unclear which of the alternatives is worst in Elena's opinion. In a similar vein, Elena's reactions to how Katherine pinches her nipples conflate pain and pleasure: "Exactly hard enough, Elena thinks, and why don't boys know this stuff? Why are they always either too gentle, or too rough?" Besides underscoring that Katherine is better than male partners (that her HoHaa is Mighty, indeed), this line makes clear that she is not "too rough" but just right; not sadistic but dominating in a pleasurable way. The power inequalities thus consistently function as an excuse for Elena to surrender, to give up the good girl act and give in to what she perceives as dark and forbidden pleasures.

The description of Elena as a submissive but consenting victim requires an explanation as it goes against the portrayal of her in the canon where she frequently stands up to vampires, hybrids and other supernatural beings despite not being able to match their strength. In *Lessons*, Elena's non-mainstream sexual tastes are hereditary: her biological mother Isobel was also Katherine's lover and she enjoyed bondage and humiliation. Elena's desires are thus about "genetics. Can't be helped," as Katherine laconically states. Genetics constitutes another force which similar to Katherine's strength cannot be resisted and which, also similarly, removes responsibility on Elena's part. This removal evokes the seduction/rape scenario in popular romance novels, especially captivity novels, which feature the abduction and "vigorous seduction" of the heroine. A common explanation to the appeal of such narratives draw on psychological models of how women are restricted to conventional passive roles which hinder them from being subjects of desire. The sex-by-force scene, turning rape into release of thitherto unknown passion which develops into great sex, is thus a way of exploring female desire and fulfillment thereof without transgressing the purported taboo of female willingness.

To an extent, this conservative pattern is recycled in the 2012 femslash fanfic, but added is an emphasis on the love Katherine feels for the woman she dominates and humiliates which allows for explorations of what each of them truly wants. Discussing slash in general, Anne Kustritz claims that the text form is not about "ideal image[s]" but about "an individual's desire to be recognized completely by another, to drop the pretense of an image, and to be accepted as a total human being, complete with imperfections and infractions" (379). The graphic sexual power play we are concerned with here similarly depicts characters as finding and sharing a true self. For Elena, who at the end of the story "knows she'll never lock the window," the relationship thus makes clear what she really wants, and she is safe in the knowledge that Katherine will accept her not in spite of, but because of her desires. Within the realm of a dub-con "at worst" story, the author explores the ambiguities linked to sexual practices and desires outside of the norm by stressing Elena's shame at being aroused by humiliation, dominance, restraint and other rough treatments which she clearly enjoys sexually. By freeing her from the responsibility for this "abnormal" desire, pleasebekidding indicates a way for "good girl" Elena to enjoy the acts without shame; a way out of another kind of closet. This can be read as an attempt to normalize or at least rid of shame certain forms of desire apparently considered as problematic.

It is not only vampiric paranormal competencies which are used to create a bond out of the ordinary in fanfic. The problematic issue of imprinting, which we touch on in chapter three and explore further in chapter five, fills a function that on some levels can be equated with vampiric mind-manipulation and blood bonds as it removes the issue of free will, however, significantly also on the part of the imprinter. In Maranda's *Facing the Music*, Jacob unexpectedly and against his wishes imprints on Edward. At the start of the fanfic, a straight Jacob is in love with the unattainable Bella and thinks of Edward as "a monster who disguised himself as a human, [...] the thing [Jacob is] born to destroy." The destruction of Edward is foremost on Jacob's mind as he waits in the meadow which in the canon is a significant place to Bella and Edward. When the vampire appears, however, Jacob is struck by his beauty, feeling "as if a chain had been wrapped around my heart pulling me towards him." Jacob flees the scene, shocked as much by the inevitability of imprinting as by the fact that the individual he has become irrevocably tied to is a sworn enemy, a rival, and a man. Potential reactions from the other members of the werewolf pack; to the homosexual desire as well as to the attraction to a "leech," make Jacob withdraw and the process of coming out, if only to himself, is filled with shame, fear and pain. But as in the canon, imprinting works both ways, and Edward, who feels the same instinctual pull, leaves Bella. At a second meeting between the males in the meadow, Edward tells Jacob that the unexpected pain is "excruciating" and, in a double entendre, "I'm not supposed to feel this way." Their ontological differences are paired with their biological similarities, both making the relationship unacceptable, however, the paranormal indestructible bond of imprinting render both differences and similarities moot. The sex which follows convinces them both of the impossibility of resisting, and although the fanfic ends in the immediate aftermath, both Edward and Jacob have transitioned into a new state in which they are absolutely committed to each other.

The stories analyzed in this section (along with the other fanfics discussed in this chapter) feature sex as the driving force and aim specifically at exploring foreplay and intercourse in graphic detail with particular focus on vampiric prowess and competencies; vampire lovers' Mighty Wangs and HooHas. They share in this focus a similarity with vampire erotica in general, which, according to Bosky, does not represent a departure from earlier, less graphic vampire fiction, but which rather "explore[s] the same sexual issues ... only making explicit what has been implicit" (217).[12] The sexual promises the traditional vampire has been seen to offer, that is, are met and realized in vampire erotica and sexual meetings with all these entail of transgressions of physical, moral and emotional boundaries. Whereas vampire erotica in this way picks up on and expands latent themes, they do so by envisioning new contexts and new characters; fanfic revisions, on the other hand, make explicit and alter desires in the preexisting canons. The starting point in the canons means that fanfic labels such as Porn Without Plot, attached to many slash and femslash fictions as well as fanfics featuring heterosexual pairings, become misleading as the canon background precludes reading the characters as completely divorced from context. Some form of plot, that is, is always already there.

* * *

The general focus on sexuality in fan fiction is connected to the centrality of pairings, and to canons in which romance, and thereby at least the promise of eroticism, is central. The vampire protagonists are simultaneously depicted as "overtly sexual" themselves, a development connected to general sociocultural changes with concomitant "ever-loosening sexual mores," and as objects of sexual lust since the gaze in all three canons is female (Overstreet 4). The close connection between the vampire and past and contemporary culture entails transgressions of different, historically situated, sexual norms and varying degrees of resistance to human-constructed categories; varying degrees of vampiric queerness.

Fanfic authors add sex where the canon enforces chastity and suggest that the denial of the physical side to relationships is deluded and unhealthy. Same-sex desires are envisioned and explored by fanfic characters who dream, fantasize, or have left homoerotic encounters in the past, as well as by those who are initiated into and remain in committed relationships. Other writers still take inspiration from other narratives and genres and recuperate the vampires' transgressive and queer potential in stories which question sociocultural constructions and test the limits of pain and resilience. The organization of this chapter has not intended to signal a movement from "innocent" to "extreme" subversion. Each fanfic is a response to or a reinterpretation of a canon event or characterization, and in this way, Bella and Edward having vanilla sex is just as subversive as Eric sexually dominating Bill. Each addition to the archive holds a power to influence future readers.

The absence of premarital sex in Twilight inspires fanfic authors to imagine Bella and Edward being sexually intimate; fanfic depictions of this intimacy influence how the Twilight canon is (re)approached. The Vampire Diaries stresses the importance of heterosexual monogamy within the given relationship; fanfic renderings of threesomes and same-sex sibling incest draw attention to this stress in the very act of subversion, reading the potential for alternatives between the lines of the canon texts. The conflicting tensions between margin and center are made explicit in True Blood through the depiction of vampires as a new minority group; in fanfic these tensions are recast as clearly sexual differences. Fanfic renderings of both hetero- and homosexual identities and practices are not illustrative of a complete resistance to the canon texts; rather, authors pick up on and subvert elements which already in the canon invite alternative interpretations.

Questioning the abstinent or heteronormative norms of the canons, fanfic authors expand the archives with depictions of characters who want to have sex before marriage, who want to experiment with same-sex partners, and who want to explore alternative, lemony, sexual practices far removed from what is perceived as vanilla representations. In the process, they add connotations to agency, equality, consent and gender reversals which, although figured in sexual terms, connect to more general themes in the canon narratives. Fanfic portrayals which subvert Twilight's norm of abstinence, for example, often illustrate how the equality which eludes Bella and Edward in the canon, can be attained when the sexual desires of both parties are acknowledged and met. Not only confined to Twilight fanfic, the agency of the female protagonists is also expanded in many sexually graphic stories, as is the need for informed choices and responsibilities. When situating same-sex encounters in the realms of fantasies, dreams or in the past, authors may on one level express a certain hesitation to envisioning a successful continuation into the now of the canon narratives, and into the characters' futures. However, this aspect of the text does not preclude them from making important contributions to the archives, and they hold possibilities of altering connotations to characters and to same-sex desire in the same way as the fanfics analyzed which depict established relationships.

In different ways, the studied fanfics illustrate a continued attraction to the marginality and queerness of the vampire, and reclaiming aspects connected to transgressions of sexual norms, the authors demonstrate the adoption of interpretative lenses which forge links with other vampire narratives. Aspects connected to danger and pain are likely to surface in these processes, the vampire figured as both distributor and recipient. These threatening but thrilling aspects combined with the longevity of the revenant and its ontological distance from human norms entail that alternative associations of erotic or familial constellations are added to the archives.

5. Something Wicked This Way Comes: Ethics, Monstrosity and Issues of the Soul

Eternallybills' fanfic *Hunger* develops events in *True Blood*'s first episode "Strange Love," and provides an inside view of monstrosity and blood-hunger. In contrast to the canon text where Bill at this early stage and through Sookie as focalizer is presented as a gentleman vampire, unfairly at the mercy of the vampire drainers the Rattrays, the fanfic's point of view reveals that he sees his fate as a "fitting end ... to a brutish and violent journey." He has enjoyed killing innocent humans, it is said, and struggles to mainstream in the post–Revelation days. *Hunger* exemplifies several themes which are at focus in this chapter: explorations of monstrosity, the issue of free will, metaphysics, and ethics connected to diet choices. In the story, Bill repeatedly refers to himself as a monster, questions choices made, and muses on the potential existence of his soul. On the topic of the synthetic blood substitute he says, "I *drank* it, but I did not *like* it, and some days, it simply was not sufficient." Eternallybills' fanfic was published June 6, 2010, about a week before the third season of the TV series was aired on HBO and when the two previous seasons had already complicated notions about the initially good vampire. The author may have found inspiration in the later storylines in the show, or in Charlaine Harris' series where ten novels had been published at this point. Still, the anchoring of the story in the TV series' first episode means that the character can and should be read from inside this specific situation. The desire is to present him as only masquerading as a regular citizen and to explore the true nature of the monster.

In this chapter, we are concerned with how questions of evil and monstrosity are introduced and explored by fanfic authors, thereby forging links to other (past and contemporary) vampire narratives, how canon character traits are picked up and exaggerated, and how canon norms concerning ethics are subverted.[1] While not consistently corporeally monstrous (nor seen as monsters by the female protagonists), the canon vampires still illustrate and emphasize forms of Otherness which remain threatening even (or especially) when they move in next door. Our fanfic analyses do not illustrate a progression from less to more evil forms of vampirism, rather, we are interested in how fanfic representations are variously distanced from the canon norms which are policed in order to underline ethical and moral choices. Diet choices and turning processes are examples of practices stressing these choices, and alternative fanfic renderings create more menacing vampires, often with the end result that romance is effectively killed (figuratively or literally). Fanfic depictions of a monstrous liminality illustrate forms of resistance to canon norms, particularly when the narrative perspective is shifted to the monster. The canon vampires' morals, guilt and worries about redemption gloss over the human/vampire difference and seemingly problematize the notion that the Otherness of the monster can illuminate deeply human issues connected to ethics, sin and good and evil. In fan fiction, the vampires' more threatening traits connected to blood lust and their supposedly true nature compete with explorations of their metaphysical plights and allow quite other questions to be raised.

Tradition and the Contemporary Vampire

When Bill reveals to Sookie that he cannot fly, levitate, turn invisible or even transform into a bat her reaction is the somewhat disappointed statement: "You don't seem like a very good vampire" (*True Blood*, 1:2 "The First Taste"). Like readers/viewers of True Blood, Sookie has pre-conceived ideas about what a vampire ought to be able to do and become, influenced by the many representations in literature and culture and, in this particular canon, by media-broadcasted information about vampires who have more traditional competencies. Because of the proliferation of textual representations, each canon delineates and presents its own variations on the vampire trope, often by the inclusion of exposition scenes (where the vampire volunteers information) or in musings from the perspective of the narrator. It is not uncommon that several myths are busted along the way and the process of creating a unique vampire entails a great and inventive variation. True Blood is paradoxically the most traditional canon in the depiction of vampire lore since they are killed with a stake through the heart or exposure to the sun. Religious paraphernalia, on the other hand, does not affect them in the slightest. True to form, the media formats in The Vampire Diaries canon present different variations on strengths and weaknesses. For example, vampires are unable to cross bodies of running water in the novels, whereas this limitation is not brought up in the TV series. What both written and visual texts have in common is that vampire destruction commonly involves some kind of mythical and hard to come by object, such as a dagger made of a particular kind of tree, and magical rings enable them to roam about outside in the daytime. The vampires in Twilight have exceptionally strong bodies and dismemberment (by other, paranormally strong vampires) is the most effective killing method. Further, they are merely beautified by the sun and they have lost the once defining element of the vampire: its fangs.[2]

As Nina Auerbach has famously claimed "every age embraces the vampire it needs," and every age has its own fears and desires, delineated in part by what the vampire can and cannot do (145). Our intention in this section is not to reiterate the comprehensive discussions about vampire narratives which precede our study, and which testify to the fact that each scholarly field seems to embrace the vampire *it* needs.[3] Rather, we will focus on a selection of traits that are used to de-familiarize the vampire in ways which exacerbate the horror and fear it can produce. Seeing the canon vampires in relation to both traditional and contemporary counterparts complements our discussions about the relatively friendly vampire next door in chapter one, and creates a backdrop for the ensuing analyses of fan fiction in which authors recuperate a bite that in many cases is taken from other, more menacing portrayals.

The romance genre's incorporation of themes and motifs from other genres, and specifically the paranormal element in the canons which opens for issues of a frightening Otherness, make us turn initially to horror. In his comprehensive delineation of a "philosophy of horror," Noël Carroll's definition of monsters is that they "are identified as impure and unclean" (23). Impurity and uncleanliness here refer to the transgression of boundaries meant to keep things separate, in the case of vampires most prominently the boundary between life and death. Along with other monsters who violate this or other boundaries, the vampire becomes a disturbing "fusion figure ... a composite that unites attributes held to be categorically distinct and/or at odds in the cultural scheme of things in *unambiguously* one, spatio-temporally discrete entity" (Carroll 43). The absolute coexistence of the categorically separate life and death makes the vampire upsetting to another degree than figures of "temporal fission," such as werewolves, in which "[t]he human identity and the wolf identity ... are sequenced" (Carroll 46). Fissured figures, by this logic, can be perceived as less monstrous, less frightening, because there are moments, often extended periods of time, when they are fully human. Noteworthy is of course that all three canons feature fissure-figures: werewolves in The Vampire Diaries and Twilight, and a host of were varieties in True Blood, and thus highlight the tension and difference between fusion and fissure. The latter is often presented as a more stable (but less thrilling) choice as a romantic partner for the female protagonist.

Uncleanliness and impurity often figure in more literal ways in traditional vampire narratives, with *Dracula* as a prime example, and depict the vampire as corporeally aberrant. When Jonathan Harker first describes the Count, his ears are pointy and his mouth "cruel-looking," and his hands give even more cause for alarm with "hairs in the centre of the palm" and fingernails "cut to a sharp point" (Stoker 23–24). Even at this early stage, small details give away the Count's Otherness, which is then underscored by his animalistic behavior — moving "down the castle wall [...] just as a lizard" — and Harker's increasing panic (Stoker 39). When Harker attempts to escape Dracula's castle, another description draws further attention to uncleanliness and excess. Having just fed, Dracula is resting in his coffin and "[i]t seemed as if the whole awful creature were simply gorged with blood; he lay like a filthy leech, exhausted with his repletion" (Stoker 53). The leech metaphor is of course appropriate given the emphasis in Stoker's novel on a potentially draining threat from the outside and on Dracula as a danger not just to Harker but to the stability of Victorian life and humanity at large.

In contemporary vampire novels such as Justin Cronin's *The Passage* and Guillermo del Toro and Chuck Hogan's *The Strain* (as well as in the sequels to both), vampirism is represented as horrific pandemics, clearly harkening back to *Dracula*'s figurations of contagion, and vampires are depicted as literal aberrations. The de-humanized vampires in *The Passage* are suitably referred to as "virals," and in its last moments, the viral Babcock, after feasting on a sacrificial human, is described as "all throbbing light and eyes and claws and teeth, its smooth face and long neck and massive chest bibbed in blood. Its body looked swollen, like a tick's" (Cronin 591). Here, the vampires/virals represent a manifest threat of draining, having almost depleted their food source: humanity. Like Dracula's association with vermin, vampires in these narratives are further "*surrounded* by objects that we antecedently take to be objects of disgust and/or phobia" in a form of "horrific metonomy" (Carroll 51). In *The Strain*, one of the vampire hunters is, in fact, an exterminator of vermin, a rat catcher, which brings home the association. In this novel, vampires are confined to dark, damp spaces such as sewers and subway tunnels, and are consistently metonymically linked to dirt and animality. The description of newly fed vampires as "ticks" returns and the character Ansel Barbour, infected with the titular strain, chains himself to "a dog's stake" that had previously kept his dogs "leashed during a summer thunderstorm" (del Toro and Hogan 548, 246). When Barbour's wife later sees him, he is "crouched in the dirt, naked ... his pale blue-veined body filthy from sleeping—hiding—beneath the dirt like a dead thing that had burrowed into its own grave" (del Toro and Hogan 290). Both in appearance and behavior, vampires in these novels sever ties with their human lives, although they, like folkloric revenants, still obey impulses to return home.

Vampires in our selected canons are neither manifestly monstrous nor metonymically associated with monstrousness via objects denoting disgust or contagion.[4] Rather, they are described as unusually beautiful and glamorous consumers with fancy cars, expensive clothes and designer homes. While hailing from temporally, and in some cases geographically, distant places, they are not, like monsters in Carroll's discussions, "native to places outside of and/or unknown to the human world" (35). Like many of their both traditional and contemporary counterparts, they exist in recognizable settings which increase possibilities for using them as illustrations of non-fictional fears and desires. Still, the worlds depicted in the canons have not changed sufficiently to completely accommodate the monster, and their Otherness is never completely removed or accounted for. The impurity of their fusion of life and death remains and, particularly in True Blood, it is used to demarcate them from other, "normal" citizens. The Fellowship of the Sun maintains the image of the vampire as a "bloodsucking abomination" (*True Blood*, 1:12 "You'll Be the Death of Me") and in the fifth season, vampires' physical difference from humans, their deadness, is continuously used as rhetoric in a mounting war between groups. In The Vampire Diaries and Twilight, rather than having humans pronounce them as aberrations, the vampires do so themselves. When Stefan reluctantly tells Elena about his past, a narration which reveals to her what he really is, he refers to himself as "a creature" and claims that "[t]he same darkness" that is in Damon resides in him (Smith, *The Awakening* 174, 181). Edward draws attention to the impurity of his existence and repeatedly tries to instill fear in Bella: "You don't care if I'm a monster? If I'm not *human?*" (Meyer, *Twilight* 161).

This admission of Otherness on the part of the vampire may seem completely at odds with proclaiming them as monstrous. In the foreword to *Speaking About Monsters*, David J. Skal argues that "the less a monster explains itself, the more likely we are to get involved, start talking to ourselves and among ourselves, looking for our own meanings and explanations," conversations which, by extension, give rise to fear (xi). The information the canon vampires so readily dispense, and which fixes them in categories, likewise seems to set them apart from monsters generally. Jerome J. Cohen maintains that the "refusal to participate in the classificatory 'order of things'" turns monsters into "disturbing hybrids whose externally incoherent bodies resist attempts to include them in any systematic structuration" (6). Jointly, Skal and Cohen thus draw attention to how monsters remain unknowable or in excess of knowledge, which the canon vampires seemingly resist when identifying as monsters.

However, the distribution and control of knowledge is eluded in the canons in ways which align them with traditional narratives and complicate easy assignations. Carroll argues that monsters in the horror genre are "cognitively threatening. They are threats to common knowledge [and] tend to render those who encounter them insane, mad, deranged" (34). In John Polidori's "The Vampyre," for example, the human protagonist Aubrey is the only witness to several revelations about vampire existence and the reader may be left questioning his sanity and the reliability of his sense-making process. "Aubrey has no one to consult with about vampires," Ken Gelder notes, and, corroborating Cohen's argument, concludes that "there is no available symbolic ... through which the vampire can be diagnosed and managed" (*Reading* 50).[5] In The Vampire Diaries, we are faced with an individual's attempt to classify or diagnose the vampire, and the threat is clearly cognitive. When Elena starts piecing together the puzzle that is Stefan and finds him feeding off doves, "[h]er mind refused to make sense of what her eyes were seeing. [...] She wouldn't believe this, she wouldn't *believe*" (Smith, *The Awakening* 162–163). In *Twilight*, Bella is alerted to the paranormal Otherness of the Cullens through Jacob and the Quileute legends about "the *cold ones*" (Meyer 107). Jacob's narration is undercut, however, as he refers to the old stories as "[p]retty crazy stuff" and Bella alone continues to gather knowledge (Meyer, *Twilight* 109). However, Bella's Internet research does little but make her doubt what her senses tell her, because no myth or tradition fits the Cullens. In this sense, the Twilight vampires' human-resembling ways exacerbate the cognitive instability of Bella's world to the point that she thinks "I couldn't even believe myself; anyone I told would have me committed" (Meyer, *Twilight* 120). Even after the vampires' admission of their ontology, these protagonists continue to struggle with a sense of disbelief, and true vampiric nature continues to elude them.

Whereas traditional narratives commonly feature the compilation of vampire knowledge for the purposes of having the revenant destroyed, the paranormal romance format entails a lack of *will* to have them defeated. Although unsettling, amassing vampire knowledge rather reflects the female protagonists' desire to connect with and understand the dual nature of the loved one. Elena,

Bella and Sookie may become experts on vampire nature in time and through close association, but in the early stages, they are not and there is no van Helsing-like character in any of the canons who can mediate knowledge and determine what is true or false. This leveling out of hierarchies is noted by Rosi Braidotti who, moving outside fictions about vampires, claims that "scholarship about monsters blurs the distinction between 'high' or learned and 'low' or popular culture" (137), and by Gelder who maintains that in contemporary popular culture texts, knowledge is embodied "by those who understand and respect folk or popular culture [...] the more 'lore' one knows" the better (*Reading* 35). While readers and viewers might be more versed in this lore than the characters, the canons' exposition scenes and the protagonists' research land audiences on the same page as Bella, Elena, and Sookie. Further, Gelder observes that "[s]ome recent vampire fiction ... depends on the *frustrating* of the kinds of 'lore' one would assume would work," which enables vampires to "have a *disillusionary* function" overthrowing established paradigms of interpretation (*Reading* 35). In self-reflexive, postmodern gestures, vampires in the contemporary canons are often aware of the classification projects and seemingly consciously perform the function of disillusion. In True Blood, vampires withhold certain aspects of the truth, for example their vulnerability to silver. As Bill tells Sookie: "We don't like for our weaknesses to be made public knowledge" (*True Blood*, 1:1 "Strange Love"). In *The Vampire Diaries*, Damon sarcastically comments, when noting that Elena's friend Caroline reads *Twilight* and wonders why he does not "sparkle," that "I live in the real world where vampires burn in the sun" (*The Vampire Diaries*, 1:4 "Family Ties"). While each canon is disillusionary in distinct ways, many explanations and revelations, while demystifying vampire existence, also serve to maintain an inherent threat to the female protagonists. The vampires simultaneously do away with and enhance their Otherness in these conversations.

The sympathetic, known and categorized vampire is at times derided precisely because the lingering threat is implicit rather than explicit. Jules Zanger argues that

> the construction and popularity of the "new" vampire represent a demoticizing of the metaphoric vampire from Anti-Christ [Dracula], from magical, metaphysical "other," toward the metonymic vampire as social deviant ... eroding in that process of transformation many of the qualities that generated its original appeal [17].

We do not subscribe to the notion that this shift demotes or trivializes the new vampires, to which Stefan, Bill, and Edward certainly belong, rather we would contend that quite different, and equally disturbing, questions about good and evil can come to the fore. Paradoxically, Zanger himself seems to imply this. He states that Dracula's "absolute evil implied and depended on the existence of an absolute good," the lack of which results in "new, diminished vampires" (26, 25). What seems to be missing in this write-off is the frightening loss in contemporary society of this "absolute good." While a focus on this aspect does little to re-vilify vampires or restore Dracula's extravagant (and somehow meaningful) violence, it does raise the equally horrifying possibility that vampires are not always the true monsters, that there may be something worse. The "anthropomorphic standpoint" adopted by contemporary authors evaluates the actions and reactions of vampires against "the evil perpetrated by humanity," and the latter is seldom seen as more benevolent (Carter 166). Further, canon authors do not seem any less interested in questions about good and evil than their historical counterparts were when they created more clearly religiously defined evils, pitted against clearly defined good.

In a response to Zanger, Gelder acknowledges the potential ordinariness that may come with the vampire's disappearing Otherness, but adds: "if the vampire really does live next door" as the subtitle of Zanger's article suggests, "then its otherness is perhaps more unsettling than it ever was" ("Our Vampires" 36). The Gothic threats of upsetting the domestic sphere and of the past returning find literal outlets when revenants become neighbors. Mainstreaming or "vegetarian" vampires work to blend in and in doing so they come disturbingly close to mortals in ways which make them figuratively invisible. Perhaps the most dangerous aspects of the canons' main vampires is that their desire is not primarily to drain all humans of blood but to protect the protagonist, watch over her and, ultimately, (symbolically or literally) marry her. The vampire as lover works his way into the female protagonist's heart while draining her of choices outside of the relationship.

Ethics: Vampire Diets and Processes of Turning

The anthropomorphization of the canons' vampires entails evaluations based on human norms. Killing humans and turning involuntary humans into vampires are seen as unquestionably evil acts. Using paranormal competencies for evil ends is deplored, and manipulating minds is considered a transgression of boundaries.[6] The foregrounding of free will and active choices further align vampires with the humans who are judged on the same grounds. The move from fictional constructs to non-fictional moral questions may seem unproductive, and Colin McGinn notes that "potential contributions of literary fiction" to discussions about moral philosophy "have been systematically neglected" because traditional methodologies have been difficult to apply to texts (vi). In his own project, however, he argues that in engaging with fiction

> we have ethical experiences, sometimes quite profound ones, and we reach ethical conclusions, condemning some characters and admiring others. We *live* a particular set of moral challenges (sitting there in our armchair) by entering into the lives of the characters introduced. [...] Stories can sharpen and clarify moral questions, encouraging a dialectic between the reader's own experience and the trials of the characters he or she is reading about [McGinn 174].

The "affective as well as cognitive" reactions which are produced by the immersion in a fictional world can be both meta-ethical in the abstract sense (interrogating ethical value in general) and normative, in the sense of evaluating "what is right to do in specific concrete circumstances" (McGinn 3, 1). The canons' meta-ethics — what is represented as good and as evil in the fictional worlds — is not divorced from non-fictional meta-ethics (killing, coercion and sadism is condemned also outside the texts). Normative ethics in given situations likewise have correspondences in non-fictional contexts and the reader is invited to respond to options the characters face and reach conclusions about what is right and wrong.

McGinn discusses depictions of mainly human characters (Frankenstein's monster is the exception), but contributions to the anthologies *Twilight and Philosophy* (2009) and *True Blood and Philosophy* (2010) suggest that the canons are well suited to ponder issues of good and evil, moral responsibility and choice, perhaps even more so than less fantastical narratives because of extreme versions of eternal love, un-death and Otherness.[7] Ethics and morality are examined through themes connected to the transformation of human into vampire, the invasion of bodily space for the taking of human blood, and the invasion of psychological space through manipulation of human minds. These practices are regulated in all our three canons, and judged as either good or evil, externally by the depicted society, and internally by vampires themselves or their human love interests. To lead morally responsible, ethical lives, the vampires' active choices are foregrounded (just as human free will is underscored in less paranormal moral discussions), but choices are made more complex by vampire nature since a diet of blood is a biological necessity, since turning processes are sometimes logical options, and mind-manipulation is a psychological competency. Bill and Eric, Stefan and Damon, and Edward and the Cullens may consequently elect to be ethically sound but this choice does not necessarily negate their competencies and urges.

Diets are foregrounded as affording choices in all three canons and veering away from human blood denotes sacrifice. The sacrificial aspect is underscored not only because human blood is a particularly rich source of sustenance but also because exchanges are linked to intimacy. In L.J. Smith's novels, the taking of blood is clearly sexual as the initial pain is "replaced by a feeling of pleasure that made [Elena] tremble" (*The Awakening* 186). In Twilight, blood lust and sexual desire enhance each other, and the intermingling represents the reason for Edward's insistence on abstinence. The fine line between desire and threat negates depictions as pleasurable as in Smith's novel, but Edward repeatedly refers to the satisfaction and mindlessness human blood can produce. In True Blood, Sookie's part-fey blood is intoxicating, unlike anything Bill and Eric have ever tasted, and reciprocal exchanges establish close bonds between lovers.

Alternative sources of sustenance are featured in all three canons and choosing them determines the moral fiber of vampires. Choosing to be good, however, often comes at a cost. Many vampires in True Blood mainstream with the help of Tru Blood, but it is indicated that the synthetic drink is inferior to the real thing and removes the thrill of authentic feeding. Initially depicted as a sinister and more evil vampire, Eric feeds on willing humans and quips about Tru Blood, "It'll keep you alive, but it'll bore you to death" (*True Blood*, 1:9 "Plaisir d'amour"). The initial division into good and bad symbolized by the abstaining from human blood crumbles as Bill resorts to taking it as well to become stronger when needed (Harris *Dead Until Dark* 167). In The Vampire Diaries, the taking of human blood similarly starts off as a definition of evil but the alternative — Stefan's initial diet of rabbits and birds — results in lack of physical strength and diminished paranormal Powers. Alone among the canons, Twilight features not only dietary choices as a sacrifice but a corresponding exteriorizing of virtue. This aspect aligns the canon with vampire narratives exhibiting links to melodrama, a genre which Milly Williamson notes "is concerned with articulation, with exteriorising ethical conflict and making it legible, so that the signs of innocence and virtue are made visible" (42). The Cullens are continuously represented as battling their natural urges for human blood, but as an "inside joke" opt to be "vegetarians" (Meyer, *Twilight* 164).[8] They live off animal blood and to boot hunt predators with a "focus on areas with an overpopulation" to not upset the ecological balance (Meyer, *Twilight* 188).[9] Their responsible choices result in beautiful golden eyes, contrasted to rogue and Volturi vampires whose moral corruption and human-based diet is made corporeally manifest in blood-red eyes.

Fanfic depictions of attitudes to dietary choices move in different directions, with some authors emphasizing the reduction of the supposedly true vampire nature which comes with rabbits, predators or the individual choice of blood type in a bottle, and others enforcing the close links between blood lust and physical desire. In stories of a deeply sexual nature (discussed further in chapter four), the vampire's fangs become stand-ins for or complements to the penetrating penis, and the bite is targeted at sexually charged areas: breasts and necks, but commonly also the inside of thighs or even genitalia. In these depictions, sustenance is not the projected outcome of the vampiric bite, and blood is figured rather as enhancing the pleasure (for both vampire and human). Other authors extrapolate the canon idea that both vampires' and humans' true nature can be revealed through and by blood. For example, in levitatethis' *Aberration*, Bill experiences mainstreaming as tragic and unnatural and the synthetic blood as unpalatable, the taste reminding him of what he should have, what his true nature demands. To completely abstain from human blood, "[t]o deny a basic tenant [sic; tenet] of his re-existence is a statement, bold and deluded," still, to abandon this choice would change him in ways he cannot accept. In this story, Tru Blood is described as "generic" whereas real blood connotes an "intimacy of the connection" which can give Bill something in return for his lost soul. Human blood is more than just sustenance; it also entails memories and experiences Bill incorporates until each human he has drunk from "is a part of him in some way." Vampire blood also carries individuality, and Bill remembers Lorena's "tainted poison copper overload" and Eric's "bold and strong" blood. Both human and vampire blood are here depicted as powerful drugs that reveal who you are and which enhance the experience of (un)life.

The Cullens' vegetarian diet raises suspicions not only in readers and critics, but in characters in fanfic. Carson Dyle's Twilight sequel *Morning*, which we discussed in detail in chapter three, features an interesting take through the outside perspective of Rupert French, a character who has a diametrically opposed view of strengths and the true nature of the revenant. He makes several comments to the effect that Edward's distaste for blood is "[a] disgrace to immortals everywhere," and that the Cullens are "faux vampires" who prevent Bella from reaching her full vampiric potential. Familial bonds are in general very important in this fanfic, and the sire/sired relation between Edward and French provides them with a twist. "You think I like admitting my creator chases animals?" French asks. "I have to lie just to save face." His view of true vampirism makes him ashamed of his lineage, and evil, in human terms, is his raison d'être. In fact, evil vampirism is figured as a particular kind of masculinity. French taunts Edward by telling Bella that he can show her "what a real vampire, a real *man* could offer" her. Edward's particular brand of defangedness, his vegetarianism, is thus constructed as emasculation.

In fanfic creations of more menacing vampires, the taking of human blood carries quite other connotations. In socact's *Invitation*, the fated Twilight romance is replaced by a biological need; Edward wants Bella not because of love, but because she is a "vessel of the blood" which is absolutely essential to his survival. The author cites Dracula as her vampire role model in her paratextual notes, and this inspiration entails both traditional limitations (Edward cannot enter Bella's house without the titular invitation), and a view of his own damnation. However, even if "the fire of a thousand hells" will one day consume him, there is no alternative to human blood: "without it we would die." The fact that Bella's blood is unusually delicious makes Edward return repeatedly to drink from her until she is hospitalized, suffering from "profound anemia." The slow but steady siphoning of her strength is one-directional and complemented with other essences Edward draws from her, such as a reconnection with emotions he thought he'd lost. McGinn points out that "we risk not naming it correctly if we think that evil must always involve a desire to kill" (69). In *Invitation*, Edward keeps Bella alive because he "want[s] to drink from her for all eternity." Selfishness and sadism thus enter the equation, and exacerbate his evil, making him a character who responds to rather than suppresses his natural vampiric urges.

Edward's alternative dietary choices can be construed as evil not only because he is a self-professed monster in socact's fanfic, but because Bella for a long time does not actively consent to him taking her blood. Rather, he does so when she is sound asleep. Issues of consent figure prominently also in renderings of vampiric evil in connection with turning. Christopher Robichaud argues that, although exceptions can be envisioned, "explicit, informed, noncoercive consent" is required for a vampire to have the moral right to turn a human (15). In fanfics that to a great extent participate in the paranormal romance genre, transformation is not necessarily presented as negative and destructive as it entails an eternal togetherness, but without consent and in stories that have closer affinities with the horror and the Gothic, the process is clearly monstrous.

Two short fanfics revolving around Elena's turning draw attention to how she is stripped of choice not only as regards the process, but in how to continue to exist.[10] In stainofmylove's *Hungry Again*, Elena has been killed by Katherine, in Sandrine Shaw's *Barefoot on Broken Glass*, Klaus' dagger pierces her heart as the story begins. To refuse vampire blood in order to avoid death is not an option in either fanfic but the choice is still difficult. So is the next step in the process: to feed off human blood to still the hunger. Young women brought in by the male vampires are the victims in both fanfics, the two Elenas unable to stop drinking until it is too late. In *Hungry Again*, Elena is encouraged by Stefan to make a different choice following her first kill, but microwaved blood tastes "off," and edged on by Damon, she kills again. Her humanity is still very close, her moral free-fall shames her, and she realizes that she has selected Damon as her companion because "[h]e wouldn't judge. He couldn't. He's a *monster*, through and through." In *Barefoot on Broken Glass*, Elena does not have Stefan's dubious moral compass to guide her, but even removed from her normal context she imagines the reactions from her former friends and realizes that her human life is over. "How can she go back to her life when every second is a struggle not to kill and every cell in her body is craving violence and destruction?" In similar ways as Damon helps the Elena in stainofmylove's fanfic, Klaus helps her here by making her understand the truth about vampire existence. "I'm not one of your little tame pet vampires," he snarls at her. "I'm not hiding a tender, emotional side underneath the monster. The monster *is* me." In both stories, Elena's hunger for blood will never abate and the only choice she can make is to give in to her new urges which, in turn, will circumscribe the choices of her future victims. Her involuntarily transformation and close associations to human mortality also entail that Elena continues to think of herself as a monster, continues to evaluate herself in relation to the human norms that have guided her.

Liminal Monsters

The liminal stage, in Victor Turner's phrase the "betwixt and between" threshold in rites of passage, is in teratological discourses often translated to a state or a subject position (93–111). Braidotti, for example, notes that "[t]he monster is neither a total stranger nor completely familiar; s/he exists in an in-between zone" (141). The undead state of vampires and the shifting corporeality of fission figures would seem to indicate a continuous occupation by these figures of a liminal role in the canon narratives, but some characters (sometimes at demarcated moments) highlight liminality even further. Bill has a particular position between humans and vampires, Stefan's as a Ripper illustrates a temporal liminality, and Renesmee represents a physical liminality in her hybrid state. In his adoption of "[l]iminality as a queer analytical tool," Benny LeMaster argues that even when vampires (in our discussions also other paranormal characters) are humanized, "liminality highlights moments of resistance to assimilation, essentialism, privacy and heteronormativity" (108), moments which in connection with Stefan, Bill and Renesmee are picked up and extrapolated by fanfic authors.

Assimilation and essentialism are in True Blood figured as push and pull processes by which vampires either choose to mainstream and take part in human society or form smaller enclaves of their own. At times, Bill performs a human identity for reasons of self-preservation, at other times, the performance comes as a result of Bill's lingering wish to *be* human. These conflicting movements place Bill in a position between vampires and humans that "allow[s] [particular] kinds of questions to be asked about liminality, and about repeated but failed attempts to belong" (Lindgren Leavenworth and Isaksson 245). The previously discussed fanfic *Aberration* along with the stories *Dismantled* and *Strange Infatuation* by the same author, levitatethis, draw out the implications of Bill's position and the internal tug-of-war. His self-perception of "[e]xisting between two realms" is connected to the contrasts between mainstreaming and taking human blood, between the monster Bill believes he is and the human he wants to be (*Aberration*). The constant push and pull from both realms make it impossible for him to fully inhabit either, trapping him in a liminal state which brings danger to humans, vampires, and to Bill himself. In *Dismantled*, Bill deals with the aftermath of his relationship with Sookie, ended because of his betrayal, and struggles to maintain the veneer of civilization.[11] The pull from the vampire side has become harder to resist and he has let "his baser instinct desires run wild," resulting, it is implied, in the taking of human blood (*Dismantled*). The pull away from mainstreaming and towards the alternative is represented as a threat to how Bill wants to be perceived and as a metaphysical struggle, and Bill fears that losing the battle (completely giving in to the bloodlust) will cause "midnight black [to spill] across the plains where his soul once dwelled" (*Dismantled*).

There is a sense of playacting involved in keeping up the pretenses of a human life, "less natural with each day that passes" which suggests the idea that the longer the vampire existence is, the more difficult it is to retain the human veneer (*Dismantled*). *Strange Infatuation* continues this idea through the depiction of the considerably older Eric and through his views of what a vampire should be. The story is based on the idea that Eric and Bill have been lovers in the past and the shared intimacy makes the former remember "the old Bill with a certain fondness" particularly because Bill "used to be almost uncaringly sadistic, [...] capable of utter cruelty against the human population, unapologetic in the taking of what he wanted." As an older vampire, less preoccupied with passing as a human and potentially unable to do so considering the suggestion that mainstreaming becomes harder and harder with time, Eric resents what Bill has become; a contrast to Bill's conviction that mainstreaming and peacefulness represent salvation. The idea of past transgressions guiding his conscientious lifestyle and making Bill consistently punish himself connects all three stories and Bill's carefully-mastered monster becomes a triple threat. Existing on the threshold between vampire and human, Bill oscillates between good and evil, the former threatening vampire existence, the latter a danger to humans. This double threat as well as his inability to be either good or evil in turn threatens his continued peaceful existence.

When Stefan is turned into a Ripper at the end of the second season of *The Vampire Diaries*, he initially seems to enter into a state which holds none of the affordances of liminal resistance. He severs his ties with humanity, flips an emotional off switch and relishes in his murderous state, a state the viewers learn is part of a cyclical process. The vampire Lexi identifies him as a Ripper in a flashback scene set during the Civil War (*The Vampire Diaries*, 2:15 "The Dinner Party") and Damon tells Elena that "I've seen it happen before," and confides in Alaric, when human casualties start piling up, that the state of the bodies signals Stefan's "signature. [...] He feeds so hard he blacks out, rips them apart, but then when he's done, he feels remorse. It's the damnedest thing. He puts the bodies back together" (*The Vampire Diaries*, 3:1 "The Birthday"). The faint trace of remorse resulting in reassembled bodies is paired with small but reoccurring gestures of humanity, mainly produced by Stefan's lingering love for Elena, and in this combination of traits Stefan becomes a liminal fission figure. The ultimate evil represented by the murderous state is not consistently maintained as his old self surfaces and makes it impossible for him to completely inhabit his new persona. The liminal state the Ripper existence consequently comes to represent is used by fanfic authors to various ends, several of them focusing on internalized musings similar to Bill's in levitatethis' stories, but very often ending with Stefan leaving the liminal state.

In Bogwitch's *Blood, the Tooth and the Claw*, Stefan wakes up in a room full of dismembered bodies and his mind snaps open to the all-consuming thought of blood, the "lust for stolen life drumming in his head like a borrowed heartbeat." Although he attempts to cling on to what he has been — "the good brother" and "the hero"— the lives he has stolen and borrowed are truly what makes him come "alive" and his struggle to resist Klaus, the Original vampire who precipitates the Ripper state, is in vain. "He's been starving for decades and he's never even known." As a Ripper, Stefan is brought closer to his true self, making him realize what he has forfeited, playing human. A similar situation is depicted in Chiyoku Shibata's *Stefan's Thoughts*, where his resistance to Klaus is substituted with "love for the man who had brought me back from the husk of angst that I'd been for decades." Here too, Stefan tries to cling on to memories of his past existence and to worries about what will happen to those he has left behind. However, the smell of blood and the pull of his true self distract him, and he cannot "concentrate long enough to become *angsty, serious* Stefan." These two short fanfics linger on Stefan's first liminal moments as a Ripper, when his human emotions are still close, and in both, emphasis is on the notion that he knows how he ought to respond, that he should resist Klaus as well as the blood lust because those are the norms he has lived by. The overwhelming thirst and his need to kill to feel alive are considerably stronger however, and both fanfics remove Stefan from the in-between state and leave him unequivocally a monster.

The potential for liminal resistance is retained in Eleai's *Absolution* where Stefan thinks back on his previous periods as a Ripper. In this fanfic, Stefan fears the titular forgiveness because it glosses over the terrible deeds he commits in his violent state. He has tried to live well according to human norms in the time period since his last bout of mayhem, but since Lexi forgave him then, he now worries that, if he returns to Mystic Falls, "Elena and Damon will divide him in half, 'new Stefan' and 'old Stefan,'" and thus negate the possibilities of him truly atoning for his sins. The mindless Ripper surfacing at the end of Bogwitch's and Chiyoku Shibata's fanfics is replaced by a character thoughtfully examining his actions, concluding that despite all the labels that can be placed on him, and all the excuses that can be made for him, he will still be "just Stefan." Human and vampire absolution would enable him to assimilate and to suppress his monstrous side, but his choice is to stay away and let all identities, ranging from lover and brother to Ripper and killer, remain part of who he is and who he will stay. In this story, consequently, Stefan makes an active choice to remain in the liminal state and continue to be punished for his transgressions.

The collapse of distinctions between human and monster can result in a sometimes physical, sometimes moral, hybrid. Cohen argues for a particular Otherness associated with this type of liminality: "a form suspended between forms that threatens to smash distinctions" (6). Bella and Edward's daughter Renesmee is half-human, half-vampire and consistently represents a threat to vampire ontology as well as a concrete danger to her mother's body before birth.[12] Ashley Donnelly describes her as "the first character on the side of 'good' in the series that has potential to cross boundaries. She is ... monstrous in her unabashed desire for blood [...] dangerous and unstable" not only as a vampire, but in the interim before she is born (190). Her very conception is puzzling and although Bella refers to the fetus as a he, the other characters use the term "it." In Carlisle's research into "ancient stories and myths" which may help explain the inexplicable, "it would appear the *creatures* use their own teeth to escape the womb" (Meyer, *Breaking Dawn* 276, our italics).[13] The fetus presents a literal internal threat to Bella's body not only at birth, which effectively ends Bella's human life, but during pregnancy. Jacob, whose narrative perspective guides parts of *Breaking Dawn*, is horrified at the sight of Bella's belly covered with "bruises" he at first takes for "big splotches of purple-black ink" and is convinced by her waning strength that what the thing inside her wants is "death and blood, blood and death" (Meyer 178, 218). After Renesmee's birth, mother and daughter are separated as the Cullens suspect Bella's blood thirst as a newborn will overpower her and although they are wrong about this, Bella is still shocked at the first sight of her child, growing at an increased rate and exhibiting the paranormal gifts of projecting thoughts and entering even shielded minds like Bella's. All these disruptions of the norm suggest a continuous need for policing where Renesmee is concerned to ensure safety. Her liminality is not done away with, rather she continues to straddle the border between the strange and the familiar. She remains throughout the canon narrative a somewhat puzzling and distant character, giving the reader few opportunities to access *her* mind.

In two short fanfics, *Seven* and *Eighteen*, Estora gives the reader precisely such access and adds troubling associations to liminality to the Twilight archive. The stories' titles refer to Renesmee's ages, she is seven in human years, eighteen according to her accelerated growth rate and both fanfics represent the same event: her seventh or eighteenth birthday. This day is not covered by the canon text — when *Breaking Dawn* leaves off Renesmee is only six months old — but it is foreshadowed at the very end of the novel when Edward notes that "Nessie will be fully matured in just six and a half years," a cause for parental concern as she will then pursue, or be forced to pursue, the relationship with Jacob who imprints on her the moment she is born (Meyer 695). The issue of imprinting is central in Estora's fanfics as well, with connotations to pedophilia featured in both. The first story, *Seven*, is told in a chillingly childish language and by a Renesmee who wishes for "princess dresses" for the birthday party but who is discouraged from wearing such clothes. "Daddy says I look eighteen. Eighteen's a big number. That's how old mommy is." Renesmee wants all the colors, tastes and experiences that come with childhood but the presents she receives reflect the other characters' perceptions of a young woman rather than a child. She gets sexy lingerie, "a wedding magazine," a fancy ink pen and a car from her father that she "can't drive. I'm only seven. Silly daddy." As disturbing as these gifts are, they pale in comparison with the "gift" Jacob is intent on giving her, being left alone with Renesmee at the end of the party. Jacob caresses and undresses her, actions which represented from this child's point of view are incomprehensible. He is "Uncle Jacob," a trusted and loved adult who is overstepping boundaries Renesmee has been instructed he can cross, even if "it hurts." The trust that Jacob is invested with by the other adults surrounding Renesmee lays the foundation for what in the story is depicted as the rape of a child.

Eighteen, Estora writes in her author notes, is "*a canon version*" of the previous story, not because it corresponds to depicted events, but because

Renesmee here has matured according to plan: "I'm a woman, despite having only seven years of life." She is nevertheless deeply uncomfortable with imprinting and its consequences. Although Jacob is a very good friend, and "a good dog," she cannot equate him with a lover, rather she finds revolting the idea of being intimate with someone "who changed [her] diapers" and read to her when she "was two. Or six-ish." Renesmee knows full well what is expected of her and cannot help but see the similarities between her prospects and her parent's life. She is to be "the perfect imprintee — submissive and angelic, never questioning him, always at his whims. Much like mom is to dad." The consistent presence of these problematic role models along with her increasing sense of unease make Renesmee reevaluate what she needs to do. It is also another imprinted couple: Jacob's friend Quil and the nine-year-old Quileute girl Claire that makes her see the extremity of her situation and the situation of every girl who stands in a completely dependent relation to someone else. In reference to Claire she thinks: "She doesn't need a grown man as her babysitter, intent on grooming her to be his life partner." Renesmee has had ample time to think about what will happen to her: that Jacob, no matter how tender and protective, is only waiting until the day comes (her birthday) when he can claim her. The reference to grooming comes back as Renesmee takes off in her new car with Claire, intent on saving her, and addressed explicitly in relation to pedophilia. Imagining the conversation she would have liked to have had with Jacob, Renesmee thinks: "*Child grooming means actions taken by an adult to form a trusting relationship with a child with the intent of later having sexual contact. Sound familiar, Jacob?*" By removing all romantic connotations to imprinting as a fated, soul-deep connection between individuals, Estora depicts it as a situation of child abuse, a process of "brainwash[ing]." She further draws attention to how the process is consistently represented from the point of view of the agents in the canon — the males who imprint rather than the children they imprint on — and to how the story is significantly different when this perspective is reversed.

Hybridity consistently features in the canon as a source of anxiety and Donnelly claims that Renesmee, the product of Edward and Bella's carnal desire, is "a monstrosity" (191). In Estora's fanfics, on the other hand, the process of imprinting is monstrous and the rape of a child (committed or projected) is unquestionably evil. Critics discussing imprinting have drawn attention to several problematic issues that are raised concomitant with it. On the one hand, imprinting plays into the stereotypical representation of the Quileute werewolves, enhancing their connection with animalistic and uncontrollable urges, on the other, it features into the lack of agency as "women ... are marked — often from birth — as the mate of a particular werewolf" (Taylor

44, note 5). Lydia Kokkola argues that "the series strives to clarify [that imprinting] is a perfect love, unclouded by petty concerns like sexual desire" and that it is conveniently used to dissolve the triangular love between Bella, Edward and Jacob (171). Importantly, however, the literal consequences of Jacob's imprinting on Renesmee are elided in the canon since she never comes of age within the narrative. Estora's two darkfics, on the other hand, add important associations to the chilling implications of a female lack of agency and a male inability to resist to the archive. In *Seven*, Renesmee not only lacks agency because of the inevitability of imprinting, she does so because her accelerated growth rate does not correspond to a psychological maturation, and the lack of understanding from her surroundings limit her even further. In *Eighteen*, both her body and mind have matured but the surroundings are as non-sympathetic to her desires as in the first fanfic. Imprinting here does not have the effects it is supposed to have and Renesmee is unable to see Jacob as other than her uncle, with the added connotations to incestuous pedophilia. Lack of agency is in this story reversed, although it comes at a price; the only way Renesmee and Claire can escape imprinting and the males who imprint is to give up life as they know it.

The Nature of the Beast and Monsters in the Mirror

"Damon Salvatore, vampire sociopath extraordinaire, reads self-help manuals," writes Spikey44 in *Big Brother Vampire*. He has "an inferiority complex the size of Everest," an intense jealousy directed toward Stefan, "zero impulse control, numerous anti-social personality disorders and a rampant drinking problem." His father has been instrumental in forming his ill-adjusted personality and Damon is now "a lonely insecure little man searching for meaning in all the wrong places." When vampires in fanfic retain their human characteristics, it is of course but natural that they would turn to human psychological models and human avenues for help in processes of self-examination. When Damon scrutinizes himself in Spikey44's story, he sees a monster, but also the way to change: awareness is the cure. The blurred boundaries between human and monster may consequently lead to self-reflexive considerations as the vampire "is the monster that used to be human; it is the undead who used to be alive; it is the monster that *looks like us*" (Hollinger 201). In all three canons, these blurred boundaries are explored when the vampire characters reflect on issues connected to their own monstrosity, often in contrast to their lives before they were turned. Similarities as well as tensions between human and vampire are explored as the vampires remember their past (pre-turning), and worry about sin and redemption connected to the potential loss of soul. The monsters that look like us are remarkably often recognized by the monsters themselves, and no more so than when fanfic authors shift perspectives and use menacing vampires as focalizers.

Ellen Smithee's *Lead Me Not into Temptation* outlines a process by which human norms necessarily need to be abandoned for Caroline to reach a state of self-fulfillment. This *The Vampire Diaries* fanfic starts with Stefan approaching the female vampire, intent on persuading her to join him and Klaus and to embrace her true, dark nature. He plays on Caroline's insecurities, arguing that her failed relationships and broken friendships would mean nothing to her in a new existence and that he can offer something else: "They don't see the real you, not like I do." Despite the promise this seems to offer, Caroline clings on to who she is and resists being part of the new constellation which transgresses norms not only concerning ethics, but familial structures and sexuality as well. Although she too is a vampire, she sees Klaus as thoroughly "evil." When Stefan replies that he is, but "[o]nly by human standards," her first thought is "*What other standards do we have?*" That both Klaus and Stefan are indeed evil becomes clear as they have kidnapped Caroline's friend and former boyfriend Matt as well as her mother, and Caroline is at first desperate to save them. Like other vampires in this canon, close associations with humans make her unwilling to act according to her vampire nature and to follow other rules, but coerced into killing Matt, she changes her views. Her insecurities are gone and her lack of fulfillment is amended as she after ingesting Matt's blood feels "*satisfied*, deep down to her bones, for the first time in her life." This experience makes her revaluate her view of norms and rules, and not even her own mother's blood on Klaus' mouth is a deterrent. Embraced by Stefan and Klaus at once, "[a]t long last she was where she belonged." Caroline has seen a monster in her figurative mirror since her turning, but embracing violence and bloodlust and accepting murder (even of friends and family) is represented as liberating, as the only path to happiness.

Many fanfics that draw out the implications of the conflation between blood lust and sexual desire in Twilight end with a very literal death of romance. We will return to stories of this kind at the end of this chapter, but here focus on an example which features an unusual depiction of the reflection of the monster. TwifanUK's *Fragile Monster* outlines how Edward loses his self-control and kills Bella on their wedding night, and introduces the idea that his lack of power is attributable to a concrete inner monster. This monster has controlled Edward once before and led him down a path dangerous to both himself and others. The author here refers to the period in the canon when Edward was less than enchanted with Carlisle's "life of abstinence" and even harbored some resentment towards his adopted father's attempts to "curb [Edward's] appetite," resulting in a period of time spent apart (Meyer, *Twilight* 298). In the fanfic, intimacy with Bella conjures forth the monster once again and although it certainly can be read as part of Edward, it is also disassociated from him. Edward and the monster communicate, which confuses Bella as she can only hear Edward's incoherent answers, and Edward is disturbed by the thought that the monster can see them, and Bella in particular, naked. At the same time, there is a progressive sense of conflation between them. What starts as crude interjections from the monster, and commands such as "*Claim her. You know you want to*" give way to non-italicized, internal fantasies of Bella's broken body. "I held onto her tighter and felt the feint pop of ribs cracking under my grip, followed by a pained gasp from Bella. [...] My teeth pierced the soft, delicate flesh of her neck as I drank greedily from her." Edward is pulled back to the reality of his relatively unharmed bride but the temporary fantasy becomes chilling reality as Edward is overtaken by the monster, or, alternatively, the side of him he has tried to repress. "The monster rose. His appetite insatiable. Clawing, gnarling and hissing as he ascended through my body towards my head; his snapping cross-hairs aimed directly at my mouth." The conflation between monster and Edward seems at this point absolute, prefaced as it is by Edward's increasingly destructive thoughts. However, Edward is figured as another victim in the process, powerless against the invasion of his body, and the italicized interjections return, enforcing the notion that a part of Edward is still himself. But the part of him that loves Bella and wants to protect her is overcome, and all that finally remains is Bella's dead body.

There is a narrative silence on the part of the monster after Bella's death, suggesting that with both blood lust and sexual desire sated, it has no power anymore. But there are, it turns out, other feelings the monster can relish in, and it taunts Edward: "The monster sang in mockery, taking delight in my despair and feeding off it." Emotions and actions depicted as negative — in the canon and in this fanfic — such as insatiable desire, excessive force, and despondency, fuel the monster but they are never completely divorced from Edward's character: they are excesses and lacks which he also harbors. The competing tendencies of conflation and disassociation enable both an internal and external look at evil. The monster looks at Edward with disappointment, seeing only unfulfilled promises; Edward looks at the monster and shudders in fear.

As a consequence of his (and the monster's) actions, Edward moves towards an uncertain future since the carefully constructed norms of his particular vampire family have been irrevocably transgressed. In the canon, the most manifest threat to the Cullen's way of life is Jasper. Albeit far less destructive than Edward's inner monster's attack in *Fragile Monster*, it is his reaction to Bella's paper-cut that forces the canon relocation of the entire family (Meyer, *New Moon* 26–27). Jasper struggles harder than the others to control his blood lust and his past is full of violence. As a human soldier in the Confederate army and as a fighter for his sire Maria who creates an army of newborns in her attempt to gain land in the South, Jasper has been instructed to kill by both human and paranormal superiors, the former instruction naturalized in times of war. Telling Bella about his past, he concedes that because he had "lost nearly all of [his] humanity [he] was undeniably a nightmare, a monster of the grisliest kind," and that meeting Alice and later the Cullens has brought him peace and "hope" (Meyer, *Eclipse* 266, 268). To author faithunbreakable, however, Jasper's life with the Cullens is nothing but a charade and he can never escape what he truly is, nor does he necessarily want to. "He doesn't hate himself enough to deny everything he is," as the author phrases it in *Swansong*, indicating that the Cullens' way of life is based on a destruction of their own true identities, and that Jasper is the only one who on some level can embrace the monster he sees in the mirror.

In *The Lepidopterist* by the same author, Jasper experiences an identity crisis precipitated by a meeting with a young woman at a bar he frequents to find new victims. The woman recognizes him as a vampire, but welcomes him to her table, and later follows him out into an alley behind the bar, where he violently takes her body as well as her life. Retaining his canon competency of empathy, Jasper can heavily influence individuals and he fills the woman with desire and pleasure to lessen her mortal fear but to his amazement realizes that she wants him to kill her. "She was using him as a one way ticket out of this world." The meeting with the woman and her death shake his world. He has been used to anguish and pain even in the victims he has lulled with positive emotions, but she has merely welcomed death and Jasper finds it hard to reconcile the part of him that wants to be feared with the part who wants to be accepted for what he is. "She'd been the first person, human or vampire, that had looked into his eyes, looked at the monster that slept there, and not been afraid," he thinks. "And he'd killed her."

Except she is not dead at all, indeed she cannot die, and apologizes to Jasper for involving him in her suicide when they later meet again. "Nothing I do has consequences," she says and like a vampire's longevity, her endless existence is driving her insane. Her unnatural cursed state means that at regular intervals she needs to die, by her own hand or by someone else's, and come back. This inevitability forges a deep link with Jasper who likewise cannot alter what he is. Like in the fable of the scorpion and the frog, which Jasper alludes to when he kills her in the alley: "Nature is nature. The scorpion killed the frog even knowing that it would kill itself, too, in the process, simply because that was what it was." The further implications of the fable are clear in Jasper's case, since killing the young woman kills the monster he is: "his stinger was broken and his venom spent." This development in turn means that he needs to find yet a new purpose in his life, leaving all his past identities behind.

The story's epilogue, set in the now of the canon novel *Twilight*, comes with a twist as Jasper meets the young woman a third time, sixty years later. He is now part of the Cullen family and has consequently established a new identity, and the woman is his brother's girlfriend and no longer nameless. "Bella. Isabella," Jasper thinks, doubting "that was her real name." The past events played out between the characters remain secret to the rest of the Cullens, but Jasper is obsessed with the past and how Bella has destabilized the monster he used to be. The epilogue points forward to a central event in *Twilight*: Bella's near destruction at the hands of the rogue vampire James, but given the twist, Bella will willingly go to meet her fate since it is time for another of her life-spans to come to its end. Jasper ponders that maybe she has been drawn to Edward "for the danger he represented" but in the end, who kills her does not matter. Since Jasper has killed her once before, Bella challenges him to do it again, not seeing that he is no longer able. The experiences they have shared have humanized him and broken the monster inside, whereas she stays the same, a "*deathless* girl," whose suicides ruin those around her. "She was the mother of all scorpions," Jasper concludes, but since she can reinvent herself in each new life, her spent venom and broken stinger have no consequences.

Swansong and *The Lepidopterist* are not explicitly linked and present different sequences of events, yet the portrayal of Jasper is consistently drawn, signaling the author's interest in the violent aspects of his past, how these experiences have formed him, and how they have created a true self in which good and evil necessarily need to remain competing. This idea is particularly evident in *Swansong*, where ignoring the past is likened to building a house without a foundation. Even if this foundation in Jasper's case is based on killing and violence it is still part of who he is and any attempt to change it is the real aberration. Bella as Other is also featured in both stories, albeit with the crucial difference of being benevolent in *Swansong* and malevolent in *The Lepidopterist*. The former story, in which Bella has a paranormal ability that enables her to foresee information vampires require and supply it when asked, ends with her human death. This death follows logically on the romance format, the implication being that she will be with Jasper for all eternity.

Swansong also includes several references to healing and transformation connected to romance themes. Bella will "fix" the broken Jasper and the vampire state will turn her from "caterpillar" to "butterfly." In *The Lepidopterist*, the fact that she cannot die is her tragedy, and distinct from canon–Bella as the human norm, she is represented as more monstrous than vampires. "Utterly broken," Jasper thinks. "Utterly mad." Inventing a tangible reason for Bella's involvement with the undead, the author does not offer hope through transformation into a more beautiful state (the lepidopterist looks in vain for this), rather she gestures to the dark implications of endlessly repeated cycles of destruction.

The beast can sometimes be intensely tired of these cycles of destruction, without being able to change its true nature and with no power to affect the surrounding world. In *Waters Will Keep Running, Rivers Will Turn*, exeterlinden explores Godric's forays across Europe and across history. As he moves through ages and places, worldviews change and with them Godric's sense of place and purpose. Initially, and despite already existing for a long time "Godric still believed that he was a death spirit, and he was still at peace," but when the gods he has believed in are revealed as false (and when new ones take their place), this peace of mind crumbles. Intermittent meetings with Eric illuminate different stages in the process of disintegration. In 12th-century Bremen they meet as Godric has just killed a family, without feeding from them. "The sun rose because the gods were pleased with our tributes," he muses, "the cult dances made the seasons turn, we inhabited the night to bring death to the deserving.... But it isn't so, is it?" Godric becomes a symbol for changed beliefs, for the various positions the vampire has occupied, and for the diminishing trust in the balance of nature. He shifts back to a more hopeful state the next time Eric sees him, in Florence where Godric has just made the acquaintance of Leonardo da Vinci. Humans are no longer just victims to him, but beings with the power to change the world. "We were never their gods, we're merely the scavengers of their society," he says, but this realization brings a desire to also be part of human society and a view of human life as an idealized state.

Godric's conflicted soul, a consequence of the identity crisis produced by alliances and bonds formed between humans and vampires, surfaces again as he becomes convinced that his guilt can be eased if he only takes the lives of the depraved. This type of portrayal is aligned with other forms of marginalized vampire instantiations which are as likely to produce sympathy as fear. Fred Botting notes, in connection with Anne Rice's Louis, a vampire with similar quandaries about the position and function of the self:

> Existing on the borders of society, the lone predator becomes a solitary wanderer seeking companionship and security, intensely aware of his difference and fascinated by the frailty and mortality of the humans around him.... His alienation

and disquieted solitude, his love of beauty and knowledge, along with his humane concerns endow him the qualities of a Romantic self, tortured by self-consciousness and a questing spirit [77].

Godric desires what mortals have — "companionship and security" — and also the inevitability of death. Also like Louis, who for periods live off rats and small animals, Godric in exeterlinden's story tries to lessen his guilt by making well-considered choices in terms of prey. He self-reflexively notes, however, that while "killing murderers and rapists is ... a little more justifiable," the notion of humane concerns in itself "is, of course, completely illusory." The monster in this fanfic has been forced to take a long, hard look at himself and found himself lacking and with this lack comes altered views not only on humanity but on what a true vampire's nature really is.

Seven Deadly Sins

The mainly secularized canons, in which religious paraphernalia no longer can be used to quell or defeat the vampire, still include ruminations on issues of potential damnation and loss of soul. Although evil is figured in social and cultural terms, insecurity and spiritual doubt are linked to postmodern identity crises, and fears are connected to metaphysical aspects, the morally responsible life some of the contemporary vampires elect to lead is a result of their belief that the vampire state equals a loss of soul and in consequence eternal damnation. The three canons have particularly strong ties to Rice's *Vampire Chronicles* when it comes to the double issues of secularization and faith. It is especially significant that Louis before being turned has lost his Catholic faith, and is therefore familiar with the experience of *having* believed. Gelder maintains that "he both believes in nothing, and is (therefore) able to believe in *anything*, including the unbelievable — vampires" (*Reading* 111). Louis performs his own mapping of vampire history and truth in his European travels, but is unable to find anything but "vampirism [as] a mode of representation," that is, hardly something which can replace his lost faith (Gelder, *Reading* 112). In the figure of Louis, Rice on the one hand downplays religious significance in terms of lore: he is not convinced of God's existence and religious paraphernalia consequently have no effect on him. On the other hand, religion remains central as Rice's vampires struggle with the lack of faith, rendering issues of good and evil highly pertinent and relatable.

There are references to religiously connoted sin in both True Blood and The Vampire Diaries, made by institutions as well as the vampire characters themselves. In Harris' novels, the view of the Catholic Church, that vampires have forfeited their souls through the transition into undead, is reiterated by The Fellowship of the Sun's Steve Newlin: "You know, eternal life on this earth may sound good, but you'll lose your soul [and go to] true hell" (*Living Dead in Dallas* 131). Even some vampires subscribe to the same view. Godric, for example, states, "All vampires are damned, and should meet the sun" (Harris, *Living Dead in Dallas* 154). Bill, however, thinks that he cannot be damned that "[t]here is something in [him] that isn't cruel, not murderous, even after all these years," which would hint to a possible salvation (Harris, *Dead Until Dark* 53). In Smith's *The Awakening*, Stefan tells Elena that by killing Damon "I condemned him to live in the night. I took away his only chance at salvation. [...] I damned my brother to hell" (179, 180).[14] Despite these pronouncements, literal damnation is not addressed explicitly in these canons. Used rather as a figure of speech, it holds no real consequences and other threats (often human) again foreground issues of free will and choice as considerably more important than damnation due to nature. With focus on Harris' novels, Susannah Clements argues that the vampires' minority-figured difference results in an evaluation of them "in social terms rather than in theological terms" (83) and we would argue that the same can be maintained in regards also to the revenants in The Vampire Diaries. Issues of faith are not rendered unimportant but salvation comes in individual and cultural shapes.

The Twilight canon engages to a greater extent with questions regarding the potential loss of the human soul, with a starting point in Edward's conviction that the vampire state means eternal damnation. As Stefan in *The Awakening*, he connects the vampire state to darkness and it features prominently in his unwillingness to turn Bella: "I refuse to damn you to an eternity of night" (Meyer, *Twilight* 415). Carlisle later explains to Bella that he and Edward differ on the point of "an afterlife for" vampires. Whereas Edward "thinks [they have] lost their souls," Carlisle is "hoping that there is still a point to this life" and that, if they try hard enough, vampires can also be saved (Meyer, *New Moon* 33). Carlisle's views (echoing Bill's quoted above) are a clear illustration of how salvation for the contemporary vampire lies in the choices made, not in what an individual is. While Bella's "life [is] fairly devoid of belief" she can still realize that Edward's conviction makes it impossible for him to turn her: placing herself in his position she doubts whether she could ever "risk Edward's soul" (Meyer, *New Moon* 32, 35). The soul becomes deeply intertwined with love, forfeiting it being equaled to giving away one's heart. Later, Bella consequently exclaims, "I don't care! You can have my soul. I don't want it without you — it's yours already" (Meyer, *New Moon* 61). Despite the drawn-out conversations between Bella and Edward, and his continuous belief in turning equaling a forfeited soul, Twilight, like the other canons, does not represent this as a concrete possibility.

The references to potential damnation are picked up, however, by fanfic authors and we will in what follows have an exclusive focus on two Twilight fanfics, both set mainly in the past, which deal specifically with notions of a more traditional religious figuration of sin. The first, spaniard's *Purgatory*, takes the form of Edward telling Bella about the human lives of his parents and siblings, the other Cullens listening to their stories as a form of penance. Because of his "obsession with the morbid descriptions of Dante Alighieri" Edward sees strong links between the seven deadly sins and the seven members of his family, but also possibilities for redemption through the narrative journey. In the multi-chapter fanfic, Carlisle is linked to the deadly sin of pride, Alice to envy, Rosalie to (others') lust, and Jasper to gluttony, and all chapters gesture to how past sins figure into what the characters have become in the now of the canon. The sins we will predominantly discuss stress the all-important notion of taking responsibility for actions committed and are thematically linked via issues of loneliness, parents, and children.

In chapters outlining the fate of Emmett, spaniard depicts a hardworking family, and a brother who at the outset does everything to protect his younger sister. The sin Emmett embodies is greed, figured on different levels. Also in his vampire state, he depicted as a figure of *"excess,"* as a character whose *"entire existence is a quest for more,"* but in the canon (and in the now of the fanfic) these are benevolent traits. In his past, however, greed has had catastrophic results for the family who is "torn apart by" it in squabbles over property and money. When Emmett stumbles upon a small cave on his brother's land and finds gold glimmering within, his greed takes over. His sister tries to curb it, but Emmett is seduced by the precious metal, and whereas he is too large (too excessive) to fit into the small aperture they have found, she can squeeze into it. In the canon, Rosalie finds Emmett as he is mauled by a bear, and while this plot element is found also in the fanfic, his sister is the bear's first victim as the cave they find is the predator's lair. The newborn vampire Emmett returns to the forest and discovers his sister alive, but in the attempt to turn her he cannot control his bloodlust — another form of greed — and he kills her. In the aftermath, Emmett realizes that he has to make a choice in what to become. The excess which has characterized his whole existence is amplified in the vampire state and could easily lead him into "madness" and "rage." Remembering his sister's love for him, however, he chooses to become the hero she has seen him as. This choice logically leads to the canon characterization of Emmett as protector and playmate of Renesmee, but invests it with a considerably darker undertone.

The protectiveness and unconditional love represented by Esme in the canon is in *Purgatory* explored through a focus on the pieces of her soul that one by one have gone missing. Esme's deadly sin is sloth, which, in accordance with *The Divine Comedy*, is to be interpreted as "despair so uncontrollable that life is rendered useless." The fanfic outlines Esme's life as a series of losses. Her sister dies as an adolescent, leaving their mother heartbroken (filled with sloth) and years afterwards, the mother dies from an overdose of laudanum, prescribed to Esme after an accident. Esme's marriage to an abusive man causes another piece of her soul to wither away, and after her escape, and after having lost her newborn baby, the destruction seems complete. The sloth-chapters are prefaced by one entitled "Through the Forest," the author noting that in Dante's work, victims of suicide are transformed into trees. One tree in particular connects Esme's fate to this intertextual link. Her sister has committed suicide by jumping from it and it is falling from the tree that causes Esme's accident (leading to her mother's death). As but one sign of her husband's evil, he takes the tree down, and it is no longer there when Esme decides to take her own life. When she returns to (un)life, she recognizes Carlisle as the doctor who once treated her broken leg, feels an immediate connection with him and instantly forms a motherly attachment to Edward. When her human husband steps "into the clearing that he had created by cutting down her tree," Edward's instinct is to kill him for the suffering he has caused, but Esme stops him because she does not want Edward to commit this evil — succumbing to the sin of wrath. The protective and self-less character traits persist in her vampire existence in the canon, and at this point in the fanfic, Esme is as innocent as Alice, despite the action she has taken to end her own life.

Of all the evils, Edward considers his crimes the worst, because some of them are based in a desire for revenge and because he has more to atone for than what is readily apparent. More is known about Edward's past than the other vampire characters, still, it is a quite sketchy picture he paints in response to Bella's questions in the canon. Readers and viewers are told that he died of the Spanish influenza at the beginning of the twentieth century and that his mother asked Carlisle to save him. We are also told of his "rebellious adolescence" when he questions his maker's choice of life (Meyer, *Twilight* 298). To rebel presupposes a previous existence when one complies with parental wishes, but spaniard gives a slightly different image of Edward's childhood. He has a talent for music, but is not too fond of practice, and on the day that will change his life forever, he is full of "trivial complaints" and is the reason he and his mother miss a car which is to take them to the conservatory. Walking there, they are attacked by a man with a knife, and Edward's heart is pierced by the blade. He has a brief glimpse of the attacker, can hear his mother scream at a distance, but remembers nothing else until he wakes up at a hospital. "Neither of us ever fully recovered."

In his mother, the attack causes a sloth-like state; she has lost the baby she has carried and her faith in mankind. In Edward, it causes a chronic heart problem, and "a nearly uncontrollable rage." He is not only filled with anger because he perceives of himself as responsible for the attack, but because his debilitated state will bring even further grief to his mother. "My death would kill her as well. In the end, time would succeed where our attacker had not." But Edward does not die. Carlisle, the family doctor, has saved him once already, and does so again when, true to the canon, Edward's whole family is dying from the influenza. As all newborn vampires in the Twilight canon, Edward struggles to maintain self-control, and Carlisle abandons his job and travels with him to less populated places, something which increases Edward's guilt, "knowing how many lives he could have saved without me by his side." The fanfic replays the last events narrated in Esme's chapters, and the relationship with his new parents temporarily abates Edward's anger. He too wants to be able to abstain from revenge, just as Esme has. However, attempting to turn a new leaf and asking Carlisle about the truth, Edward learns that his mother had not just been attacked all those years ago, but tortured during the three days her son had lain unconscious. The realization pushes him over a brink. "I was Wrath. And they would all pay now." In this way, spaniard creates a detailed image of Edward's years of barely kept self-control, and invents a very tangible reason for his rebellion against the peaceful ways of Carlisle and Esme.

In Chicago and later in New York, Edward goes on a rampage among criminals in pursuit of his mother's torturer. Although spaniard stays close to the canon in her portrayal of a "predator among predators" and of Edward as a being whose monstrosity seems tempered by the fact that he kills "other monsters," other lives are lost in the process. Along with thieves and serial killers, Edward also becomes "a killer of innocents." The threatening decent into madness the killing of children represents makes Edward again reach out to his parents and when he encounters the man he has sought, he is not alone. In an unexpected twist, which adds another layer to Edward's guilt, he is not the one to kill the attacker. Rather, to save her son from accumulating more blood on his hands, the man becomes Esme's "first and only victim." A deep love here results in a taking of a life which the narrative paints as deserving of this fate, but the author importantly does not alter the character's own view of the deed committed. Esme makes a choice, but it is not one she will ever condone.

While *Purgatory* somewhat simplistically ends with Bella offering forgiveness and Renesmee redemption, the fanfic in complex ways plays with the notion of sin. In some cases, the characters themselves have not committed the sin, but it is figured in relation to their deaths. Rather than working solely from the premise that the taking of a life is by nature evil, spaniard shifts and changes associations to what evil means and to how sins are conceived. The chapters also go a long way in establishing how the vampires came to be the ones they are in the canon, foregrounding issues of free will and choice. Without their experiences and ruminations on their fates, it is suggested, they would be unable to practice the control which characterizes them in the now. Like other prequels, discussed in chapter three, there are thus gestures towards the future canon-state in all chapters. By locating traditionally figured and religiously connoted sins in the past, the fanfic also conveniently avoids dealing with the canon's secularized now.

Carlisle's past, temporally longer than the other vampire characters' in Twilight, is explored with emphasis on a particular kind of monstrousness in TWBB's *The Canonical Five* and plays heavily on notions of sin and salvation. The title refers to the number of human victims Carlisle kills, but more specifically to the women killed by Jack the Ripper in the 1880s. Carlisle's medical profession in the canon, along with the fact that the Whitechapel murders remain unsolved, make him a good candidate for Jack the Ripper's true identity, and TWBB adds a carefully explored motive for his murderous acts.[15] In the story, Carlisle has for a long time contemplated creating a companion for himself, and found an ideal candidate in a young man named Joseph. Joseph, however, dies from syphilis contracted from his associations with "[a] woman of the night." Before this event, Carlisle has tried to live by the same dietary ethics that guide him in the canon, but his grief alters his view of humans and prostitutes in particular whom he not only kills for vengeance, but for sustenance. Deranged by sadness, Carlisle thinks he hears the voices of both his father and Joseph, guiding him to the victims "deserving" of the fate of death, the killings designed "to grant lasting peace to [Joseph's] soul" but also to put an end to the women's own sinful lives and give them a chance of heavenly forgiveness.

Another sin, however, intrudes on Carlisle's project when he comes to experience desire in his proximity to the women. As "sexual fulfillment" has been Joseph's "downfall" and as Carlisle has been instructed to read any kind of physical sexual release as a sin, he tries to fight his carnal urges but succumbs to the seduction of his last victim. Physical pleasure and vampiric needs combine and the blood he sucks during intercourse gives him "the reach" required to climax, and in the aftermath he realizes that he has completely destroyed his lover, even taken her heart out of her body (this, of course, in line with what is known about Jack the Ripper's last victim). The sin of physical desire is also combined with the sin of selfishness. As Carlisle tells the suddenly appearing vampire Aro, a friend from his more peaceful, vegetarian life: "The others were for *him*. [...] But she ... she was for me." Aro tries to assure Carlisle that he has "broken none of our [vampire] laws." He has followed his instincts and while not laudable, the taking of human lives does not represent a transgression. Carlisle, however, does not agree with this interpretation which would absolve him from guilt. Rather he sees his masking of the paranormally induced deaths through his deftly handled scalpel as making the grisly murders even more evilly corrupt. His father's religious instruction also remains a powerful influence. Revenge, murder, desire, deception and selfishness are thus used to paint a picture of self-inflicted judgment reliant on religiously connoted sins.

The morally responsible life the Cullens elect in the canon and the emphasis they put on free will and choice (relating to both themselves and to their potential victims) are in these fanfics a consequence of past offences. In this, they corroborate the canon to a great extent since the vampires there as well make references to dark pasts and to actions that need to be atoned for. Clements argues that while the characters in Stephenie Meyer's series "speak occasionally about being 'damned' for being what they are, nothing in the novels supports this as a genuine reality" (111). Somewhat ironically, despite recuperating and elaborating on elements which are figured in clearly theological terms, the fanfics reiterate a similar hesitancy. By setting the stories in the past, deadly sins and the thought of hell figure as realities, but only in a temporally limited sense. In the secularized now, the characters are in no danger of being damned to hell as long as they stick to conscientious choices and altruistic approaches.

Monstrous Misogyny

When transforming characters into monsters, or when exaggerating the monstrous aspects of them, one development presents a particular problem: when the monsterization in fanfic becomes bound up with misogyny and abuse, often featured in the form of rape. Fanfic-authors are naturally not alone in the construction of this scenario, rather, their depictions can be tied to discourses in other genres and media formats. In discussions about horror films, Harry M. Benshoff argues that "a function of the genre [is] to displace 'real life' rape or abuse onto fictional monsters, [and that] such a displacement is also an invitation to take pleasure in such images" (142). That is, there is a disconnect between non-fiction and fiction; projected onto a screen, events become even further distanced from the horror and pain of the victim, even as these emotions are part of the viewing pleasure. Benshoff further sees the horror discourse as connected to "our patriarchal culture's relative comfort with that process when those abused bodies are female, that is, 'acceptable' objects of the straight male gaze" (142). Processes of naturalization of violence are seen also in romance novels. In "bodice rippers," non-consent gradually gives way to consent and it is invariably the female character who protests the hero's often violent seduction. Captivity romances likewise carry connotations to issues of consent and a dehumanization of the female protagonist. The hero forces the heroine "into docility [and] the woman is reduced to animal status; she must be brought to submission" (Kaler 93). Both bodice rippers and captivity romances have decreased in popularity and Linda J. Lee argues that "sexual brutalities have become anathema" in romance fiction since the late twentieth century. However, she also points out that "the only mainstreaming romance subgenre in which sexually violent elements are likely to appear is the paranormal romance" due to the unrealistic setting which "is subject to a different set of rules and expectations than contemporary Western culture" (55). Explicit abuse is with one exception (which we will return to) not featured in the canon texts, but the complex relationship between power and agency in human/vampire relationships still complicates notions of consent. The vampire is older, more experienced and possesses paranormal abilities that gives him access to the female protagonist's mind. Even if kisses and other forms of intimacy are represented as romantic in the canons, there are instances of mind-manipulation and other forms of psychological transgressions which uncomfortably straddle the border between assent and violation.[16]

In the previously analyzed fanfic *The Lepidopterist*, faithunbreakable's emphasis on Jasper's paranormal competency has the effect of degrading the humans whose psyches he controls. He exaggerates the desire in women and makes men afraid and his victims become "[g]ood little dogs," easily mastered and controlled. Eternallybills includes internal musings on Bill's part concerning the dubiousness of using mind control in *Hunger*. In the days before the Revelation and the option of Tru Blood, Bill reflects, "[t]he cruel and reckless killed; the more prudent and benevolent glamoured." Glamoring is not a practice Bill wants to engage in, however, since "[i]t seemed only like a kinder, gentler rape, if such a thing were possible." Physical and psychological transgressions of boundaries are equated, and carry the same connotations to lack of choice and protection on the part of the victim. In these fanfics, the vampires alternately practice or resist psychological manipulation, but their competency is depicted as a truly monstrous trait. Issues of non-consent or dubious consent also feature into our discussions about vampire ethics. In socact's *Invitation*, for example, Edward takes the blood of a sleeping Bella which precludes her active consent to the process. In *Barefoot on Broken Glass* by Sandrine Shaw and *Hungry Again* by stainofmylove, Elena's transformation into a vampire is involuntary and her mindless hunger in turn limits the choices of her victims. These victims are significantly female and anguish and pain are projected onto them, even if their emotions remain obscured through the focalization on Edward and Elena, respectively. In these stories as well, an exaggeration of monstrous character traits follows tendencies in both horror and romance. When not kept in check by human norms and conscientious choices, vampiric monstrosity flourishes (the point in these and other fanfics) and a diminished humanity of the victim is the consequence.

Dubious consent and non-consent, in fanfic terms dub-con and non-con, are warnings fanfic authors can attach to their stories to signal sexualized dark contents. Several of the fanfics mentioned contain warnings either in pre-set tags or in paratextual notes. *Hungry Again*, for example, comes with the archive warning "graphic depictions of violence." *The Lepidopterist* is published on FanFiction.net, a site which allows authors to file their stories according to genre but which does include non-con or dub-con as pre-set tags (Archive of Our Own, in contrast, has the archive warning "rape/non-con" as an option). In her paratextual notes, however, faithunbreakable includes a warning to her readers. Her fanfic contains "[v]ampires behaving vampire-ish" and there are, she cautions, "[t]iny consent issues." Readers who are uncomfortable with either exaggerated vampiric traits or dubious consent are encouraged to stop reading: "I won't hold it against you," the author writes. While dubious consent is featured in the fanfic, it is used as a vehicle for Jasper's ruminations on his own monstrosity, and deemed as evil. In other fanfics, similarly, abuse and misogyny comingle with monsterization and become consequences of exaggerated monstrous character traits rather than being monstrous in and of themselves. This is not without problems.

In *Scream* by NykkiLeighVampireHeart, readers are presented with a Damon in full-blown killer mode in which he has not only turned off his human emotions but "shut off his humanity." The author writes in the notes following a prologue that her main aim is a depiction of Damon's "mind spiraling out of complete control!" The prologue, in which canon events are quickly covered, thus reads as a fast forward and it is indicated that the author wants to take questions of potential evil considerably further than the canon text (the TV series). She creates a dangerous and selfish monster by intertwining the killing of a woman with rape in the ensuing chapter and later making Elena a pawn in Damon's sadistic power games. In connection with the unnamed first victim, the author writes that Damon "knew that in her mind, she wasn't enjoying this, but her body was" and in the forced intimacy, Elena is "torn between feeling very frightened of this monster Damon had become, and becoming aroused at what he was doing to her." The involuntarily pleasure the victims take in the abuse has an obvious connection to the disturbing romantic staple of the heroine protesting the hero's kiss or seduction, being betrayed by her own body, and to vampire narratives where "the deepest fear behind the vampire's kiss [is] not that the victims are taken against their will, but rather that the vampire's kiss releases the hidden desires that the will would repress" (Haggerty, "Anne Rice" 16). However, in contrast to both traditional romances and the allure of the vampire's embrace, the pleasures the female characters experience in the fanfic in no way lessen the fear they feel; there is no turning point at which horror is overcome. Further, the focalization on Elena removes any distance from the events and also translates her terror to the unnamed first victim. The reader cannot access this woman's mind, but may realize, with experience of Elena's, the horror and pain she is in.

The pleasure Damon is represented to find in rape, abuse and sadism, finds an unsettling counterpoint in Elena's view of him. Clinging to memories of Damon, humanity retained and tender towards her, she thinks she will be safe with him. Even being raped by him the first time, she "imagin[es] the way it would feel if he did this while he was still the way he used to be." The unexpected pleasure, that is, would be enhanced, more meaningful, if love featured into the equation. It does not, as Elena comes to realize. "Everything she ... loved about him was gone. He was now a monster." In this reflection is the sense that Damon has changed; he has become a monster rather than reverting back to any natural vampiric state. The monsterization featured in this fanfic is on one level figured in human terms as he is vilified as any human would be because of his actions. On another level, it is connected to vampirism as it is Damon's supernatural powers and strength that enable him to dominate the human victims. Mind-manipulation is brought into the equation as Damon compels Elena to forget about the sexual abuse, but not completely. Although Stefan will not see the bruises and "never wonder why Elena would feel slightly frightened by the [sexual] act" it is suggested that there will be lingering traces of fear, although Elena will never be able to identify the source of it. In discussions about sadism, McGinn argues that "[i]t is not merely the power of life and death" that drives the sadist, "it is the power to make someone invert the values they assign to these two conditions" (77). Value-inversion produced by the sadist is thus featured in several forms in the fanfic: Elena is made to want Damon despite being raped by him, is made to fear sex with Stefan (previously linked to emotional intimacy and love), and made to prefer death over life.

As *Scream* is published on FanFiction.net it comes with no tags signaling that rape is featured (it is filed with the genre labels Horror/Tragedy) and no paratextual warnings alert readers to the story's dark and abusive contents.[17] There are ongoing debates about the use (and misuse) of warning labels and in *Eric the FanFiction Rapist*, Thyra10 comments metatextually on these and other issues connected to rape-fics. In this True Blood fanfic, a dazed Eric wakes up in a room with glass walls, and is informed of recent textual developments by the fairy Claudine who admonishes him for his behavior against Sookie whom he is "not treating ... very well" in fanfic. Eric needs to be educated about the text form and particularly about how he has been coopted by fans in constructions of abuse. Eric vehemently protests, asking: "Why is anyone writing me as a rapist? Don't they know that I myself have been.... Don't they know I would never do this?" His own experiences at the hands of his maker Ocella (the fanfic works from Harris' novels) make it unthinkable that he would put anyone else through such an ordeal, but matters become even worse when Claudine tells him that Sookie will "always love you in fanfiction even if she starts out hating what you're doing to her." What Claudine (and Thyra10) is referring to here are the many fanfics in which rape is either not seen as abuse — as Claudine suggests many "probably don't realize that they are writing rape fics," which gestures towards an uncomfortable normalization process — or where Sookie (and other female characters) are depicted as loving the abuser fiercely.

Both tendencies are of course prevalent also in traditional romances, and rape is featured in the canon itself, rendered in ways which gel with how Claudine in the fanfic laments depictions of sexual abuse. In *Club Dead*, after a period of imprisonment and starvation, Bill is locked into a car trunk with Sookie.[18] His hunger for blood makes him oblivious to her pain and to the threat inherent in taking too much, and the violence of the feeding turns into another kind of mindless attack. "[H]e entered me with no preparation at all. I screamed, and he clapped a hand over my mouth" (Harris, *Club Dead* 223). In the aftermath, Bill is horrified at what he has done, but the violent blood sucking and rape are downplayed to an extent because he has not recognized his victim as Sookie. The implication seems to be that his remorse is merely an effect of their association. Sookie feels guilty for not feeling "all right" since "[a]fter all, it was Bill who'd been held prisoner and tortured" and is hesitant to label the event as rape (Harris, *Club Dead* 223). In a later situation of lovemaking she feels betrayed by her own body when "[i]t seemed to be blacking out Bill's mindless attack" (Harris, *Club Dead* 235). Although the events take place towards the end of Bill and Sookie's relationship, it is not the rape in itself that causes her to stop loving him and

Bill's condition is to an extent used to mask his actions as something other than sexual abuse.

In Thyra10's fanfic, two groups of women have gathered outside the building, some advocating the right of free speech, others demanding that warnings are attached to fanfics that portray abuse and rape. Claudine believes that some fanfic authors "want to test out new waters when it comes to their writing — explore the dark closets, so to speak" whereas others want to depict abuse to garner reviews; something which they paradoxically are less likely to get if attaching a warning label to their story. Creative freedom is to be protected, on this Claudine is clear, but she is concerned that readers with a history of abuse or memories of a traumatic event will have devastating reactions when coming across rape in a fan fiction (just as Eric has when coming across himself as a rapist). Eric's comment that perhaps such readers should "just stay away from those fics" brings the question back to the lack of warnings. Claudine asks: "How can they stay away from the rape fics if neither you nor the writer tell[s] them that you're going to rape Sookie in the story? When you pretend it's a romantic story and suddenly the readers have a rape smack in their faces?" The fan fiction Eric, she thereby suggests, should give a shout from within the story to warn readers although he is powerless against the depictions of him as an abuser.

When distancing the vampire from human norms by exaggerating or inventing monstrous traits, one effect is the dehumanization of the human victims. While depictions of rape and other forms of sexual abuse may naturally sit uncomfortably with many readers, they are not divorced from portrayals in which humans are killed, tortured or coerced into value-inversions of other kinds. Somewhat paradoxically, however, fanfic authors who subvert one set of norms, established by the canons, often end up supporting another; in the case of rape-fics or stories of a dub-con nature, the patriarchal view of the female body as a dispensable form on which to project dark fantasies.

The Death of Romance

We will end this chapter and our analyses of fan fiction by returning to the centrality of the canon romances, but investigate what happens when fanfic authors construct fanged and menacing versions of the male protagonists, often by extrapolating their canon competencies, ethics and behavior. The logical conclusion in stories like these is the death, destruction or involuntary turning of Bella, Sookie and Elena effected by the monster. Love is not necessarily absent in fanfics of this kind, on the contrary, it often works to emphasize danger and threat. It is, however, commonly represented as some form of corrupted love — too excessive, too unconditional — and in this way questions the romance gloss of the canons. In other stories, fanfic authors resist incorporating tender emotions altogether, instead underscoring that the vampire/human relationship can never be figured in terms of either romance or love.

The fated canon love between Edward and Bella is retained in 4theluv ofMary's *Magic in the Midnight Sun*, but is too strongly conflated with bloodlust and, thus corrupted, it follows another logic.[19] The fanfic, told from a third-person perspective, retells events in Twilight, and begins in biology class where Edward's urge to attack Bella is becoming stronger and where collateral damage in the form of the other students would be unavoidable. Helpless in the face of these urges, Edward and Alice go on the run to find Edward other victims, sometimes human sometimes animal, but the memory of Bella pulls at him and they return to Forks. As in the canon, Bella is different; her scent is unusually delicious and he does not have access to her mind, finding "solace in [her] silence." As Edward's bloodlust increases, so does his sexual desire which, as in the canon where he is represented as virginal, is a novelty: "a desire for flesh, not to consume but be consumed by." The new carnal desire is coupled with increasingly warmer feelings for Bella and a return, albeit brief, to his "long, lost dormant human side." Despite the obstacles they face, and Edward's half-hearted attempts to think about Bella in terms of love rather than in terms of a food source, they finally find themselves alone together. They kiss, but a small cut in her tongue makes him taste her blood, "his quest for humanity was lost" and intimacy turns into "a feeding frenzy." The strong instincts override Edward's vague awareness of Bella's increased fear and pain: "[b]ones broke under him, her body stilled." The death of Bella is presented as inevitable through the careful construction of Edward's monstrosity and natural vampiric urges. It comes at a price, however, which is likewise illustrated by the focus on his internal battle. In the aftermath he mourns the destruction of "the one he should've had as a mate."

Author Llwy imagines a similar end to Bella's life in *all lost*, although the route taken there is different and romantic love is emphatically removed. An altered point of view to an omniscient stance, exemplified by references to "our protagonist," produces an immediate distance both to Bella and to the grisly events depicted in the story. It also finds a parallel in the distance between humans and vampires which, albeit featured also in the canon, is enhanced here. When Bella first sees the Cullens, she notes that although attractive, they are "beautiful in the way a painting was, lifeless and unchanging. They were cold, they didn't belong." There are affinities between this fanfic and Lisse's *Moves in Mysterious Ways*, discussed in chapter two, that partly come from the depiction of the vampire as inherently "eerie" (the corresponding word in Lisse's fanfic is "creepy"), partly because of the emphasis on realism, however, the outcome of the two stories is very different. Llwy writes, "Maybe if Bella's association with the Cullens had ended there," after her first glimpse of them in the school cafeteria, "this would be an altogether different tale." Like the unnamed boy in *Moves in Mysterious Ways*, Bella could then have gone on to college and to a career; she may have married, had children and grandchildren, and enjoyed the natural course of a lifespan. "But," the omniscient narrator states in *all lost*, "that's not the tale I'm telling." Instead, what unfolds is a tale of Bella beset with nightmares of Edward invading the "haven [which] to all teenagers [is] their bedrooms," watching her, immobile, while she rests; of sleeplessness and gradual disintegration, of accidents which may be explained by her clumsiness but which are not. Like Lisse's fanfic, this is all but a love story, because Edward is a vampire and Bella is a human.

Llwy also alters other characters' reactions and imagines chilling fates for some. Bella's father, for example, does not protest against his daughter's new boyfriend, a changed characterization that removes the protection he offers in the canon, although it is there rather figured as an obstacle the couple has to overcome. Correspondingly, and in line with the portrayal of a menacing vampire figure, Carlisle, who treats Bella after an accident which lands her in hospital, is far from the benevolent healer in the canon. In a disturbing scene, Bella thinks she is having another nightmare in her hospital bed when Carlisle and Edward enter, the former drawing blood from her arm. Given the syringe, Edward "place[s] the end in his mouth, depressing the plunger to deposit roughly half of the fresh blood in his mouth, before passing it to the other Cullen to do the same." The distance created by the altered narrative perspective and by the pronounced difference between human beings and unchanging vampires finds an effective parallel in this depiction of blood taking: there is no close proximity between vampire and human, and the intimate bite is replaced by a disinfected hypodermic needle. When Edward and Carlisle become partners in crime, Bella is further left utterly helpless. Not even the thought that it has all been a dream offers any solace, because "real life isn't a dream" and when waking up for real the next morning, the bruise on her arm testifies to the concreteness of what has happened.

Bella's sojourn in the hospital has a correspondence in the canon, but is here rendered in far more sinister terms. Other canon events are also included, such as Edward saving her from a stranger in Port Angeles, and Bella initiating a relationship with Jacob. In the fanfic, however, Bella learns that the stranger has been brutally killed. Further, her first date with Jacob is on a "Friday night. By Sunday morning Jacob Black was dead." One by one, sources of support are taken from Bella, and it is only too late that Bella realizes the paranormal reason for the deaths, disappearances and Edward's Otherness. For a long painful time she rather wrestles with the sense that her sanity is slipping away, which adds sadism to Edward's character and underscores the instability of Bella's cognitive world. When, in the last meeting between them, she understands that he has no need to draw breath, that his smile is merely him "showing his teeth," and is helped to fathom his true nature by a revelation of paranormal speed and strength, the realism of her own life (and the insistence on it in the fanfic) collides with the impossible. "[A]pparently hell was empty and the monsters were all here," Bella thinks in horror, "because one of them was stroking her cheek gently with the frozen fingers of a corpse." The story comes to its logical end with the death of Bella, written off as the consequences of a predatory attack in the woods. In contrast to Lisse's story which, due to the responsibility the vampire shoulders as the stronger counterpart, ends with the prospect of a happy future for the boy, Llwy effectively kills the romance before it has even begun.

A particular threat to Stefan and Elena's relationship in the televised instantiation of the canon appears when Stefan becomes a Ripper at the end of the second season. In terms of behavior and ethics he is at this point far removed from his previous humanized state and human emotion and consequently also from Elena. When his Ripper period is featured in fan fiction, a consequence of the emotional rift between the central characters is often that Stefan is paired with someone else, seen as more compatible with his more clearly vampiric state. In *The Cautionary Tale of Unconditional Love*, by SweetWillowTree, Elena remains with Stefan also after his change, the author exploring what their relationship would be like with his changed persona but with unconditional love still intact. As the title indicates, this is indeed a tale of caution, because Stefan's violent tendencies are taken out on Elena and she accepts this because she loves him. The story starts with Elena tending to her physical wounds and thinking about a newly acquired habit of going back to her diary entries from when she first met Stefan. "She likes the simple romance of that story," SweetWillowTree writes, but can now, a few years into the future, only pity the young girl who walked into a relationship with a vampire convinced "that she would be his rock, his tether, forever" without realizing what forever really means. Their lives together now is one of constant threat erupting in physical abuse, Stefan's taking of her blood, and his guilt.

The fanfic paints a painful portrait of the consequences of following the canon logic of fated love. Here, Elena does not distance herself from Stefan when he becomes a Ripper, but instead, with full knowledge of what he now is "kiss[es] him hard, trying to *bring him home*." The love that can overcome all odds, that can anchor the wayward, is paired with her reflection: "when had she ever listened to that voice in her head that told her to run?" Elena's canon behavior; being headstrong and following through even when all signs tell her not to is in this way carried over into the fanfic, but given the AU element of retaining the pairing even in Stefan's violent state, the consequences are significantly altered. Elena's tendency to protect others in the canon is also used as she "changes from the passive collector of Stefan's transgressions to an active thief of them." She can sense when his bloodlust becomes overpowering and puts herself in other victims' place. However, the progressively more destructive relationship, following "a pattern" of lies, omissions, moments when Elena has "schooled herself to keep her voice quiet, to remain passive" contrasted with outbursts of violence, brings a sense of pleasure also to her. "She loves him too much, and has become addicted to blood and bruises, deep gashes and broken bones."

In volatile situations, Stefan repeatedly takes Elena's blood, but her injuries are at times too severe for her to be able to cover them up or manage. As a result, she is forced to ingest Stefan's blood to heal. In a final situation, when Stefan has seemed to calm down in accordance with the cyclical Ripper state, his threats and physical proximity cause her to take a step too far backwards and she falls down a flight of stairs. When she wakes up, "her heart is not beating." Dying with a bodily system full of vampire blood entails the beginning stages of vampiric transformation in The Vampire Diaries and somewhat ironically it is an accident caused by the threat of violence rather than literal violence that in this way takes Elena's human life in the fanfic. The final step in the turning process is not featured, but Elena's brother Jeremy is waiting outside the door which suggests he will be the human she drinks from to complete her transition. She will do so because she has no other choice and because it will ensure that she will continue to be with Stefan. Despite abuse and insecurity, love is not absent in this fanfic, rather it is corrupted by being, precisely, unconditional, and theirs is a "twisted fate." A human can love a vampire in SweetWillowTree's darkfic, but there are severe consequences when there are no limits to this love.

Similar to Elena in The Vampire Diaries, Sookie in the canon protests against the fate of being turned even if such an act could potentially ensure an everlasting happiness with one of her suitors (or someone else of the vampire persuasion). Many fanfic authors who envision a vampiric existence for Sookie focus on such a successful outcome, whereas for others, the situation becomes fraught precisely because Sookie's canon resistance is retained. In vic_vega66's *A lose, lose situation*, Sookie has been lured away from Bon Temps by Eric and has been turned against her will. Returning on a plane, she reflects on Eric's betrayal: in exchange for information about her missing lover Bill, "she would spend a month with [Eric] and be at his call" around the clock, particularly when it comes to sexual favors. Although she has enjoyed parts of the sexual intimacy there has been "no one to say enough, no one to say stop," and Sookie has been completely at Eric's mercy.

The author presents images of Eric as power-hungry, materialistic and cynical, and of vampire existence as shallow, filled with political intrigue and where "despising humans would be the norm." Sookie, who wants to grow old and have a family, and importantly enjoy "free will and choices" has no tender feelings at all towards Eric and deeply resents the way she has been forced into a new state of being. "Romance is dead," she says. "Boy doesn't meet girl anymore and fall in love with her. Now he kidnaps her and turns her into a vampire." The only benefits she can see with the vampire existence is that her telepathic ability has been lost and that she can shield her own mind from Eric's prying thoughts. It is, however, her ability to also lift this shield that brings her salvation in the end. Without access to her emotions, Eric cannot fathom why she would protest against a future with money and power, but when she lets him see that in her eyes he is "a monster," not for being a vampire but for robbing her of her life, he grudgingly releases the power he has over her as maker. Sookie's last action, illustrating the return of free will and choice, is to step out of the plane into her "first and last sunrise." Romance remains a fond but distant memory for Sookie in this fanfic and her own two deaths, as a human and as a vampire, are consequences of its death.

* * *

The alternative or exaggerated renderings of evil, morally corrupt monsters in fan fiction can be seen as a reaction to the general humanization of the vampire in contemporary texts and to the paradox inherent in this development. The sympathetic vampire's metaphysical plights have become more applicable to the human state and consequently present options to explore human evil through the vampire. But increasingly humanized vampires mean diminished opportunities to investigate forms of evil that in the words of Joan Gordon and Veronica Hollinger, can "provide guidelines *against which* we can define ourselves" (5, our italics). Fan fictions analyzed in this chapter demonstrate desires to reinforce the human/monster boundary in order to effect other lines of questioning than the canons seem to allow. The selected stories reclaim the threat and danger traditionally associated with the vampire trope; they ask important questions about what it means to be evil, what consequences there are, and what happens when monsters, once again, are clearly monstrous.

McGinn argues, "We are [the monsters'] creators, the source of their monstrosity; they have the attributes we give to them" and while the canon creators invest the vampires with particular characteristics and particular forms of monstrosity, so do fanfic authors (144). The majority of the stories analyzed in this chapter does not negate the vampires' canon competencies, but rather exaggerate these in depictions of blood hunger and transformational processes. It is predictably on the level of ethics that the stories transgress the canon norms when the vampires next door become more menacing and guided by their true nature. In all cases, however, the fan fictions expand their respective archives with suggestions of alternative developments and characters' fates. In fanfic, revenants hunt for both blood and sport, unapologetically so because blood lust is a part of who they are; they have been reduced by the "unnatural" choices previously made. The shifted narrative perspectives illustrated by the majority of stories entail that the monsters look into their mirrors and see themselves. Processes of recognition are sometimes painful, sometimes liberating, but foregrounded is that the canons' human norms are seen as limiting and constrictive, post-transformation or in the embracing of the vampire state.

Conclusion: The Vampire Archived and Re-Fanged

I own nothing, I just borrow occasionally. Okay, so I borrow a lot, but I always give back. —Beckylady, *Six Degrees of Separation*, story notes

We will never be able to return to Meyer's Twilight series or the film adaptations and see Edward Cullen only as the romantic and sparkling gentleman-cum-superhero Bella falls for. There will always be traces of fanfic versions of Edward adding layers of interpretation to his personality. We now know that he is capable of enough self-restraint to give Bella the kind of intimacy she is longing for; or that in his heart, he actually dreams of a future with one of the muscular werewolves Seth or Jacob. We have also learned that the Salvatore brothers are driven by desires not always explored in The Vampire Diaries. Damon's tormented thoughts about his traumatic background and father issues affect future readings of him, as do the details about his monstrous cruelty which will also remain connoted to this character. Stefan, we have come to understand, is not only convinced that the vampiric state is damning, but is also exceedingly bored with it. And when encountering Bill Compton and Eric Northman again, the canon depictions of them as more or less evil will compete in our minds with images of intense soul searching or a past existence in which vampires did not mainstream but unapologetically took what they desired. The canon texts provide a background and a filter, but the fanfic renditions, those discussed in this book, and the countless others we have read over the years, accompany us when we return to the canons. The archives of Twilight, The Vampire Diaries and True Blood are endlessly and continuously expanded.

Abigail Derecho argues that

> to write or read or study fanfic is to admit that the text is never stable, that virtualities inside source texts are perpetually in the process of becoming actual-

ized, that between texts in a given archive there is repetition with a difference, and that the interplay between the texts can never be solidified and stilled, for fear of losing the difference, the spark, the chaos that is invention and innovation [75].

The somewhat schizophrenic situation outlined above, where Edward is simultaneously faithful to Bella and acting on his homosexual impulses, where the Salvatores are monstrous, conflicted, and tender at once, and where Bill's and Eric's past and present experiences exist simultaneously, one as real as the other, is a result of fanfic authors upholding a creative chaos. The multitude of associations point, precisely, to the fact that as long as texts are interacted with, they are alive and can continue to contribute meaning, and that the parts are as important as the whole. Rather than fixing meanings, identities, bodies, and words, these are in a state of flux, and each new interpretation, inspired and affected by the canon, affects the canon in turn.

The endless possibilities that each archontic text holds, and which are invoked by the simple question "what if?" are concretely made manifest in fanfic. Authors' interest in what the story would be like told from another perspective result in varied new associations to minor characters and new views on the canons' narrators and focalizers. Curiosity about what happened before Forks, Mystic Falls/Fell's Church, and Bon Temps became homes to vampires adds detailed examinations of the vampires' backstories, as human and as newly turned, to each archive. And what if the story does not end where the canon creator has left it? What if the characters move on to new adventures, battling new unforeseen threats, or explore a new relationship? Unencumbered by the necessity for plot and character consistency and chronological developments, fanfic associations, readings and alternatives are inserted in the gaps of the canon text, ignoring some plot developments and exaggerating others. The continuous play with characters, plot strands and narrative elements, while not automatically subversive or resistive, ensures that meaning is always in a state of flux. Subversion and resistance are more clearly illustrated in the fanfics analyzed in the last two chapters, and demonstrate to a higher degree that authors also move outside the canon texts and find inspiration in other narratives and other genres, inspiration which is used to fill some gaps and to create others.

It is in fanfics which depict a transgressive sexuality and sexual practices, and which explore questions of monstrosity with emphasis on horror and damnation, that the vampire is most clearly re-fanged, figuratively or literally. Contesting the canons' sexual ethics — monogamy, abstinence or heteronormativity, whatever the case may be — fanfic renditions of characters who are sexually experimental, who inflict or receive pain, who are exaggeratedly skilled in the arts of seduction and giving pleasure, recuperate figurative fangs in the return to a vampirism which is sexually threatening and brings out the victim's latent desires. The blurred lines between vampires and humans are redrawn in fanfics which literally bring the fangs into play; when vampires are re-monsterized and recognize themselves as truly Other, and when they abandon their diets and go for the jugular. The paranormal romance genre in which the canons are situated, and which forms one structural part of the archontic text, becomes increasingly promiscuous. Sexually graphic fanfic features elements from erotica and pornography and in stories in which the monster is let loose, aspects from the Gothic and horror cast a new gloss on both characters and romance.

The vampires in the canon, romantically attractive neighbors, have in our discussions about genre, sexuality and teratology (chapters one, four, and five, respectively) seemed far removed from their precedents in the literary tradition. While they remain Other in some respects, and are never completely at home next door, there are tendencies in the canons to fix them into set positions and to make them fully understandable to the female protagonists who are irrevocably drawn to them. On the subjects of monsters, Rosi Braidotti claims that their

> [d]ifference will just not go away. And because this embodiment of difference moves, flows, changes; because it propels discourses without ever settling into them, because it evades us in the very process of puzzling us, it will never be known what the next monster is going to look like; nor will it be possible to guess where it will come from. And because we *cannot* know, the monster is always going to get us [150].

Fanfic ensures that the archontic text will never come to rest, and fanfic processes of re-fanging means that the monster will become what Braidotti envisions, even when it originates in a canon which desires to calcify its meaning. While some characterizations return in sexually graphic and horror-influenced fanfic, the multitude of representations adds to the archive an endless variation. When starting to read a fanfic, it is impossible to determine what shape the monster will take, or, indeed, where it will come from; sometimes, as we have seen, it is the female protagonists rather than the vampires who are the real beasts. Consequently, even if the canons set boundaries and make definitions, the ever-expanding archives ensure that the monster *will* get us.

As particularized written readings of the canons, fan fictions thus illustrate how readers and viewers of these contemporary popular texts interact with them; how they comply with some messages, intended or not, and how they resist others. The variation illustrated by the selected stories analyzed in this book further shows how details which are seen as insignificant by many (perhaps even the canon creators) can acquire a profound meaning for an individual reader. By moving fanfic texts into the same neighborhood as printed intertextual fictions, be these earlier derivative texts or contemporary mash-ups and "co-authored," spiced up classics, this play with levels of signification is clearly demonstrated. And by borrowing methods and theories from the field of literary studies, like fanfic authors we give something back: an expanded knowledge of a form of intertextuality that is archontic rather than hierarchical and of the function fanfic fills in studies of contemporary, literary creativity.

Chapter Notes

Introduction

1. Stoker's novel is published in the e-book series Clandestine Classics. Readers are reassured on the publisher's website, "You only pay for the words our authors have added, NOT for the original content" (Total E-Bound Publishing, "Dracula" n. pag.).
2. The relatively new e-format has been mentioned as a reason for the texts' success as it enables readers to peruse them on tablets and e-readers without a revealing cover, and thus immerse themselves in the raunchy "mommy porn" without divulging this to fellow morning commuters (see Schwartzbaum n. pag.).
3. Formatting in all quotations correspond to the original unless noted.
4. Bronwen Thomas' short article "What Is Fanfiction and Why Are People Saying Such Nice Things About It?" (2011) provides a brief overview of these stages, and the introduction to the anthology *Fandom: Identity and Communities in a Mediated World* (Gray, Sandvoss and Harrington 2005) offers a more comprehensive account.
5. Later surveys point in the same direction regarding gender, some giving even higher percentages of female fans and fan writers in fandoms (see, for example, Brooker 134, and Cicioni 154).
6. Moretti's discussion is found in *Signs Taken for Wonders*, 24–27.
7. There are two grammatically distinct ways in which the term canon is used, the most common within fandoms being an adjectival meaning. A statement such as "Edward's golden eyes are canon" exemplifies this adjectival use: something, that is, can be described as *being* canon. This usage naturally means that the plural form (canons) is not employed. In our analyses and discussions, we will use the noun form, the canon, to denote the concrete textual artifacts fan fiction stands in relation to. The statement above would in this usage be transformed into "Edward's eyes are golden in the canon." Since we are concerned with three textual universes we will also employ the noun in the plural form (canons).
8. We have opted to designate the True Blood canon as such despite the fact that Harris' novel series which forms such an integral part of it has a different name. In contemporary discussions, True Blood is in a similar way often used as an umbrella term, for example in the volume *True Blood and Philosophy* (2010) in which authors still extensively discuss Harris' novels.
9. In November 2012, Wikipedia lists around sixty ongoing series, both adult and juvenile ("Vampire literature").

Chapter 1

1. There are numerous websites the reader can consult for more comprehensive summaries of each of the canon works, such as Wikipedia and IMDB, author and production company sites, and individually maintained homepages devoted to specific canons, or specific characters.
2. The potential for promiscuity is used in contemporary publishing and marketing, in attempts to appeal to as wide an audience as possible. On Barnesandnoble.com, in December 2011, the first of Charlaine Harris' Sookie Stackhouse novels *Dead Until Dark* is

described as "a delightful hybrid of mystery, science fiction, and romance" ("Sookie Stackhouse series" n. pag.). This hybridity is emphasized by the number of categories in which the novel is placed: in "Vampire Thrillers" and "Mystery & Crime" as well as in the Fantasy sections "Contemporary" and "Epic," and in the Crime Fiction category under both "Women Sleuths" and "Psychics & Supernatural Sleuths." Finally, they are found in the sub-category "Vampires" under "Paranormal & Fantastic Romance," the latter, in turn, found under Romance and Science Fiction, and Fantasy & Horror. The categorizations of the *True Blood* DVDs suggest a more limited range of generic belongings: in December 2011, Amazon.com associates it with "Horror," "Fantasy," and "Romance" (with the added label "Drama" for the fourth season). It can be argued that there is an element of randomness in categorizations of both written and visual materials, which is arguably connected to commercial concerns, but taken together they on the one hand demonstrate the porosity of the genres in question (and of their definitions), and on the other provide readers and viewers with various interpretative grids.

3. Nor is it only ritual in the twentieth-century romantic suspense novels Regis discusses (150).

4. The lack of parental authority is lessened even more in the TV series *The Vampire Diaries*, where Elena's Aunt Jenna is only a few years older than herself.

5. Harris has published several short stories set in the "Sookieverse." Her collection *A Touch of Dead* (2009) features many, but not all, of them.

Chapter 2

1. Pairings as a term is linked to another: ships (relationships), but was originally not thought to have the same romantic connotation. There is quite a lot of confusion here, as is evident, and some terms have come to stand for other things than they originally did. Pairing suggests that the story should be about couples (twosomes), but as fanfic authors have started inserting the slash or the ampersand merely to signal what characters are featured, pairings also run the risk of becoming ineffective in searches.

2. The title calls to mind the Irving Stone biography of Michelangelo (1961), although no explicit reference is given by Cavalier Queen. The chapter is the penultimate in the version published on Archive of Our Own. On FanFiction.net, three chapters are posted after it, but the final two contain additional information about the author and about her upcoming fanfics, and do not continue the story.

3. In the A/Ns for chapter 19, Cavalier Queen states that she has not "read past book 2" in Harris' series and in these novels as well as in the seasons of the TV series aired at this point, the canon pairing is Sookie/Bill.

4. It should be noted that fanfic authors are not the only ones writing themselves, or improved versions of themselves, into an existing canon. J.R. Ward, for example, conducts interviews with vampire characters from her series The Black Dagger Brotherhood on her homepage ("The Brothers").

5. The difference between various forms of originality is highlighted by the emphasis on the inclusion of a disclaimer in connection with each fanfic. It is suggested in the submission guidelines that authors use a version of the following text: "All publicly recognizable characters, settings, etc. are the property of their respective owners. The original characters and plot are the property of the author. The author is in no way associated with the owners, creators, or producers of any media franchise. No copyright infringement is intended."

6. Real Person Fiction (RPF) predictably centers on actors, artists, or celebrities rather than on fictional characters.

7. Gwenllian Jones' definition of a "virtual universe" encompasses "industry and production conditions, cast, crew and creators, fandom and fan-produced texts, publicity and promotional material, and merchandise. It extends its embrace to include the histories, myths, religions, customs and timescapes invoked by the series, as well as its actual and fictional geographies" ("Starring" 10).

8. It should be noted that the term fic is commonly used as an abbreviation and does not automatically signal a distance from the fan aspect.

9. Smith's novels of course predate Twilight and so cannot have been inspired by the latter in featuring the rampant-running theme.

Piper's comment rather indicates that she has become increasingly aware of this theme through her acquaintance with Twilight.

10. The situation further corresponds to a scene in which Bella cuts herself in order to distract attacking vampires, thus imitating "the third wife" of Quileute legends (Meyer, *Eclipse* 212–236, 478). Using Shakespeare rather than Quileute mythology as a model for the human protagonist, Lisse forges yet another link to the canon, while giving it a twist.

11. When turned in the canon, Bella presents a more literal threat to humans even if she is able to control her bloodlust. By holding her breath as she encounters hikers during her first hunt, she is able to refocus and instead feed off a mountain lion and a deer (Meyer, *Breaking Dawn* 385–392).

Chapter 3

1. There is a fourth strategy: to fill in narrative gaps in the canon without expanding on or influencing events that come before or after them. While stories about these kinds of missing moments often fall into the switched perspective category of transformation, there are also those which retain the narrative voice found in the canon. Examples of these kinds of stories are rare, however, as most authors exhibit an interest in developing or altering aspects of the canon.

2. We want to remind the reader that the label fan fiction can be misleading, as in some instances authors are clearly not fans of the canon they use as a starting point.

3. Derecho's "history of archontic literature as a medium of political and social protest" takes its starting point in female-authored 17th-century texts connected to Sir Philip Sidney's *The Countess of Pembroke's Arcadia* (67).

4. Questions of ownership are sometimes raised by canon authors and a well-publicized example is Anne Rice's message on her home page in April 2000: "The characters are copyrighted. It upsets me terribly to even think about fan fiction with *my* characters" ("Anne Rice on Fan Fiction," our italics). In an interview on the site Twifans.com Stephenie Meyer voices a similar view of ownership when stating, in connection with authors of Twilight fanfic, "I think it's sad to spend so much energy on something you can't own" ("Stephenie Meyer on fan fiction"). However, her own attempt to enter the fanfic contest "Take a walk in my shoes" with a story from Rosalie's perspective seems to indicate that her attitude towards both fans and fanfic is benevolent, and she includes numerous links to fanfic sites on her homepage.

5. Derecho's discussion builds on Glissant's *Poetics of Relation* (1990).

6. The nine parts were originally published on FanFiction.net between December 2008 and February 2009 and only a week after the last installment as one text on EricNorthman.net, a site launched in January 2009. It is the latter version we have used in the analysis. At this point, only one season of *True Blood* had been aired, but eight novels had been published in Charlaine Harris' series. On FanFiction.net, *The Deep* was filed in the book section, but on EricNorthman.net, there is no division between books and TV series, rather, authors file according to category. *The Deep* is categorized as Drama.

7. Although *The Deep* was originally published in the book section of FanFiction.net, it should be pointed out that the eleventh episode of the first season of *True Blood*, aired in November 2008 (before the publication of the fanfic) is entitled, precisely, "To Love is to Bury."

8. Recollected conversation is represented in italics in the fanfic.

9. Fanfics about Bill's past reflect these more difficult relationship dynamics and often include the dissolution of the maker/child bond, necessary for Bill's character development. In Eternallybills' *Hunger*, for example, he reflects, "She [Lorena] made me forget my humanity, but I battled my way back to it over the decades since my release."

10. A one-shot is a fanfic consisting of only one chapter. It is not uncommon for one-shots to be combined, as Beckylady's, to form a longer text in which each part is freestanding.

11. In an interview on the Twilight Lexicon site Meyer simply states that Bella's mother's maiden name was Higginbotham, which Beckylady then uses in her fictive time-traveling.

12. It is thus a sequel to this season, but not to the canon generally.

13. There is a natural comparison here

with Twilight in which Bella and Edward similarly are thought unable to procreate. In line with *The Vampire Diaries*' reflexive stance, badboy_fangirl has Elena's college roommate Lydia exclaim: "Elena! Are you going to have a demon baby, like Bella and Edward?"

14. Parrish notes that only "about one tenth … a surprisingly low percentage" of the stories she has examined feature the pairing (182).

15. Burke's use of the term "Indian" is deliberate because of Meyer's reliance on the homogenous "American construction of Indianness" rather than an acknowledgement of the heterogeneity of First Nations (208). It should also be noted that although Meyer refers to shape shifters rather than werewolves in the novels, the shape they do shift into is invariably that of wolf.

16. The notion of teams is not confined to Twilight, although subsequent references are derived from fanfic connected to this canon, and also in other fandoms it is not uncommon that fans profess their allegiance to several, and include discussions about how their own choices have shifted and changed.

17. The publication of eight novels in Harris' series before the TV series' first season makes analyses of fanfic more complex as authors, even when stories are filed in the TV section (on sites which permit this), may be influenced by plot developments in the written canon texts.

18. Fanfic crossovers naturally abound with characters who have never encountered each other before, but this text form is not considered further in what follows.

19. In September 2012, there were two fanfics based on the novels which have Caroline as a tag on Archive of Our Own, and in both stories, centered on other pairings, she is a minor character. On Fell's Church Library there were three, but here as well, she is not part of the central pairing. TwilightTales, exclusively devoted to book fanfic, featured three stories with Caroline, but the only specifically romantic/erotic pairing is with Meredith in a femslash fanfic. On FanFiction.net, there were three romance stories ostensibly based on the novels and featuring Caroline, but narrative details and characters' names (Tyler Lockwood, for example) show that they are based on the TV series and thus misfiled (Tyler's last name in the novels is Smallwood).

20. We discuss fanfic renderings of mind-manipulation in chapters four and five with emphasis on how it represents a transgression of physical boundaries leading to issues of non-consent. In *Forget Me Not*, Tara not only consents to having her memories erased and her attitude to vampires shifted, but asks to be glamoured.

21. The inconvenient fact that Sam also in this fanfic has imprinted on Emily, and misses her when the story starts, is dealt with as Emily has a rather realistic reaction to being hurt by him which contributes to Sam's vulnerable state. Sam tells Bella that he has visited Emily at the hospital after the traumatic event and offered to kill himself. Her response is "I hope you burn in hell, but I'm not going to send you there." Sam continues by saying, "She sent me away, though, and it was almost the same thing. She broke the imprint. It's supposed to be unbreakable but it's also supposed to be whatever she needs, and she needed me gone, so I went. But doing it almost ended me."

Chapter 4

1. In fanfic discussions in general, the terms are becoming more rarely employed. In connection with fanfic working from our three canons, however, they still seem to be viable and meaningful terms and are at times complemented with others, similarly taken from the world of citrus fruits. The "Citrus Scale" indicates levels of sexual intimacy with "citrus" merely denoting that sex is featured, "Orange," "Lime," and "Lemon" indicating increased sexual contents, and the rarely occurring "Grapefruit," finally, signaling "X-rated or truly bizarre lemons" (Wikia, "Citrus Scale" n. pag.).

2. In *Dead Until Dark*, Sookie muses, "I was beginning to see that the ability to have sex for several centuries leaves room for lots of experimentation" (Harris 114) and in *Club Dead* she concludes, "Vampires seem, as a whole, to be extremely tolerant of any sexual preference; I guess there aren't that many taboos when you've been alive a few hundred years" (Harris 182).

3. Despite Twilight's Young Adult label, it is widely appreciated also by adult audiences, as evidenced for instance by sites like Twilightmoms.com.

4. Beds and bedding are similarly casualties of Edward's lapsed self-control in the canon (Meyer, *Breaking Dawn* 81, 99).

5. LaTessitrice originally published a short version of *The Courtyard* on Twilighted.net (2009) and under the pseudonym La_Tessitore, which we have analyzed in more detail in "Gazing, Initiating, Desiring" (2011). In the version we have used here, the original text is featured as the first of fifteen chapters.

6. Discussions in various fan forums show a consensus regarding Edward's virginity before meeting Bella, although Meyer's novels do not state this explicitly. This is rather inferred from his statements about not having met the right girl until he found Bella. Lydia Kokkola, evincing a reading similar to those in fan forums, writes: "Edward is still a virgin. Despite several female vampires' attempts at seducing him, he has remained chaste, waiting for someone he can truly love" (171).

7. Many of the fanfics discussed in the later sections of this chapter bring alternative choices and desires into the present and examine lasting relationships between same-sex partners.

8. This girlish and innocent behavior ties back to the title of the fic, *Cherry-flavored lip gloss*, which is an intertextual play on a line from Katy Perry's song "I Kissed a Girl (and I Liked It)," in which one of the things the singer claims to have liked is "the taste of her cherry Chapstick."

9. See Pam Keesey's anthology *Daughters of Darkness* (237–43) for a more complete filmography/bibliography.

10. It should be noted that Brite's depiction of vampire propagation can be read as despondently misogynistic, as the women who give birth to vampires invariably die and that other women are featured mainly as sources for amusement and pleasure. Trevor Holmes, among others, notes this as a distinct problem in the novel, "although one not without precedent in the real world" (182).

11. The couple agrees on a safe word at a later stage in the fanfic, and in a play on the animosity between Eric and Bill, and their different approach to most things, it is "Bill Compton."

12. Among the examples of the vampire erotica and pornography (she does not make a distinction) Bosky analyzes are Pat Califia's "The Vampire" (1988) and stories from Cecilia Tan's anthologies *Blood Kiss* (1994) and *Erotica Vampirica* (1996).

Chapter 5

1. As was made clear in the "Interlude," processes of normalization underlie our discussions about both canon and fanfic, but are not explicitly addressed in each instance. We refer to vampires as evil and monstrous either when they behave in ways which go against the canon ethics, or when they are described as such by canon and fanfic authors.

2. The loss of fangs sets the Twilight vampires apart but there are, of course, several depictions of a literal defangedness. In Suzy McKee Charnaz' *The Vampire Tapestry* (1980), Weyland has no fangs as he has adapted to fit into society to more easily be able to hunt. In Dan Simmons' *Carrion Comfort* (1989) vampires control minds and feed off of feelings of hatred and violence rather than blood. A literal absence of fangs does not mean that the vampire's threat is diminished or that draining cannot be featured in more symbolic forms.

3. Ethnographers and anthropologists have been interested in "real" vampires (people exhibiting physical signs and ailments aligning them with vampirism) and trace how the vampire is figured in folk lore (for example Summers, *The Vampire in Europe*). Scholars focusing on the Gothic or horror have situated the vampire within these genres and thus seen the figure as part of larger structures (see Punter, *The Literature of Terror* and Jones, *Horror*). The revenant has also been studied from psychoanalytic perspectives with emphasis on what fears and desires it embodies (see Rickles 1999). The vampire's place within general literary history has also been exhaustively analyzed with particular stress on what contemporary issues it can be said to address (in, for example, Gelder, *Reading the Vampire* and Gordon and Hollinger *Blood Read*).

4. The only link to the issue of contagion is True Blood's play with the figuration of "[t]he politically correct theory" of the vampire as a "victim of a virus that left him apparently dead for a couple of days and thereafter allergic to sunlight, silver, and garlic" (*Dead Until Dark* 2). However, details are sketchy and depend on the news source and the vampirism-as-virus explanation is soon

abandoned in favor of a more traditional transformation based on blood exchange.

5. The quest for Dracula, in contrast, is performed by the Crew of Light (whose members can substantiate each other's discoveries) and falls into general classification projects of the Victorian era, as well as into the period's allocation of power and knowledge according to gender and class.

6. In situations where vampires are pitted against each other, rules are considerably different. As a minority community in True Blood, vampires perform sanctioned destructions of each other using traditional means (exposing the victim to sunlight) and their use of powers is naturalized. Since the vampire secret is fiercely protected in Twilight and The Vampire Diaries, vampires can kill other vampires without anyone noticing or condemning them, and using paranormal powers on each other is part and parcel of their existence.

7. We have not found any indications that a corresponding volume connected to our third canon is in the works, but the majority of anthologies published so far deal with paranormal popular culture texts. Among the examples are *Superman*, *The Hobbit*, and *Game of Thrones* (Wiley, "The Blackwell Philosophy and Pop Culture Series").

8. In his analysis of Anne Rice's *Interview with the Vampire*, David Punter foreshadows the inside joke by likening Louis to "a kind of vegetarian bloodsucker" because of his animal diet (*The Literature of Terror: The Modern Gothic* 161).

9. One meaning of the last name of Meyer's vampires naturally connects to this approach: they cull the flock of animals in an eco-friendly way to maintain its size. Another meaning of to cull is to select the best examples from a sample, resulting in a better-than-average group, which, it can be argued, is what Carlisle has accomplished.

10. Both fanfics are published before Elena is turned in the canon.

11. The story, filed in the TV section at Archive of Our Own, is published after the second season and Bill's betrayal has not yet been revealed. The author takes inspiration from Harris' novels in her portrayal of this narrative element.

12. There are other hybrids featured in Twilight, more specifically a coven in South America to which the Cullens turn after Renesmee's birth. Among these is Nahuel who, until meeting Edward, Bella and Renesmee, has seen himself as "inherently evil ... because ... half immortal." His birth killed his mother and he was afterwards raised by his maternal aunt whose love for her dead sister "shaped his whole perspective" (Meyer, *Breaking Dawn* 696). There is thus an implicit linking of hybridity and liminality with evil, even if this is later refuted.

13. Despite presenting very different takes on both vampire myths and romance, there is a parallel here with vampire procreation in Poppy Z. Brite's *Lost Souls*, which is similarly achieved at the cost of the human mother's life and represented as the vampire baby clawing or biting its way out of the womb.

14. In this scene, Stefan also draws attention to the ironic fact that his last name should make him a figure of salvation rather than damnation (Smith, *The Awakening* 179).

15. Jack the Ripper features into another contemporary vampire text, Kim Newman's metatextual novel *Anno Dracula* (1992), in which Victorian England is ruled not only by the Queen, but by the Prince Consort, Count Dracula. The Whitechapel murders are here similarly carried out by a medical professional, Doctor Jack Seward.

16. In analyses of Buffyverse slash, Virginia Keft-Kennedy argues that rape is "a seductively aestheticised fantasy ... discursively constructed through the literary tropes of the vampiric" (60). The vampire's bite as an analogy for rape is one such discursive component, as are violence and preternaturally strong bodies. In Keft-Kennedy's discussions, the receptor and distributor of pain are often both vampires.

17. Neither, it should be pointed out, do epitextual comments suggest discomfort with the depicted events; rather, readers profess their attraction to the evil and dark Damon.

18. A corresponding situation is featured in the *True Blood* episode "Hitting the Ground" (3:7) although the issue of rape is downplayed.

19. The fanfic's title intertextually references Meyer's novel draft *Midnight Sun* in which events in *Twilight* are narrated from Edward's perspective.

Works Cited

Primary Sources

Fan Fictions

Many of the accessed fan fictions are intended for mature readers and require verification that the reader is over eighteen, a verification which becomes part of the URL. This verification is removed in the entries below. In cases where fanfics have different publishing dates and update dates, we refer to the latter.

badboy_fangirl. *Saved by Grace. Archive of Our Own.* 23 Dec. 2011. Web. 5 Apr. 2012. http://archiveofourown.org/works/300586.
Beckylady. *Six Degrees of Separation. Twilighted.* 28 Feb. 2009. Web. 10 Sept. 2012. http://twilighted.net/viewseries.php?seriesid=212.
Bogwitch. *Blood, the Tooth and the Claw. FanFiction.net.* 4 June 2011. Web. 15 Nov. 2012. http://www.fanfiction.net/s/7050945.
Carson Dyle. *Morning. Twilighted.* 5. Nov. 2011. Web. 7 June 2012. http://www.twilighted.net/viewstory.php?sid=14562.
CatsOnMars. *The Golden Phase of Dying Leaves. Archive of Our Own.* 24 Jan. 2012. Web. 6 Sept. 2012. http://archiveofourown.org/works/326660.
CavalierQueen. *Paradise Within: Happier Far. FanFiction.net.* 16 Nov. 2009. Web. 20 Feb. 2012. http://www.fanfiction.net/s/5009969; *Archive of Our Own.* 5 Sept. 2010. Web. 20 Feb. 2012. http://archiveofourown.org/works/112383.
Chiyoku Shibata. *Stefan's Thoughts. FanFiction.net.* 12 May 2011. Web. 15 Nov. 2012. http://www.fanfiction.net/s/6986285/.
colacherry. *Castration Frustration. FanFiction.net.* 26 July 2009. Web. 6 Nov. 2012. http://www.fanfiction.net/s/5251175.
CrowX. *Love Is Not Consolation. FanFiction.net.* 7 July 2011. Web. 3 Nov. 2012. http://www.fanfiction.net/s/6812233.
cyclogenesis. *Demons. LiveJournal.* 16 Feb. 2012. Web. 5 Nov. 2012. http://cyclogenesis.livejournal.com/147275.html.
Daddy's Little Cannibal. *When Life Gives You Lemons. FanFiction.net.* 17 July 2008. Web. 18 Sept. 2012. http://www.fanfiction.net/s/4250523.
DCWriter16. *The Deep. EricNorthman.net.* 9 Feb. 2009 Web. 3 May 2012. http://www.ericnorthman.net/fanfic/viewstory.php?sid=35.
dreaming in black and white. *Alice, Interrupted. Twilighted.* 10 Jan. 2012. Web. 12 Sept. 2012. http://twilighted.net/viewstory.php?sid=16080.
Eleai. *Absolution. FanFiction.net.* 25 May 2012. Web. 6 Dec. 2012. http://www.fanfiction.net/s/8057957/.

Ellen Smithee. *Lead Me Not into Temptation.* FanFiction.net. 23 June 2012. Web. 15 Nov. 2012. http://www.fanfiction.net/s/7109436/.

EricBonesVladCurran. *Aftermath.* FanFiction.net. 20 Aug. 2009. Web. 27 Sept. 2012. http://www.fanfiction.net/s/5317593/1/.

Estora. *Eighteen.* FanFiction.net. 23 Mar. 2009. Web. 30 Oct. 2012. http://www.fanfiction.net/s/4942443/1/.

———. *Seven.* FanFiction.net. 30 Sept. 2008. Web. 30 Oct. 2012. http://www.fanfiction.net/s/4567400/1/.

Eternallybills. *Hunger.* FanFiction.net. 19 June 2010. Web. 14 Nov. 2011. http://www.fanfiction.net/s/6031096/1/.

———. *No Thrill Left in Feeding on the Willing.* Wiki'd Women. 29 May 2010. Web. 18 May 2012. http://billswikidwomen.wetpaint.com/page/No+Thrill+Left+in+Feeding+on+the+Willing.

exeterlinden. *Waters Will Keep Running, Rivers Will Turn.* Archive of Our Own. 20 Dec. 2010. Web. 10 Nov. 2011. http://archiveofourown.org/works/142159.

faithunbreakable. *The Lepidopterist.* FanFiction.net. 9 July 2011. Web. 10 Dec. 2010. http://www.fanfiction.net/s/7162585/1/.

———. *Swansong.* FanFiction.net. 31 Dec. 2010. Web. 10 Dec. 2011. http://www.fanfiction.net/s/6222044/1/.

fembuck/Janine. *Damsel.* FanFiction.net. 24 May 2009. Web. 14 Oct. 2011. http://www.fanfiction.net/s/5084157/1/.

———. *The Edge.* LiveJournal. 14 Oct. 2008. Web. 28 Oct. 2011. http://fembuck.livejournal.com/204275.html?mode=reply.

———. *A Girl Like You, A Place Like This.* Dreamwidth. 26 July 2011. Web. 6 Nov. 2012. http://fembuck.dreamwidth.org/21629.html.

Finta. *Secrecy.* Twilight Tales. 2 Dec. 2004. Web. 4 Apr. 2012. http://www.ttales.net/fic/finta/secrecy.txt.

flute_genevive. *In the Land of One Thousand Years.* Twilighted. 23 Dec. 2008. Web. 11 Sept 2012. http://twilighted.net/viewstory.php?sid=1521.

4CullensandaBlack. *There's Always Room for More.* FanFiction.net. 22 Nov. 2011. Web. 15 Oct. 2012. http://www.fanfiction.net/s/7572076.

4theluvofMary. *Magic in the Midnight Sun.* FanFiction.net. 26 Sept. 2010. Web. 9 Nov. 2011. http://www.fanfiction.net/s/6353530.

glitter and stardust. *Lullaby.* FanFiction.net. 18 Aug. 2009. Web. 16 Aug. 2012. http://www.fanfiction.net/s/5312532/.

havocthecat. *Nothing of the Kind.* Archive of Our Own. 22 Dec. 2010. Web. 5 Nov. 2012. http://archiveofourown.org/static/collections/yuletide2010/works/142867.

Heyl13. *The Blue Book of Pain.* Archive of Our Own. 10 June 2012. Web. 13 Sept. 2012. http://archiveofourown.org/works/430213.

jazzywazzy08. *Contact.* The Writer's Coffee Shop. 7 June 2012. Web. 27 Sept. 2012. http://www.thewriterscoffeeshop.com/library/viewstory.php?sid=6496.

jenny_haniver. *Opus.* Archive of Our Own. 24 May 2011. Web. 17 Dec. 2012. http://archiveofourown.org/works/203745.

Lady Dragoncrow. *The Beauty of the Dark.* Fell's Church Library. 3 May 2011. Web. 4 Oct. 2012. http://fanfic.vampire-diaries.net/viewstory.php?sid=293&warning=4.

L'amante di Destino. *True Twilight.* FanFiction.net. 29 Sept. 2009. Web. 15 Mar. 2012. http://www.fanfiction.net/u/1851965/.

LaTessitrice. *The Courtyard.* Archive of Our Own. 6 Oct. 2011. Web. 1 Nov. 2012. http://archiveofourown.org/works/261487/.

Lenore. *Lessons in Being Inhuman: Two Vignettes.* Archive of Our Own. 1 Sept. 2011. Web. 10 Nov 2011. http://archiveofourown.org/works/247426.

levitatethis. *Aberration*. Archive of Our Own. 5 Sept. 2009. Web. 10 Nov. 2011. http://archiveofourown.org/works/56914.
———. *Dismantled*. Archive of Our Own. 22 Sept. 2009. Web. 10 Nov. 2011. http://archiveofourown.org/works/56913.
———. *Strange Infatuation*. Archive of Our Own. 13 Mar. 2010. Web. 10 Nov. 2011. http://archiveofourown.org/works/70076.
light4dawn. *Chains*. Archive of Our Own. 9 Nov. 2011. Web. 6 Sept. 2012. http://archiveofourown.org/works/375752.
———. *Masks*. Archive of Our Own. 28 Oct. 2011 Web. 6 Sept. 2012. http://archiveofourown.org/works/375738.
lil_utterance. *Order Up*. Archive of Our Own. 28 Dec. 2009. Web. 31 Oct. 2011. http://archiveofourown.org/works/40429.
linaerys. *Human Things*. Archive of Our Own. 23 Dec. 2010. Web. 10 Nov. 2011. http://archiveofourown.org/works/143137.
LingeringLuminosity. *Ownership, Apologies and Being Kicked In The Nuts*. FanFiction.net. 30 Oct. 2008. Web. 30 Oct. 2012. http://www.fanfiction.net/s/4625431/1/.
Lisse. *Moves in Mysterious Ways*. FanFiction.net. 18 June 2008. Web. 17 Feb. 2012. http://www.fanfiction.net/s/4333491/1/.
lit_chick08. *The Past is Prologue*. Archive of Our Own. 6 Dec. 2011. Web. 10 Sept. 2012. http://archiveofourown.org/works/289427/.
LJ Summers. *Adeste Fidelis*. Twilighted. 13 Feb. 2012. Web. 12 Sept. 2012. http://twilighted.net/viewstory.php?sid=16179.
Llwy. *all lost*. Archive of Our Own. 22. Mar. 2012. Web. 7 Sept. 2012. http://archiveofourown.org/works/367480.
Lunar Siren. *Alice Smiled*. Twilighted. 12 Feb. 2010. Web. 12 Sept. 2012. http://twilighted.net/viewstory.php?sid=10372.
Maranda. *Facing the Music*. Twilighted. 10 Sept. 2011. Web. 12 Dec. 2012. http://twilighted.net/viewstory.php?sid=15581.
Megi. *Empty Sex*. Twilighted. 30 Sept. 2009. Web. 10 Sept. 2012. http://twilighted.net/viewstory.php?sid=7769.
MeraNaamJoker. *Holding Sam*. Archive of Our Own. 16 July 2011. Web. 13 Sept. 2012. http://archiveofourown.org/works/429518/.
midnightquiver. *Strong Enough*. FanFiction.net. Web. 1 June 2010. Web. 13 Sept. 2012. http://www.fanfiction.net/s/6015945/.
mneiai. *Needful Things*. Archive of Our Own. 21 Nov. 2009. Web. 31 Oct. 2012. http://archiveofourown.org/works/17554.
MyTwiDreams. *A Pre-Wedding Day Dream*. FanFiction.net. 26 Dec. 2011. Web. 6 Nov. 2012. http://www.fanfiction.net/s/7675839/.
NykkiLeighVampireHeart. *Scream*. FanFiction.net. 24 Feb. 2011. Web. 9 Nov. 2011. http://www.fanfiction.net/s/6462082/.
oliviacirce. *Show Me Your Teeth*. Archive of Our Own. 11 June 2010. Web. 12 Dec. 2012. http://archiveofourown.org/works/93859.
Piper. *The Most Impulsive Thing*. Archive of Our Own. 1 Jan. 2011. Web. 10 Nov. 2011. http://archiveofourown.org/works/146646.
pleasebekidding. *Cherry-flavoured lip gloss*. Archive of Our Own. 24 Nov. 2011. Web. 31 Oct. 2012. http://archiveofourown.org/works/282953.
———. *Lessons*. Archive of Our Own. 10 Mar. 2012. Web. 16 May 2012. http://archiveofourown.org/works/359670.
prelives. *Practice Run*. Archive of Our Own. 6 Apr. 2011. Web. 3 Nov. 2012. http://archiveofourown.org/works/178476.

psychobabblers. *The Haunting. Archive of Our Own.* 26 Mar. 2012. Web. 20 Sept. 2012. http://archiveofourown.org/works/369359.
Queenhaq. *And the Dead Keep on Living. FanFiction.net.* 17 Aug. 2009. Web. 27 Sept. 2012. http://www.fanfiction.net/s/5310488/.
Red. *On Our Way To Hell. LiveJournal.* 10 Feb. 2009. Web. 5 Nov. 2012. http://ljslash.livejournal.com/2240.html.
Roman. *The Child. Archive of Our Own.* 25 Nov. 2009. Web. 6 Aug. 2012. http://archiveofourown.org/works/20898.
———. *White Nights. Archive of Our Own.* 6 June 2006. Web. 6 Aug. 2012. http://archiveofourown.org/works/92503.
Sandrine Shaw. *Barefoot on Broken Glass (One Step at a Time). Archive of Our Own.* 21 May 2011. Web. 15 June 2011. http://archiveofourown.org/works/202707.
———. *Future Imperfect. Archive of Our Own.* 16 Feb. 2012. Web. 31 Oct. 2012. http://archiveofourown.org/works/341199.
sciphile. *Patience. Twilighted.* 3 Dec. 2009. Web. 6 Sept. 2012. http://twilighted.net/viewstory.php?sid=5885.
shoefreak37. *The Strange Design of Comfort. Twilighted.* 2 Dec. 2009 Web. 14 Aug. 2012. http://www.twilighted.net/viewstory.php?sid=9167.
smc-27. *So Cold, So Cold. FanFiction.net.* 30 Oct. 2009. Web. 27 Sept. 2012. http://www.fanfiction.net/s/5476854/.
socact. *Invitation. FanFiction.net.* 27 June 2010. Web. 3 Dec. 2012. http://www.fanfiction.net/s/6091157/.
some_stars. *What falls away. Archive of Our Own.* 20 Dec. 2009. Web. 3 Nov. 2012. http://archiveofourown.org/works/33225.
someryn. *Consolation. Archive of Our Own.* 28 Aug. 2012. Web. 6 Sept. 2012. http://archiveofourown.org/works/491480.
spaniard. *Purgatory. Twilighted.* 29 Nov. 2011. Web. 12 Sept. 2012. http://twilighted.net/viewstory.php?sid=479.
Spikey44. *Big Brother Vampire. FanFiction.net.* 5 Jan. 2011. Web. 10 Nov. 2011. http://www.fanfiction.net/s/6598465/.
stainofmylove. *Hungry Again. Archive of Our Own.* 9 Nov. 2010. Web. 5 Dec. 2010. http://archiveofourown.org/works/132417.
Suki59. *Dark Fic. FanFiction.net.* 6 Mar. 2012. Web. 28 Sept. 2012. http://www.fanfiction.net/s/7901494/.
SweetWillowTree. *The Cautionary Tale of Unconditional Love. FanFiction.net.* 10 Oct. 2011. Web. 29 Oct. 2012. http://www.fanfiction.net/s/7425691/.
Taia. *The Experiment. Twilighted.* 23 July 2010. Web. 18 Sept. 2012. http://www.twilighted.net/viewstory.php?sid=12286.
TammyDevil666. *Crave. FanFiction.net.* 17 Aug. 2009. Web. 16 Sept. 2012. http://www.fanfiction.net/s/5309681/.
Thyra10. *Eric the FanFiction Rapist. FanFiction.net.* 3 Mar. 2012. Web. 24 Oct. 2012. http://www.fanfiction.net/s/7892060/.
TWBB. *The Canonical Five. Fanfiction.net.* 17 June 2010. Web. 12 Sept. 2012. http://www.fanfiction.net/s/6060489.
22wolf. *Eric's Gift. FanFiction.net.* 14 Sept. 2010. Web. 26 Sept. 2012. http://www.fanfiction.net/s/6325068.
TwifanUK. *Fragile Monster. FanFiction.net.* 2 Nov. 2010. Web. 9 Nov. 2011. http://www.fanfiction.net/s/6447079/.
urban_folk_girl. *Human-Girl. LiveJournal.* 5 Sept. 2010. Web. 24 Apr. 2012. http://femslashheaven.livejournal.com/5176.html.

vic_vega66. *A lose, lose situation.* Archive of Our Own. 1 June 2012. Web. 29 Oct. 2012. http://archiveofourown.org/works/419230.
Winter Ashby. *Cliff Diving.* FanFiction.net. 27 Apr. 2007. Web. 17 Sept. 2012. http://www.fanfiction.net/s/3510642/.
wisedec4u. *Forget Me Not.* FanFiction.net. 4 Dec. 2010. Web. 17 Sept. 2012. http://www.fanfiction.net/s/6496192/.
_____. *Little Red Riding Hood.* FanFiction.net. 6 Oct. 2010. Web. 17 Sept. 2012. http://www.fanfiction.net/s/6350547/.
_____. *Save Me.* FanFiction.net. 26 June 2011. Web. 17 Sept. 2012. http://www.fanfiction.net/s/6901273/.
Yodigittyyoyo. *My Last Sunrise.* Archive of Our Own. 21 June 2012 Web. 25 Sept 2012. http://archiveofourown.org/works/439955.

Canon Texts

Breaking Dawn—Part 1. Dir. Bill Condon. Perf. Kirsten Stewart, Robert Pattinson, and Taylor Lautner. Summit Entertainment, 2011 Film.
Breaking Dawn—Part 2. Dir. Bill Condon. Perf. Kirsten Stewart, Robert Pattinson, and Taylor Lautner. Summit Entertainment, 2012. Film.
Eclipse. Dir. David Slade. Perf. Kirsten Stewart, Robert Pattinson, and Taylor Lautner. Summit Entertainment, 2010. Film.
Harris, Charlaine. *All Together Dead.* New York: Ace, 2007. Print.
_____. *Club Dead.* New York: Ace, 2003. Print.
_____. *Dead and Gone.* New York: Ace, 2009. Print.
_____. *Dead as a Doornail.* New York: Ace, 2005. Print.
_____. *Dead in the Family.* New York: Ace, 2010. Print.
_____. *Dead Reckoning.* New York: Ace, 2011. Print.
_____. *Dead to the World.* New York: Ace, 2004. Print.
_____. *Dead Until Dark.* New York: Ace, 2001. Print.
_____. *Deadlocked.* New York: Ace, 2012. Print.
_____. *Definitely Dead.* New York: Ace, 2006. Print.
_____. *From Dead to Worse.* New York: Ace, 2008. Print.
_____. *Living Dead in Dallas.* New York: Ace, 2002. Print.
Meyer, Stephenie. *Breaking Dawn.* 2008; London: Little, Brown, 2009. Print.
_____. *Eclipse.* 2007; London: Little, Brown, 2009. Print.
_____. *New Moon.* 2006; London: Little, Brown, 2009. Print.
_____. *Twilight.* 2006; London: Little, Brown, 2007. Print.
New Moon. Dir. Chris Weitz. Perf. Kirsten Stewart, Robert Pattinson, and Taylor Lautner. Temple Hill Entertainment, 2009. Film.
Smith, L.J. *The Awakening & The Struggle.* 1991; London: Hodder Children's Books, 2009. Print.
_____. *The Fury & The Reunion.* 1991; London: Hodder Children's Books, 2009. Print.
_____. *The Return: Midnight.* London: Hodder Children's Books, 2011. Print.
_____. *The Return: Nightfall.* 2009; London: Hodder Children's Books, 2010. Print.
_____. *The Return: Shadow Souls.* 2009; London: Hodder Children's Books, 2010. Print.
True Blood. Season 1. Prod. Alan Ball. 2008; HBO Home Video, 2009. DVD.
True Blood. Season 2. Prod. Alan Ball. 2009; HBO Home Video, 2010. DVD.
True Blood. Season 3. Prod. Alan Ball. 2010; HBO Home Video, 2011. DVD.
True Blood. Season 4. Prod. Alan Ball. HBO, 2011. Television.
Twilight. Dir. Catherine Hardwicke. Perf. Kirsten Stewart, Robert Pattinson, and Taylor Lautner. Summit Entertainment, 2008. Film.

The Vampire Diaries. Season 1. Prod. Kevin Williamson and Julie Plec. Warner Home Video, 2010. DVD.
The Vampire Diaries. Season 2. Prod. Kevin Williamson and Julie Plec. Warner Home Video, 2011. DVD.
The Vampire Diaries. Season 3. Prod. Kevin Williamson and Julie Plec. CW Television Network, 2011–12. Television.

Secondary Sources

Alexander, Jenny. "A Vampire is Being Beaten: De Sade Through the Looking Glass in *Buffy* and *Angel*." *Slayage* 4:3 (2004). N. pag. Web. 18 Dec. 2012.
Anatol, Giselle Liza, ed. *Bringing Light to Twilight: Perspectives on the Pop Culture Phenomenon.* New York: Palgrave, 2011. Print.
"Anne Rice on fan fiction." *Anne Rice.com.* N.d., n. pag. Web. 12 Apr. 2012. http://www.annerice.com.
Aubrey, Jennifer Stevens, Elizabeth Behm-Morawitz, and Melissa A. Click. "The Romanticization of Abstinence: Fan Response to Sexual Restraint in the Twilight Series." *Transformative Works and Cultures* 5 (2012): n. pag. Web. 31 Oct. 2012. Doi:10.3983/twc.2010.0216.
Auerbach, Nina. *Our Vampires, Ourselves.* Chicago: University of Chicago Press, 1995. Print.
Bacon-Smith, Camille. *Enterprising Women: Television Fandom and the Creation of Popular Myth.* Philadelphia: University of Pennsylvania Press, 1992. Print.
Bailie, Helen T. "Blood Ties: The Vampire Lover in the Popular Romance." *The Journal of American Culture* 34: 2 (2011): 141–148. Print.
Benefiel, Candace. "Blood Relations: The Gothic Perversion of the Nuclear Family in Anne Rice's *Interview with the Vampire*." *The Journal of Popular Culture* 38:2 (2004): 261–273. Print.
Benshoff, Harry M. "'Way Too Gay to Be Ignored': The Production and Reception of Queer Horror Cinema in the Twenty-First Century." Picart and Browning 131–144.
Betz, Phyllis M. *The Lesbian Fantastic: A Critical Study of Science Fiction, Fantasy, Paranormal and Gothic Writings.* Jefferson, NC: McFarland, 2011. Print.
"The Blackwell Philosophy and Pop Culture Series." *Wiley.* N.d., n. pag. Web. 14 Dec. 2012. http://eu.wiley.com
Bosky, Bernadette Lynn. "Making the Implicit, Explicit: Vampire Erotica and Pornography." Heldreth and Pharr 217–233.
Botting, Fred. *Gothic Romanced.* London: Routledge, 2008. Print.
Braidotti, Rosi. "Signs of Wonder and Traces of Doubt: On Teratology and Embodied Difference." *Between Monsters, Goddesses and Cyborgs: Feminist Confrontations with Science, Medicine and Cyberspace.* Eds. Nina Lykke and Rosi Braidotti. London: Zed, 1996. 135–152. Print.
Brite, Poppy Z. *Lost Souls.* 1992; New York: Dell, 1993. Print.
Brooker, Will. *Using the Force: Creativity, Community and* Star Wars *Fans.* New York: Continuum, 2002. Print.
"The Brothers." *J.R. Ward.* 2009. N. pag. Web. 5 Dec. 2012. http://www.jrward.com.
Burke, Brianna. "The Great American Love Affair: Indians in the *Twilight* Saga." Anatol 207–219. Print.
Busse, Kristina. "Crossing the Final Taboo: Family, Sexuality, and Incest in Buffyverse Fan Fiction." *Fighting the Forces: What's at Stake in Buffy the Vampire Slayer?* Eds. Rhonda V. Wilcox and David Lavery. Lanham, MD: Rowman & Littlefield, 2001. 207–217. Print.

_____, and Karen Hellekson. "Introduction: Work in Progress." Hellekson and Busse 5–31.
Calvino, Italo. *If on a Winter's Night a Traveler*. Trans. William Weaver. 1979; San Diego: Harcourt, 1981. Print.
Carroll, Noël. *The Philosophy of Horror, or Paradoxes of the Heart*. New York: Routledge, 1990. Print.
Carter, Margaret. "Vampire-Human Symbiosis in *Fevre Dream* and *The Empire of Fear*." Heldreth and Pharr 165–176.
Case, Sue-Ellen. "Tracking the Vampire." *Differences: A Journal of Feminist Cultural Studies* 3.2 (1991): 1–20. Print.
"Character Bios." *Twilight Lexicon*. N.d., n. pag. Web. 11 Sept. 2012. http://www.twilightlexicon.com.
Cherry, Brigid, ed. *True Blood: Investigating Vampires and Southern Gothic*. London: I.B. Tauris, 2012. Print.
Cicioni, Mirna. "Male Pair-Bonds and Female Desire in Fan Slash Writing." Harris and Alexander 153–177.
"Citrus Scale." *Wikia*. N.d., n. pag. Web. 4 Nov. 2012. http://ppc.wikia.com/wiki/Citrus_Scale.
Clements, Susannah. *The Vampire Defanged: How the Embodiment of Evil Became a Romantic Hero*. Grand Rapids: Brazos Press, 2011. Print.
Click, Melissa A., Jennifer Stevens Aubrey, and Elizabeth Behm-Morawitz, eds. *Bitten by Twilight: Youth Culture, Media & the Vampire Franchise*. New York: Peter Lang, 2010. Print.
Cohen, Jeffrey Jerome. "Monster Culture (Seven Theses)." *Monster Theory: Reading Culture*. Ed. Jeffrey Jerome Cohen. Minneapolis: University of Minnesota Press, 1996. 3–25. Print.
Craft, Christopher. "'Kiss Me with those Red Lips': Gender and Inversion in Bram Stoker's *Dracula*." *Representations* 8 (1984): 107–133. *JSTOR*. Web. 26 Apr. 2011.
Cronin, Justin. *The Passage*. New York: Ballantine, 2010. Print.
"Darkfic." *Fanlore*. N.d. http://fanlore.org/wiki/Darkfic. Web. 1 Oct. 2012.
Del Toro, Guillermo, and Chuck Hogan. *The Strain*. 2009; New York: Harper, 2010. Print.
"Delena fanfiction." *Blogspot*. N.d., n. pag. Web. 12 Oct 2012. http://vdfanfiction.blogspot.se.
Derecho, Abigail. "Archontic Literature: a Definition, a History, and Several Theories of Fan Fiction." Hellekson and Busse 61–78.
Donnelly, Ashley. "Denial and Salvation: The *Twilight* Saga and Heteronormative Patriarchy." *Theorizing Twilight: Critical Essays on What's at Stake in a Post-Vampire World*. Eds. Maggie Parke and Natalie Wilson. Jefferson, NC: McFarland, 2011. 178–193. Print.
"Dracula." *Total E-Bound Publishing*. N.d., n. pag. Web. 21 Nov. 2012. http://www.total-e-bound.com.
Driscoll, Catherine. "One True Pairing: The Romance of Pornography and the Pornography of Romance." Hellekson and Busse 79–96.
Dyer, Richard. "Children of the Night: Vampirism as Homosexuality, Homosexuality as Vampirism." *Sweet Dreams: Sexuality, Gender and Popular Fiction*. Ed. Susannah Radstone. London: Lawrence & Wishart, 1988. 47–72. Print.
Elliot-Smith, Darren. "The Homosexual Vampire as a Metaphor for ... the Homosexual Vampire? *True Blood*, Homonormativity and Assimilation." Cherry 139–154.
Flanagan, Caitlin. "What Girls Want." *Atlantic Monthly* (Dec. 2008): 108–120. Print.
Foucault, Michel. *The History of Sexuality. Volume I: An Introduction*. Trans. Robert Hurley. 1976; New York: Vintage, 1990. Print.

_____. *Power/Knowledge: Selected Interviews and Other Writings* 1972–1977. Trans. Colin Gordon. Brighton: Harvester Press, 1980. Print.
Fuchs, Christian. "Information and Communication Technologies and Society: A Contribution to the Critique of the Political Economy of the Internet." *European Journal of Communication* 24.1 (March 2009): 69–87. Sage. Web. 13 Nov. 2012. Doi: 10.1177/0267323108098947.
Gelder, Ken. "Our Vampires, Our Neighbours." Picart and Browning 30–37.
_____. *Popular Fiction: The Logics and Practices of a Literary Field*. London: Routledge, 2004. Print.
_____. *Reading the Vampire*. London: Routledge, 1994. Print.
Genette, Gérard. *Palimpsests: Literature in the Second Degree*. Trans. Channa Newman and Claude Doubinsky. 1982; Lincoln: University of Nebraska Press, 1997. Print.
_____. *Paratexts: Thresholds of Interpretation*. Trans. Jane E. Lewin. Cambridge: Cambridge University Press, 1997. Print.
Giffney, Noreen. "Introduction: The 'q' Word." *The Ashgate Research Companion to Queer Theory*. Eds. Noreen Giffney and Michael O'Rourke. Farnham: Ashgate, 2009. 1–13. *Ebrary*. Web. 11 Nov. 2012.
Gordon, Joan, and Veronica Hollinger, eds. *Blood Read: The Vampire as Metaphor in Contemporary Culture*. Philadelphia: University of Pennsylvania Press, 1997. Print.
_____. "Introduction." Gordon and Hollinger 1–7.
Gray, Jonathan, Cornel Sandvoss, and C. Lee Harrington, eds. *Fandom: Identities and Communities in a Mediated World*. New York: New York University Press, 2007. Print.
Grossman, Lev. "The Boy Who Lived Forever." *Time* 27 July 2011. N. pag. Web. 14 Aug. 2012. www.time.com.
Gwenllian Jones, Sara. "The Sex Lives of Cult Television Characters." *Screen* 43.1 (2002): 79–90. Print.
_____. "Starring Lucy Lawless?" *Continuum: Journal of Media & Cultural Studies*, 14:1 (2000): 9–22. Print.
Haggerty, George E. "Anne Rice and the Queering of Culture." *Novel: A Forum of Fiction* 32:1 (1998): 5–18. *JSTOR*. Web. 11 June 2012.
_____. *Queer Gothic*. Urbana: University of Illinois Press, 2006. Print.
Halberstam, Judith. "Technologies of Monstrosity: Bram Stoker's *Dracula*." *Victorian Studies* 36.3 (1993): 333–352. *JSTOR*. Web. 12 Dec. 2011.
Haraway, Donna. "Foreword: Companion Species, Mis-Recognition and Queer Worlding." *Queering the Non/Human*. Eds. Noreen Giffney and Myra J. Hird. Aldershot: Ashgate, 2009. xiii–xxvi. Print.
Harris, Cheryl, and Alison Alexander, eds. *Theorizing Fandom: Fans, Subculture, and Identity*. Creskill, NJ: Hampton Press, 1998. Print.
Heinecken, Dawn. "Changing Ideologies in Romance Fiction." Kaler and Johnson-Kurek 149–172.
Heldreth, Leonard G., and Mary Pharr, eds. *The Blood is the Life: Vampires in Literature*. Bowling Green, OH: Bowling Green State University Press, 1999. Print.
Hellekson, Karen, and Kristina Busse, eds. *Fan Fiction and Fan Communities in the Age of the Internet*. Jefferson, NC: McFarland, 2006. Print.
Herman, David. "Editor's Column: The Scope and Aims of Storyworlds." *Storyworlds: A Journal of Narrative Studies* 1 (2009): vii–x. *Project Muse*. Web. 16 Aug. 2011.
Herzog, Alexandra. "'But This Is My Story and This Is How I Wanted to Write It': Author's Notes as a Fannish Claim to Power in Fan Fiction Writing." *Transformative Works and Cultures* 11 (2012): n. pag. Web. 11 Dec. 2012. Doi:10.3983/twc.2012.0406.
Hills, Matt. *Fan Cultures*. London: Routledge, 2002. Print.

———. "Media Academics *as* Media Audiences: Aesthetic Judgments in Media and Cultural Studies." Gray, Sandvoss and Harrington 33–47.
Hollinger, Veronica. "Fantasies of Absence: The Postmodern Vampire." Gordon and Hollinger 199–212.
Holmes, Trevor. "Coming Out of the Coffin: Gay Males and Queer Goths in Contemporary Vampire Fiction." Gordon and Hollinger 169–188.
Holmgren Troy, Maria. "'Between Memory and History': The Nineteenth Century in Jewelle Gomez's Vampire Novel *The Gilda Stories* and the TV Series *True Blood*." *American Studies in Scandinavia* 42.2 (2010): 57–73. Print.
Isaksson, Malin, and Maria Lindgren Leavenworth. "Gazing, Initiating, Desiring: Alternative Constructions of Agency and Sex in Twific." *Interdisciplinary Approaches to Twilight: Studies in Fiction, Media, and a Contemporary Cultural Experience*. Eds. Mariah Larsson and Ann Steiner. Lund: Nordic Academic Press, 2011. 127–142. Print.
James, E.L. *Fifty Shades of Grey*. 2011; London: Arrow, 2012. Print.
Jenkins, Henry. "Confessions of an Aca-fan." *The Official Weblog of Henry Jenkins*. N.d., n. pag. Web. 6 Oct. 2012. http://henryjenkins.org/.
———. "*Star Trek* Rerun, Reread, Rewritten: Fan Writing as Textual Poaching." *Critical Studies in Mass Communication* 5 (1988): 85–107. Print.
———. *Textual Poachers: Television Fans and Participatory Culture*. New York: Routledge, 1992. Print.
Jones, Darryl. *Horror: a Thematic History in Fiction and Film*. London: Arnold, 2002. Print.
Jones, Miriam. "*The Gilda Stories*: Revealing the Monsters at the Margins." Gordon and Hollinger 151–167.
Kaler, Anne K. "Conventions of Captivity in Romance Novels." Kaler and Johnson-Kurek 86–99.
———, and Rosemary E. Johnson-Kurek, eds. *Romantic Conventions*. Bowling Green OH: Bowling Green State University Popular Press, 1999. Print.
Keesey, Pam. *Daughters of Darkness: Lesbian Vampire Tales*. Berkeley: Cleis Press, 1993. Print.
Keft-Kennedy, Virginia. "Fantasising Masculinity in *Buffyverse* Slash Fiction: Sexuality, Violence, and the Vampire." *Nordic Journal of English Studies* 7 (2008): 49–80. Print.
Kokkola, Lydia. "Virtuous Vampires and Voluptuous Vamps: Romance Conventions Reconsidered in Stephenie Meyer's 'Twilight' Series." *Children's Literature in Education* 42 (2011): 165–179. Web. 6 Oct. 2012. Doi: 10.1007/s10583-010-9125-9. Web. 6 Oct. 2012.
Kustritz, Anne. "Slashing the Romance Narrative." *The Journal of American Culture* 26.3 (2003): 371–384. *Academic Search Elite*. Web. 4 May 2011.
Lamb, Patricia Frazer, and Diane Veith. "Romantic Myth, Transcendence, and *Star Trek* Zines." *Erotic Universe: Sexuality and Fantastic Literature*. Ed. Donald Palumbo. Westport, CT: Greenwood Press, 1986. 236–255. Print.
Landon, Brooks. *Science Fiction after 1900: from the Steam Man to the Stars*. New York: Routledge, 2002. Print.
Le Fanu, Sheridan. *Carmilla*. *The Penguin Book of Vampire Stories*. Ed. Alan Ryan. 1987; London: BCA, 1988. 71–137. Print.
Lee, Linda J. "Guilty Pleasures: Reading Romance Novels as Reworked Fairy Tales." *Marvels & Tales: Journal of Fairy-Tale Studies* 22.1 (2008): 52–66. *Project Muse*. Web. 22 Nov. 2012.
LeMaster, Benny. "Queer Imag(in)ing: Liminality as Resistance in Lindqvist's *Let the Right One In*." *Communication and Critical/Cultural Studies* 8.2 (2011): 103–123. Print.
"Lemon." *Television Tropes and Idioms*. N.d., n. pag. Web. 17 Sept 2012. http://tvtropes.org.

Lindgren Leavenworth, Maria. "Lover Revamped: Sexualities and Romance in the Black Dagger Brotherhood and Fan Fiction." *Extrapolation* 50. 3 (2009): 442–462. Print.
_____. "Variations, Subversions, and Endless Love: Fan Fiction and the *Twilight* Saga." Anatol 69–81.
_____, and Malin Isaksson. "The Recuperated Bite and Issues of the Soul in Fan Fiction." Schott and Moffat 239–253.
Litte, Jane. "Master of the Universe versus Fifty Shades by E.L James Comparison." *Dear Author*. 14 Mar. 2012. N. pag. Web. 14 Aug. 2012. http://dearauthor.com/.
Loza, Susana. "Vampires, Queers, and Other Monsters: Against the Homonormativity of *True Blood*." Schott and Moffat 91–118.
MacCormack, Patricia. "The Queer Ethics of Monstrosity." Picart and Browning 255–265.
Magnusson, Gert. "Are Vampires Evil?: Categorizations of Vampires, and Angelus and Spike as the Immoral and the Amoral." *Slayage* 9.2 (2012): n.pag. Web. 29 Oct. 2012.
Margolin, Uri. "Character." *The Cambridge Companion to Narrative*. Ed. David Herman. Cambridge: Cambridge University Press, 2007. 66–79. Print.
Marks, Pamela. "The Good Provider in Romance Novels." Kaler and Johnson-Kurek 10–22.
Marshall, Eric. "Defanging Dracula: The Disappearing Other in Coppola's *Bram Stoker's Dracula*." *The Gothic Other: Racial and Social Constructions in the Literary Imagination*. Eds. Ruth Bienstock Anolik and Douglas L. Howard. Jefferson, NC: McFarland, 2004. 289–302. Print.
"Mary Sue." *Fanlore*. N.d., n. pag. Web. 5 Dec. 2012. http://fanlore.org.
McGinn, Colin. *Ethics, Evil, and Fiction*. Oxford: Clarendon Press, 1997. Print.
McMahon-Coleman, Kimberley. "Mystic Falls Meets the World Wide Web: Where is *The Vampire Diaries* Located?" Schott and Moffat 169–186.
Meredith, Charlotte. "Fifty Shades of Grey Becomes the Bestselling Book of All Time." *The Daily Express*. 1 Aug. 2012. N. pag. Web. 14 Aug. 2012. www.express.co.uk.
Mighall, Robert. *A Geography of Victorian Gothic Fiction: Mapping History's Nightmares*. Oxford: Oxford University Press, 1999. Print.
Modleski, Tania. *Loving with a Vengeance: Mass-Produced Fantasies for Women*. New York: Methuen, 1982. Print.
Moretti, Franco. *Signs Taken for Wonders: On the Sociology of Literary Forms*. Trans. Susan Fischer, David Forgacs and David Miller. 1983; London: Verso, 2005. Print.
Mukherjea, Ananya. "My Vampire Boyfriend: Postfeminism, 'Perfect' Masculinity, and the Contemporary Appeal of Paranormal Romance." *Studies in Popular Culture* 33.2 (2011): 1–20. Print.
Mulholland, Monique. "When Porno Meets Hetero: SEXPO, Heteronormativity and the Pornification of Mainstream." *Australian Feminist Studies* 26.67 (2011): 119–135. Print.
Nakagawa, Chiho. "Safe Sex with Defanged Vampires: New Vampire Heroes in *Twilight* and the *Southern Vampire Mysteries*." *Journal of Popular Romance Studies* 2.1 (2011): n. pag. Web. 12 Apr. 2012. http://www.jprstudies.org.
Overstreet, Deborah Wilson. *Not Your Mother's Vampire: Vampires in Young Adult Fiction* Lanham, MD: Scarecrow Press, 2006. Print.
Owen, Laura Hazard. "Erotic Novel '50 Shades of Grey,' Fan Fiction And Copyright." *PaidContent: The Economics of Digital Content*. 13 Mar. 2012. N. pag. Web. 30 May 2012. http://paidcontent.org/2012/03/13/419-erotic-novel-50-shades-of-grey-fan-fiction-and-copyright/.
Parrish, Juli. "Back to the Woods: Narrative Revisions in *New Moon* Fan Fiction at Twilighted." Click et al. 173–188.
Pearce, Lynne. *Romance Writing*. Malden, MA: Polity Press, 2007. Print.
Penley, Constance. "Brownian Motion: Women, Tactics, and Technology." *Technoculture*.

Eds. Constance Penley and Andrew Ross. Minneapolis: University of Minnesota Press, 1991. 135–61. Print.

———. *NASA/Trek: Popular Science and Sex in America*. London: Verso, 1997. Print.

Picart, Caroline Joan S., and John Edgar Browning, eds. *Speaking of Monsters: a Teratological Anthology*. New York: Palgrave Macmillan, 2012. Print.

Pugh, Sheenagh. *The Democratic Genre: Fan Fiction in a Literary Context*. Bridgend: Seren, 2005. Print.

Punter, David. *The Literature of Terror, Vol 2: The Modern Gothic*. London: Longman, 1996. Print.

Radway, Janice A. *Reading the Romance: Women, Patriarchy, and Popular Literature*. 1984; Chapel Hill: University of North Carolina Press, 1991. Print.

Regis, Pamela. *A Natural History of the Romance Novel*. 2003, Philadelphia: University of Pennsylvania Press, 2007. Print.

Rein, Katarina. "Mothers, Killers and Vampires: The Post-Familial Society in 'True Blood.'" *Popmatters*. 22 Nov. 2011. N. pag. Web. 16 June 2012. http://www.popmatters.com/pm/feature/146473.

Rickles, Lawrence A. *The Vampire Lectures*. Minneapolis: University of Minnesota Press, 1999. Print.

Robichaud, Christopher. "To Turn or Not to Turn: The Ethics of Making Vampires." Dunn and Housel 7–17. *True Blood and Philosophy: We Wanna Think Bad Things with You*. Eds. George A Dunn and Rebecca Housel. Hoboken, NJ: John Wiley & Sons, 2010. Print

Russ, Joanna. "Pornography by Women, for Women, with Love." *Magic Mommas, Trembling Sisters, Puritans, & Perverts: Feminist Essays*. Ed. Joanna Russ. Trumansburg, NY: Crossing Press, 1985. 79–99. Print.

Saxey, Esther. "Staking a Claim: the Series and its Slash Fan Fiction." *Reading the Vampire Slayer: The New Updated, Unofficial Guide to Buffy and Angel*. Ed. Roz Kaveney. London: Tauris Parke, 2004. 187–210. Print.

Schopp, Andrew. "Cruising the Alternatives: Homoeroticism and the Contemporary Vampire." *The Journal of Popular Culture* 30 (2004): 231–243. Print.

Schott, Gareth, and Kirstine Moffat, eds. *Fanpires: Audience Consumption of the Modern Vampire*. Washington, DC: New Academia, 2011. Print.

Schwartzbaum, Lisa. "Fifty Shades of Grey: Review." *Entertainment Weekly*. 14 Mar. 2012. N. pag. Web. 13 Aug 2012. www.ew.com.

Scodari, Christine. "Resistance Re-Examined: Gender, Fan Practices, and Science Fiction Television." *Popular Communication* 1.2 (2003): 111–130. *Informaworld*. Web. 9 March 2009.

Sedgwick, Eve Kosofsky. *Between Men: English Literature and Male Homosocial Desire*. New York: Columbia University Press, 1985. Print.

———. *Tendencies*. New York: Routledge, 1993. Print.

Seifert, Christine. "Bite me! (Or Don't)." *Bitch Magazine*. N.d., n. pag. Web. 10 Jan. 2010. http://bitchmagazine.org/.

Skal, David J. "Foreword: What We Talk About When We Talk About Monsters." Picart and Browning xi–xiii.

"Sookie Stackhouse series." *Barnes & Noble*. N.d. http://www.barnesandnoble.com. Web. 10 Dec. 2011.

Spooner, Catherine. *Contemporary Gothic*. London: Foci, 2006. Print.

Stein, Louisa, and Kristina Busse. "Limit Play: Fan Authorship between Source Text, Intertext, and Context." *Popular Communication* 7 (2009): 192–207. Print.

"Stephenie Meyer on fan fiction." *Twifans*. N.d., n. pag. Web. 12 Apr. 2012. http://www.twifans.com.

Stevens, Kirsten. "Meet the Cullens: Family, Romance and Female Agency in Buffy the Vampire Slayer and Twilight." *Slayage: The Journal of the Whedon Studies Association.* 29 (2010): n. pag. Web. 18 Dec. 2012.

Stoker, Bram. *Dracula.* 1897; New York: W.W. Norton, 1997. Print.

"Submission Guidelines." *Twilighted.* N.d., n. pag. Web. 12 Apr. 2012. http://twilighted.net.

Summers, Montague. *The Vampire in Europe.* London: Kegan Paul, 2003. Print.

Taylor, Anthea. "'The Urge Towards Love is an Urge Towards (Un)Death': Romance, Masochistic Desire and Postfeminism in the *Twilight* Novels." *International Journal of Cultural Studies* 15. 31 (2012): 31–46. *Sage.* Web. 3 Jan. 2012.

Thomas, Bronwen. "What is Fanfiction and Why Are People Saying Such Nice Things about It?" *Storyworlds: A Journal of Narrative Studies* 3 (2011): 1–24. *Project Muse.* Web. 14 Aug. 2012.

Toffler, Alvin. *The Third Wave.* London: Collins, 1980. Print.

"True Blood DVD." *Amazon.* N.d., n. pag. Web. 10 Dec. 2011. http://www.amazon.com.

Turner, Victor. *The Forest of Symbols: Aspects of Ndembu Ritual.* Ithaca: Cornell University Press, 1967. *Google Book Search.* Web. 5 Dec. 2012.

"Twi-Girl Revolution." *FanFiction.net.* 12 June 2010. N. pag. Web. 5 Nov. 2012. http://www.fanfiction.net/u/2330327.

"The Vampire Diaries DVD." *Amazon.* N.d., n. pag. Web. 10 Dec. 2011. http://www.amazon.com.

"Vampire Diaries series." *Barnes & Noble.* N.d. http://www.barnesandnoble.com. Web. 10 Dec. 2011.

"Vampire literature." *Wikipedia.* 21 Nov. 2012. N. pag. Web. 21 Nov. 2012. http://en.wikipedia.org/wiki/Vampire_literature.

Vivanco, Laura and Kyra Kramer. "There are Six Bodies in This Relationship: an Anthropological Approach to the Romance Genre." *Journal of Popular Romance Studies* 1:1 (4 Aug. 2010). N. pag. Web. 18 Aug. 2012. http://www.jprstudies.org.

Williamson, Milly. *The Lure of the Vampire: Gender, Fiction and Fandom from Bram Stoker to Buffy.* London: Wallflower Press, 2005. Print.

Wilson, Natalie. "Civilized Vampires Versus Savage Werewolves: Race and Ethnicity in the Twilight Series." Click et al. 55–70.

Woledge, Elizabeth. "Intimatopia: Genre Intersections Between Slash and the Mainstream." Hellekson and Busse 97–114.

Zanger, Jules. "Metaphor into Metonomy: The Vampire Next Door." Gordon and Hollinger 17–26.

Zidle, Abby. "From Bodice-Ripper to Baby-Sitter: The New Hero in Mass-Market Romance." Kaler and Johnson-Kurek 23–34.

Index

aesthetics, of fan fiction 8, 69, 71–72, 110–111
agency, of audience 7, 11–12, 44, 111; of character 6–7, 11–12, 15, 23–24, 28, 32–33, 45, 62, 67, 70, 80–81, 95, 97, 103, 122–123, 125, 130–132, 143–149, 150, 153–154, 157, 165–166, 169, 173, 175–176, 189–191, 197
AH *see* All Human
Alexander, Jenny 143
All Human 5–7, 51, 54
Alternate Universe 5, 49, 51, 54, 66–68, 88, 119, 197, 201
Alternative Universe *see* Alternate Universe
A/Ns *see* author notes
appropriation, of text 4, 13, 69–70
archive 12–13, 15, 41, 68–111, 119, 140, 142, 156–157, 174, 176, 199–203; sites 12, 45–47, 190; *see also* archontic
archontic 13, 69–73, 92, 110–111, 201–203; *see also* archive
AU *see* Alternate Universe
Auerbach, Nina 1, 119, 135, 160
author notes 44, 48–51, 54, 57–58, 63–64, 66, 84, 88, 96, 103, 123, 169, 174, 190

Bacon-Smith, Camille 8
badboy_fangirl 96–100
Bailie, Helen T. 38
Ball, Alan *see* Bill; Eric, Sookie; *True Blood*
BDSM 6, 116, 119, 142–150, 153; *see also* agency
Beckylady 84–85, 87, 200
Bella (Swan) 3, 5–7, 17, 19–22, 24–36, 42, 54–56, 58–68, 73, 84–85, 88, 92–95, 100–106, 109–110, 122–130, 135–136, 145–147, 150, 155–157, 162–164, 168–169, 173–181, 183–186, 190, 193–196, 200–201
Benefiel, Candace 139
Benshoff, Harry M. 188–189
Betz, Phyllis M. 135, 137

Bill (Compton) 17, 22–24, 26, 28, 32–34, 38–39, 42–43, 50, 64–66, 72–73, 82, 96, 105–106, 108, 127–128, 138, 145, 148–149, 151, 156, 158–159, 164, 166–168, 170, 172, 183, 189, 192–193, 198, 200–201
blood diet 165–174; bloodlust, blood-drinking 22, 26, 30–31, 35, 38, 56, 60, 66, 75, 78, 89, 96, 105–106, 123, 130–132, 134, 136–137, 139–140, 143, 145, 148–153, 158–159, 161, 177–179, 184, 187, 190–192, 194–197, 199, 207 *ch*2*n*11; exchange 119, 138; figurative exchange 4
Bogwitch 172–173
bondage 6, 154
Bosky, Bernadette Lynn 122, 155, 209*n*12
Botting, Fred 18, 181–182
Braidotti, Rosi 164, 170, 202
Brite, Poppy Z. 134, 139–140, 142, 209*n*10
Buffy the Vampire Slayer 30–31, 41–42, 143
Burke, Brianna 101, 104, 208*n*15
Busse, Kristina 8–9, 52–53, 67, 95, 140
Butler, Octavia 134

canon, delineation 10–12, 205*n*7; analysis 17–43
Carmilla see Le Fanu, Sheridan
Carroll, Noël 160–163
Carson Dyle 92–95, 168
Carter, Margaret 165
Case, Sue-Ellen 120–121
categorization 112–113; of fan fiction 45–47, 50–53; of media 205–206*ch*1*n*2
CatsOnMars 102, 105
CavalierQueen 48–50
chapter notes *see* author notes
Chiyoku Shibata 172–173
Clements, Susannah 65, 125, 144, 183, 188
Cohen, Jeffrey Jerome 163, 173
colacherry 145–146
community 44, 49, 52–53
competencies, of canon characters 54–58,

223

61–63, 65, 67, 83, 89, 93, 99, 103, 122, 143, 147, 150–152, 154–155, 159, 165–166
compliance, audience 11–12, 113, 202; canon 17
consent 123, 137, 143, 145–147, 150, 152–153, 157, 169, 189–190, 208n20; see also glamouring
contestation, audience 11, 18; in depictions 47, 68, 142, 201–202
Craft, Christopher 120
Cronin, Justin 161
crossover 54–55, 56, 62–63, 208n18
CrowX 141–142
cyclogenesis 136–138

Daddy's Little Cannibal 124–126
Damon (Salvatore) 17, 21–22, 29–30, 33–34, 36–38, 54, 57–58, 68, 89–91, 95–100, 105, 107, 121, 127–128, 132–133, 137–139, 141–142, 151–152, 162, 164, 166, 169–170, 172–173, 176, 183, 190–191, 200
darkfic 116–117, 176, 197
DCWriter16 73–78
defanging 11–12, 18, 168, 209n2
Del Toro, Guillermo 161–162
Derecho, Abigail 13, 69, 71–71, 111, 200–201, 207n3; see also archontic
derivative writing 3, 5, 71
dominance see agency; BDSM
Donnelly, Ashley 173, 175
Dracula/Dracula see Stoker, Bram
dreaming in black and white 83
Driscoll, Catherine 46
dubious consent (dub-con) see consent
Dyer, Richard 119, 121

Edward (Cullen) 3, 5–7, 17, 19–22, 24–27, 32–38, 42, 47, 54, 56, 59–62, 64–67, 72, 82, 84–85, 87–88, 92–96, 100–105, 109, 122–130, 145–146, 150, 155–157, 162, 164, 166–169, 173–180, 183–186, 190, 194–196, 200–201
Eleai 173
Elena (Gilbert) 17, 19, 21–22, 24–26, 28–34, 54–55, 57, 68, 73, 86–87, 89–92, 95–100, 105, 107, 127, 132–133, 136–139, 141–142, 153–154, 162–164, 167, 169–170, 172–173, 183, 190–191, 193, 196–197
Ellen Smithee 177
Elliot-Smith, Darren 121
Eric (Northman) 17, 22–24, 28–29, 32, 34, 38–39, 48–51, 68, 73–81, 88, 96, 105–106, 108, 116, 127–128, 130–131, 147–149, 151–152, 156, 166–168, 171, 181, 192–193, 197–198, 200–201
EricBonesVladCurran 106

erotica 6, 72, 138, 143, 202; vampire erotica 155
Estora 174–176
Eternallybills 147–148, 158, 189, 207n9
ethics, of canon, of characters 55–56, 58, 61–62, 67–68, 70, 89, 93, 96–97, 103, 108, 111, 114, 118, 124, 128, 132, 141–143, 149, 153, 158–159, 165–170, 172, 187, 190, 193, 196, 199, 201, 209n1; of fan fiction 69, 71, 110–111
ethnography 7–9; autoethnography 9
evil 65, 112, 114, 116, 165, 183, 185, 187, 200, 202 210n12; and good 4, 12, 30, 68, 96, 99, 101; vampiric evil 22, 38, 54, 79, 158–199, 209n1
exeterlinden 181–182

faithunbreakable 179–181, 189–190
fan studies 7–8, 9, 44, 127
fandom 6, 8, 10–11, 40–42, 44–47, 49, 50–53, 69, 71, 101, 118–119, 144
fanon 10, 53
female protagonists 25–33; see also Bella; Elena; Sookie
fembuck/Janine 136, 146–147, 151
femslash 56, 72, 118, 127–128, 133, 139, 146, 153–154; see also pairings; slash
fictional universe see storyworld
fidelity, to canon 12, 49, 53–56, 58, 63, 65–69, 79, 82–83, 85, 99, 108, 111, 124–126, 155, 186, 188, 194–195, 197
Fifty Shades of Grey see James, E.L.
Finta 89–92
Flanagan, Caitlin 122
Fledgling see Butler, Octavia
flute_genevive 82
focalization, focalizer 25–26, 30, 37, 68, 137, 153, 158, 177, 190–191, 201
Foucault, Michel 112–113
4CullensandaBlack 148–151
4theluvofMary 194
Fuchs, Christian 8

gay 115, 119–122, 128, 152; see also homosexuality
Gelder, Ken 18, 26, 121–122, 163–165, 182
gender roles 11–12, 35, 123, 135, 140; subversion of 70, 116, 120, 122, 127, 145–146, 157
genfic 46
genre, constraints of and resistance to 6, 11–12, 14, 17, 67 72–73, 129, 131; fanfic genres 6, 13, 44–47, 115, 127, 190, 192; genre hybridity 135, 156, 160, 188, 201–202, 206ch1n2; see also paranormal romance
Giffney, Noreen 113
The Gilda Stories see Gomez, Jewelle

glamouring 94, 108–109, 152, 155, 165–166, 189, 191, 208n20; *see also* consent
glitter and stardust 106
Gomez, Jewelle 134, 139, 195
good *see* evil
Gordon, Joan 198
the Gothic 18, 137–138, 143, 165, 169, 202
Gray, Jonathan 7–8
Grossman, Lev 4–5, 69
Gwenllian Jones, Sara 41, 45, 53–56, 11, 206n7

Haggerty, George E. 143, 191
Halberstam, Judith 114–115
Haraway, Donna 115
hard data, canon 53–55, 57, 60, 62–63, 67, 93, 131, 133, 138, 152
Harrington, C. Lee 7–8
Harris, Charlaine 10–11, 22, 24–26, 28, 38–40, 46, 49–50, 63, 79, 116, 136, 138, 158, 167, 183, 192; *All Together Dead* 11; *Club Dead* 11, 192, 208n2; *Dead and Gone* 11, 79; *Dead as a Doornail* 11; *Dead in the Family* 11, 79; *Dead Reckoning* 11; *Dead to the World* 11, 39; *Dead Until Dark* 11, 22, 28, 167, 183, 205ch1n2, 208n2, 209ch5n4; *Deadlocked* 11; *Definitely Dead* 11; *From Dead to Worse* 11; *Living Dead in Dallas* 11, 38–39, 183; *see also* Bill; Eric; Sookie; *True Blood*
havocthecat 138–139
Heinecken, Dawn 32
Hellekson, Karen 8–9, 95
Herman, David 39, 53
Herzog, Alexandra 49–50
heteronormativity 6, 11, 12, 14, 18, 56, 68, 70, 72, 109, 112, 114, 118, 120–122, 127, 129–130, 139, 157, 170, 201; *see also* normativity
heterosexuality 13, 46, 56, 72, 96, 114–115, 120, 127–129, 131–133, 135, 139, 143, 146, 150
hetfic 46
Heyl13 6–7
Hills, Matt 8, 9
Hogan, Chuck *see* del Toro, Guillermo
Hollinger, Veronica 176, 198
Holmes, Trevor 209n10
Holmgren Troy, Maria 18
homoeroticism 8, 56, 72, 127–133, 139, 141, 145, 156
homosexuality 14, 114, 119, 120–121, 127–128, 130–131, 151, 155–156, 201; *see also* gay; lesbian
homosociality 3, 56, 72, 119, 127–128, 136
horror, genre 18, 46, 47, 57, 116, 160, 163, 169, 190, 192, 202; films 188–189

humanization, of vampires 11, 14, 25, 33–39, 72, 91, 98, 106, 114–115, 170, 180–181, 191, 198, 202; de-humanization 161, 172, 179, 189–191, 193–194, 196
hybridity 98, 104, 154, 163, 170, 173, 175; of genres 13, 206ch1n2

imitation 4, 13, 69, 71
intertextuality 3, 7, 9, 13, 15, 41, 48, 50–51, 57, 60, 67, 69–73, 84, 103, 133, 185, 203
intimacy, physical 3, 20, 23, 27, 32, 35, 37, 39, 56, 64–65, 67, 89, 96, 99, 102, 105, 110, 112, 119, 122, 133–142, 146, 156, 167–168, 171, 175, 178, 189, 191, 194–195, 198, 200, 208n1; textual 44, 51
intimatopia 127–128, 136, 147
Isaksson, Malin 123, 171

Jacob (Black) 3, 7, 17, 26, 31, 94–95, 100–105, 109, 126–128, 150, 155, 163, 173–176, 195, 200
James, E.L. 5–7, 144
jazzywazzy08 107
Jenkins, Henry 7, 8, 62
jenny_haniver 141
Jones, Miriam 139, 145

Kaler, Anne K. 93
Keft-Kennedy, Virginia 119, 127, 210n16
kink 112, 114, 118, 121, 125, 143, 150; kinkfic 6, 116, 119, 143–144
Kokkola, Lydia 27, 124, 176, 209n6
Kramer, Kyra 150–151
Kustritz, Anne 9, 154

Lady Dragoncrow 151–152
L'amante di Destino 56, 62–67
Lamb, Patricia Frazer 8
Landon, Brooks 30
LaTessitrice 124, 126, 209n5
Lee, Linda J. 18–19, 23, 189
Le Fanu, Sheridan 72, 134–136, 139
LeMaster, Benny 170
lemon 118, 124, 157, 208n1
Lenore 130–131
lesbian 114–115, 128, 133–134, 137, 139, 145; *see also* homosexuality
levitatethis 168, 171–172
light4dawn 104–105
lil_utterance 138
liminality 138, 170–176, 210n12
linaerys 131
Lindgren Leavenworth, Maria 70, 123, 129, 171
LingeringLuminosity 129–130
Lisse 56–62, 67, 194–196, 207ch1n10
lit_chick08 86–87, 110

Litte, Jane 5
LJ Summers 87–88
Llwy 194–196
Lost Souls see Brite, Poppy Z.
Loza, Susana 121
Lunar Siren 82–83

MacCormack, Patricia 113
Magnusson, Gert 114
mainstream, media and messages 4–5, 7, 9–10, 12, 121, 140, 144, 189; mainstreaming vampires 38, 158, 165, 167–168, 170–171, 200
male protagonists 33–39; *see also* Bill; Damon; Edward; Eric; Stefan
Maranda 155
Margolin, Uri 39
Marks, Pamela 32
Marshall, Eric 33
Mary Sue 51
McGinn, Colin 165–166, 169, 191, 199
McMahon-Coleman, Kimberley 37, 40
Megi 110, 118
MeraNaamJoker 109, 208*n*21
Meredith, Charlotte 5
metaphysics 14, 33–35, 65, 108, 113, 158–159, 164, 168, 171, 177, 181–188, 198, 200; *see also* evil; monstrosity
Meyer, Stephenie 3, 5, 10, 20–21, 24–27, 30–31, 39, 54, 59–62, 82–84, 93–94, 101, 103, 109, 120, 123–124, 129, 162–163, 167, 173–174, 178–179, 183, 185, 188, 200; *Breaking Dawn* 3, 10, 24–27, 104, 109, 173–174, 207*ch*2*n*11, 209*ch*4*n*4, 210*n*12; *Eclipse* 10, 27, 82, 100, 109, 123, 179, 207*ch*2*n*10; *New Moon* 10, 22, 62, 93, 100, 103, 109, 124, 179, 183; *Twilight* 10, 20–21, 26–27, 59, 82, 162–163, 167, 178, 180, 183, 185; *see also* Bella; Edward; Jacob
midnightquiver 107
Mighall, Robert 119
mind manipulation *see* glamouring
misogyny 188–193, 209*n*10
missing moments, fanfic 6, 55, 73, 81, 83, 207*n*1
mneiai 128
Modleski, Tania 18
monogamy 22, 96–97, 99, 121–122, 127, 130, 141, 156, 201
monster, monstrous, monsterization 2, 14, 33, 35–36, 38, 56, 61, 93, 109, 112–114, 116, 119–120, 136–137, 141, 148, 155, 158–190, 200–202, 209*n*1; *see also* re-fanging
Moretti, Franco 10, 205*n*6
Mukherjea, Ananya 23–24, 27, 32
Mulholland, Monique 144

MyTwiDreams 129

Nakagawa, Chiho 20, 29, 34, 59
non-consent (non-con) *see* consent
normativity 12, 14, 17, 19, 24–25, 51, 58, 61–62, 67, 70, 82, 95, 99, 112–117, 120–121, 133, 154, 162, 165–166, 170, 173, 181, 190, 192, 198–199; subversion of 105, 112, 114–117, 119–122, 126, 129, 139, 142, 144, 156–157, 159, 174, 177–178, 193, 199; *see also* heteronormativity; resistant readings
NykkiLeighVampireHeart 190–192

OC *see* Original Character
oliviacirce 152–153
one-shot 184, 207*ch*3*n*10
One True Pairing 95
OOC *see* Out of Character
Original Character 51, 58, 90, 147
Otherness 11–12, 25, 29, 33, 36, 59, 80, 82, 85, 89, 101, 113–115, 118–122, 139, 142, 147, 155, 160–166, 173, 180, 196, 202
OTP *see* One True Pairing
Out of Character 50–52, 55, 110, 132
Overstreet, Deborah Wilson 18, 156
Owen, Laura Hazard 6

pain 6–7, 65, 79, 83, 104, 106, 108, 126, 155–157, 179, 189–192, 194, 196, 199, 201; and pleasure 14, 115, 122, 142–159, 153, 167
pairings 46–48, 50, 70, 88, 95–111, 115, 118, 126, 140, 156, 197, 206*n*1; same-sex pairings 8, 14, 53, 56, 56, 127–139, 153; *see also* femslash; slash
paranormal romance 3, 11, 13–14, 17–25, 38, 45, 55, 58–59, 67, 91, 95, 97, 114, 118, 124–125, 128, 133, 163, 169, 189, 202
paranormality 4–5, 7, 19–20, 23, 25, 28–32, 34–37, 59, 75, 78–79, 83, 85–86, 89, 91, 105, 109, 115–116, 122, 124, 126, 143, 151–155, 160, 163, 165–167, 170, 174, 179–180, 188–189, 191, 196, 210*n*6; *see also* power
paratext 13, 44–45, 48–50, 54, 71, 92, 115, 117, 169, 190, 192
Parrish, Juli 100, 103, 208*n*14
participation, culture 5, 8–9, 12, 71; genres 11, 14, 18–19, 32, 55, 58, 95, 169
The Passage see Cronin, Justin
Pearce, Lynne 24–25
Penley, Constance 8, 143–144
perspectival shift 6, 10, 13, 37, 55, 64–65, 68–70, 73–78, 86, 89, 137, 158–159, 174–182, 194–195, 199, 201, 210*n*19
Piper 56–58, 62, 67

pleasebekidding 132–133, 153–154
Plec, Julie *see* Damon; Elena; Stefan; *The Vampire Diaries*
point of view 64, 73, 158, 174–175, 194
porn without plot 156
pornography 72, 143, 202
POV *see* point of view
power, authorial 7, 45, 48–50; power play 119, 145, 148, 154, 190; structures 7, 34–35, 70, 112–113, 120, 124, 143–147, 150–153, 189, 210n5; *see also* paranormality
prelives 150
prequel 68, 70, 79–88, 110–11, 179–182, 184–188
prosumption 44–67, 69
psychobabblers 54
Pugh, Sheenagh 7
Punter, David 210n8
pwp *see* porn without plot

Queenhaq 106
queer 14, 113–115, 118, 120–122, 143–144, 156–157, 170

Radway, Janice A. 18
Red 140–141
re-fanging 15, 72, 193, 200–203; *see also* monster
Regis, Pamela 18–24, 31–32, 35, 95
Rein, Katarina 31, 82
resistant readings 8–9, 11–14, 17, 50, 67–68, 112–113, 120–127, 133, 156, 159, 170, 173, 176, 194, 201–202; *see also* normativity; subversion
Rice, Anne 33, 72, 134, 181–182, 207n4
Robichaud, Christopher 169
Roman 80–82
romance *see* paranormal romance
Russ, Joanna 8

Sandrine Shaw 128, 169–170
Sandvoss, Cornel 7–8
Saxey, Esther 42
Schopp, Andrew 128, 144
sciphile 103, 105, 126
Scodari, Christine 9, 113,
Sedgwick, Eve Kosofsky 113, 128
Seifert, Christine 123
sequel 68, 70, 88–95, 104, 107, 111
seriality 13, 22, 24, 26, 39–43
shoefreak37 3, 128
sites, fan fiction 45–47, 49, 51–53, 71, 83
Skal, David J. 162–163
slash 8, 46–47, 56, 72, 95, 116, 118, 127–128, 133, 143, 154, 156; *see also* femslash; pairings
smc-27 98, 105

Smith, L.J. 11, 21–22, 25–26, 29–30, 34, 36–37, 41, 56–57, 89–91, 105, 107, 120, 132, 162–163, 167, 183; *The Awakening* 11, 21, 26, 29, 36–37, 162–163, 167, 183, 210n14; *The Fury* 11, 22, 90; *Midnight* 11, 29, 57; *Nightfall* 11; *The Reunion* 11, 25, 89; *Shadow Souls* 11, 107; *The Struggle* 11, 22, 37, 90; *see also* Damon; Elena; Stefan; *The Vampire Diaries*
socact 168–169, 190
some_stars 141
someryn 101–104
Sookie (Stackhouse) 17, 22–24, 26, 28–34, 38–40, 43, 48–50, 54–55, 62–64, 66, 73–79, 88, 96, 105–106, 108, 116–117, 127, 136, 138, 145, 148–150, 158–159, 164, 167, 171, 192–193, 197
soul *see* metaphysics
source text *see* canon
spaniard 184–187
Spikey44 176
Spooner, Catherine 18
stainofmylove 169–170, 190
Stefan (Salvatore) 17, 21–22, 24, 26, 29–30, 32–34, 36–39, 57, 68, 72, 89–92, 96–99, 106–107, 127–128, 132, 138–142, 162–164, 166–167, 169–170, 172–173, 176–177, 183, 191, 196–197, 200
Stein, Louisa 52–53, 67
Stevens, Kirsten 31, 92
Stoker, Bram 4, 10, 33, 120, 134, 161, 164–165, 169, 210n5
storyworld 5, 19, 39–43, 53, 55–56, 63, 83, 111, 146, 166
The Strain see del Toro, Guillermo
submission *see* agency; BDSM
subversion *see* normativity; resistant readings; transgression
Suki59 116–117
SweetWillowTree 196–197
sympathetic vampire *see* humanization

Taia 123–124
TammyDevil666 105–106
Taylor, Anthea 18, 24, 28, 35–36, 175–176
Thomas, Bronwen 8
Thyra10 192–193
Toffler, Alvin 44
transformative works, activities 4, 68–71
transgression 3, 13–15, 69, 112, 114–115, 118–157, 160, 165, 171, 173, 177, 188–189, 199, 201; *see also* normativity; resistant readings
transmediality 13, 39–43
True Blood (TV series) 11, 17, 38–40, 42, 49, 54, 63, 73, 78–79, 81–82, 107–108, 121, 130, 136, 143, 147–149, 152, 158–159,

162, 164, 167, 207n6, 207n7, 210n18 see also Bill; Eric; Harris, Charlaine; Sookie
Turner, Victor 170
turning, vampiric 4, 14, 21–23, 25, 27–31, 33, 35, 57–58, 65–68, 73–82, 87–88, 90–91, 94, 96–99, 103, 107, 110, 119, 122, 124, 126, 132–134, 136, 139–141, 159, 165–169, 172, 176–177, 181–185, 190, 193, 197–199, 201, 207ch2n11
TWBB 187–188
22wolf 51
TwifanUK 177–179
Twilight Lexicon 84, 86

urban_folk_girl 145

vampcest 116, 140–142
The Vampire Diaries (TV series) 11, 17, 19, 22, 29–30, 34, 37–40, 54, 86, 96–97, 99, 105–107, 120–121, 132, 141, 164, 172, 206ch1n4, 207–208n13; *see also* Damon; Elena; Smith; Stefan

Veith, Diane 8
vic_vega66 197–198
virtual universe *see* storyworld
Vivanco, Laura 150–151

Ward, J.R. 128, 206ch2n4
Williamson, Kevin *see* Damon; Elena; Stefan; *The Vampire Diaries*
Williamson, Milly 10, 25, 30, 72, 134, 142–143, 167; *see also* humanization
Wilson, Natalie 101
Winter Ashby 100–101
wisedec4u 107–109
Woledge, Elizabeth 127; *see also* intimatopia

Yodigittyyoyo 88–89

Zanger, Jules 164–165
Zidle, Abby 26–27, 34–35

www.ingramcontent.com/pod-product-compliance
Ingram Content Group UK Ltd.
Pitfield, Milton Keynes, MK11 3LW, UK
UKHW041946140426
5217IPUK00014B/680